IF LOST, PLEASE RETURN TO:

_____

"This book is a stunning accomplishment. To say so much in so few words—breathtaking. . . .

Give it to the one you love and say, 'I love you like this.'

Give it to someone who has lost, or is losing, someone and say, 'It must hurt so much.'

Give it to someone who's lost himself and say, 'Live.'

Give it to someone who needs to hope, who needs to cry, or who needs to really dream—and say nothing at all."
—Keri Holmes, bookseller, The Kaleidoscope
(Hampton, Iowa)

"A novel that can be read in a single sitting of less than two hours that might continue to resonate with readers for weeks, months, even years."
—*Kirkus Reviews* (starred review)

"A gem of a book, [*The End of the Alphabet*] delivers more fable than fiction, more elongated short story than conventional first novel. Although characters, locales and comic touches will put many readers in mind of Mavis Gallant's European stories, Richardson's style is as minimalist as Norman Levine's. This is a very difficult book to put down at bedtime, even when the final page is turned. Like both Gallant and Levine, Richardson not only has an interesting story to tell, but writes with such visual and emotional density that the end of one reading readily becomes the start of another."

—*The Globe and Mail*

CS RICHARDSON

THE END OF

THE ALPHABET

ANCHOR CANADA

COPYRIGHT © 2007 DRAVOT & CARNEHAN INC.

Anchor Canada edition 2008

LIBRARY AND ARCHIVES CANADA CATALOGUING IN PUBLICATION

Richardson, CS
    The end of the alphabet / CS Richardson. — Anchor Canada ed.

ISBN 978-0-385-66341-0

    I. Title.

PS8635.I325E63 2008   C813'.6   C2007-906207-5

DESIGN: KELLY HILL
Printed and bound in Canada

Published in Canada by
Anchor Canada, a division of
Random House of Canada Limited

Visit Random House of Canada Limited's website: www.randomhouse.ca

10   9   8   7   6   5   4   3

For Rebecca . . .

T M D

Think of the long trip home

Should we have stayed at home and thought of here?

Where should we be today?

ELIZABETH BISHOP, 'Questions of Travel'

A Z
———
Z A

===

This story is unlikely.

Were it otherwise, or at the least more wished for, it would have begun on a Sunday morning. Early, as that was his best time of the day, and in April, that odd time between a thin winter and a plump spring.

He would have closed the door of his house and stood on his front step, eyeing the predawn sky. He would have given the neighbourhood stray a shove from its perch on his window ledge. The scruffy cat would have hissed and bolted across the narrow road to the park across the way. He would have hissed back, proud he had at last defeated the mangy beast, and set off. As he had every Sunday morning as far back as he could remember.

As he walked up the road, the woman from number eighteen would be retrieving the morning paper from her doorstep. The cool morning would have meant she had remembered to throw on a dressing gown. They would have traded pleasant, awkward good-mornings. He knew her to be the mother of two energetic children whose names he could never recall. She knew he worked in some sort of creative field. After a moment or two of searching for common ground, he would have asked after her children's artwork. He and his wife had no children of their own.

Farther on, he would have seen the elderly man and his tiny dog that lived at number twelve, about to begin their morning walk around the park. The pair would be waiting to say hello. The man would have tipped his cap and launched directly into an eccentric opinion about something. The tiny dog would have begun yapping at the neighbourhood stray.

He would have worried about disagreeing with the old fellow and causing offence, or starting a discussion on a topic he knew nothing about, or the soundness of his own opinion. He would have forced an agreeing laugh, wished his neighbour a good day and eyed the dog with suspicion.

He would have made his way to Kensington High Street and grumbled about the winter that had passed. He would have wished he had taken his wife to Italy. But that would have been expensive or difficult or meant a bad time at the office. He would have sighed to himself, then smiled as the London sky inched from black to grey to yellow to blue.

He would have turned in at Kensington Gardens, up past the palace and on to Broad Walk. Here he would have been happiest. He would have paused near the Round Pond, looked towards the east and the swans, and squinted in his way to watch a girl of perhaps nine or ten, her hair dark and fine and in need of a trim or a ribbon, reading a book beyond her years. He would have closed his eyes in the warmth of a sun just clearing the budding treetops.

He would have checked his watch, counted his minutes and the day's schedule in his head, and turned for home. He would have retraced his route down the Walk, past the palace, along the High Street, into his road, past number twelve and number eighteen and the cat now back on the window ledge, and through his front door.

His wife would have begun to stir in her sleep. Five minutes more, she would have mumbled, just loud enough for him to hear as he made her tea. As usual, a tepid cup with too much milk.

Ambrose Zephyr would have been content that it was Sunday and that spring had come again to that part of London and that there was no need to go to the office. He would have read a draft of his wife's latest magazine column and (as gentle readers are obliged) made one or two enthusiastic comments.

He would have wondered about the days ahead of him and, as was his habit, dreamed of doing something else. And there it would have ended.

But that is not this story.

—

On or about his fiftieth birthday, Ambrose Zephyr failed his annual medical exam. An illness of inexplicable origin with neither known nor foreseeable cure was discovered. It would kill him within the month. Give or take a day.

It was suggested he might want to make arrangements concerning his remaining time.

—

Ambrose Zephyr lived with his wife—content, quiet, with few extravagances—in a narrow Victorian terrace full of books.

He owned two bespoke suits, one of which he had been married in. The other—a three-piece linen number with lapelled waistcoat—he wore whenever and wherever he travelled: on business, on the underground, on his Sunday walk. A pocket square, discreetly puffed, always in place. He collected French-cuffed shirts as others might collect souvenir spoons or back issues of *National Geographic*. He rarely wore ties but liked them as challenges in graphic design. His footwear was predominantly Italian, loaferish and bought in the sales on Oxford Street. His watches—of which there were many—were a range of silly colours and eccentric shapes.

When cornered, he claimed to read Joyce, Ford and Conrad. Rereads of Fleming and Wodehouse were a more accurate library. His opinion of Miss Elizabeth Bennet was not favourable (though he liked Mr B and held a wary respect for Darcy). *Wuthering Heights*, according to Ambrose, was the dullest book ever written.

He had not read a newspaper in some time.

Everything Ambrose Zephyr knew about cuisine he learned from his wife. He was allowed in the kitchen, but under no circumstance was he to touch anything. He was a courageous eater, save Brussels sprouts and clams. His knowledge of wine was vague and best defined as Napa good, Australian better, French better still. Kir royale was his drink of occasion. For an Englishman, he made a poor cup of tea.

He believed women to be quantifiably wiser than men. He was neither a breast nor a leg nor an ass man; hair could be any length, any colour. Ambrose preferred the complete puzzle to a bit here, a piece there.

He stood when someone entered the room. He walked to the street side. Opened his wife's door first. He could be trusted.

Ambrose Zephyr worked as the creative wallah for Dravot, Carnehan. Ill-mannered competitors termed it the D&C. Messrs Dravot and Carnehan had long ago divested their interests in the advertising agency to a globalizing media concern. The principals then went off to seek other fortunes and left Ambrose working for a wise and exhausted woman named Greta.

Co-workers considered Ambrose to possess an inventive if journeyman approach to the creative process: on time, on budget, realistic, reasonable. He was neither star nor guru. Ambrose was comfortable with that. A client is in the business of selling something, he often said, but that something is usually not Ambrose Zephyr.

———

With his heels to the wall Ambrose stood an inch or two under six feet. Excluding the inevitable middle-years-droop of waist and waddle, his frame was thinnish. His head, well seasoned, carried the same amount of hair it did when he was a boy. His eyes were creased at the corners and as blue as the day when, fifty years before, a young and sad Queen had come home from Africa.

Those who knew him described Ambrose Zephyr as a better man than some. Wanting a few minor adjustments, they would admit, but didn't we all. His wife described him as the only man she had loved. Without adjustment.

Indeed, said the doctor. Arrangements.

Ambrose Zephyr suggested, for all in the outer office to hear, that the doctor might want to wait one damn minute before suggesting that Ambrose might want to arrange his remaining days. Days that until moments before had been assumed would stretch to years. With luck to decades. Not shrink to weeks.

If that, said the doctor.

The room filled with fog. The doctor became a

blurry lump behind the desk. The air turned as thick as custard, sauna hot. Ambrose struggled to keep his questions from spilling out with his breakfast in a puddle on the floor.

Something of a mystery, answered the doctor.

Not contagious as far as we can tell.

Fatal? Yes, quite.

Very sure.

—

Ambrose Zephyr was married to Zappora Ashkenazi, a woman as comfortable in her own skin as anyone else. She had kept her name for the apparent reasons, would have preferred to have been born a Frenchwoman, suffered fools with grace and a smile, loathed insects.

She had decorated the Victorian terrace in tastefully Swedish DIY, updating as budget and wear dictated. She was resigned to the likelihood that a *pied-à-terre* in the sixth arrondissement might not be in her future. She was content with that.

She wore the best labels she could afford and knew the mysteries that moved a £500 ensemble to the £50 rack. Red and black and white were her 'colours.' Accessorizing she considered well worth the effort, and her earrings were almost always perfect with that outfit. She owned one pair of stilettoed shoes that hurt just to look at. But Ambrose liked them. Which was enough.

She read everything. Russian epics, French confections, American noir, English tabloids had at one time or another taken their place in a wobbly pile beside the bed. Non-fiction was too much like school, she said. Experimental literature left her cold and annoyed and despairing for the so-called modern craft. She had lost count of how many times she had read *Wuthering Heights*.

She could walk into a kitchen she had never seen before and—without a recipe—plate a meal worthy of a starred review in half the time it took her husband to find an egg to boil. Her kitchen was full of cookery books that had never felt the splash of an errant sauce. She read them, she displayed them; they felt good in hand. They completed the room. Like earrings.

Men brought out her best and made her laugh. She liked most beards, hated all moustaches and furrowed her brow at the mention of tattoos. Height and weight and size didn't matter. Manners and nice shoes mattered. Doing the better thing mattered.

Her shoulder was ready when friends felt a cry coming on. She knew where to offer opinion and when to shut up. She could juggle oranges. She lied only a little, and they were always white.

Zappora Ashkenazi was the literary editor for the country's third most-read fashion magazine. Her publisher had wanted to introduce the magazine's reluctant readership to both new and classic literature, and if that literature held a passing link to couture, so much the better. It was a job with challenge: Austen, Woolf and Parker had never, so far as Zappora knew, assembled a spring collection. Yet those who read 'On the Night Stand' every month did so faithfully and first. Her writing was known for its economic style and refreshing avoidance of simile. Her husband was her first reader. Every word, every draft. You always have an interesting story to tell, he would say.

Zappora started in the fashion trade as a photographer's dresser. She flipped collars, fanned skirts, hitched pants, buttoned, tied, zipped. By the end of the first hour with her first model on her first day of her first real job she was given her first nickname.

Zipper.

She was very proud.

Zipper was not quite as tall as her husband, not quite as thin and not quite as old. Her hair was dark and fine and trimmed precisely every eight weeks. Coloured, perhaps tied with a ribbon, as required.

Her eyes were creased at the corners. She wore glasses when reading. The glasses were purchased in a small shop in Paris, around the corner from an antiquarian bookshop.

———

Zipper sat silent beside her husband, thinking how curious it was that her body had stopped working. That the doctor sounded like he was speaking under water.

She wondered what would happen if she got up and left. Better yet, hadn't come in at all. She clung to the sense of it.

I am not in the room.

Ambrose is not unravelling into the sweating, pasty stranger sitting next to me.

We are at home, preparing a meal for friends or deciding which film to see or selecting which book to curl up with or standing on the doorstep watching that annoying cat with those stupid birds.

We are not here.

None of this is happening to us.

Depending on the storyteller, Ambrose and Zipper met for the first or second time in the offices of Dravot, Carnehan. The third most-read fashion magazine in the country was at the time a fledgling and unread concept. It was being pitched to the city's advertising community in an effort to change that.

Messrs Dravot and Carnehan sat at one end of their unnecessarily long boardroom table. Ambrose stood in a corner trying to look creative.

He was the only man in the room not wearing a tie. The magazine's presentation team was led by a painfully loud publisher and trailed by a nervous junior editor, introduced as Young Ms Ashkenazi Who I Believe Will Be Heading Up Our Literary Efforts.

Ambrose would later admit to a nagging sensation of having seen this Ms Ashkenazi before. How he could not place her, but that her handshake felt small, warm, a touch damp. How he could not take his eyes off her. And how, more than once, he had narrowed his gaze to watch her, topless, eating tapas on a beach in Spain. She might have been twenty, maybe twenty-one years old. It was hard to see clearly, Ambrose would explain, what with the sun and the heat and the glare off the sea.

Zipper had an equally odd feeling throughout the meeting. She thought, but couldn't be sure, that she knew the slightly handsome man in the corner who said nothing. (What she never mentioned to anyone was the pleasant hum she felt as Ambrose spent the meeting trying not to glance at her breasts. Or that she found his periodic squint boyishly charming.)

Looking back, Ambrose and Zipper agreed the meeting could not have ended soon enough. As we'll-be-in-touch's went around the room, Ambrose complimented Ms Ashkenazi on her glasses. In that moment Zipper recalled where she had seen this man before.

Coffee? Ambrose then suggested.

It's Zappora. Zipper, actually.

But if you'd rather not . . .

Zipper smiled.

You're busy then . . . not to worry. Right. *Zipper*? Well. Yes. Lovely. Perhaps another time . . . Have we met? No, my mistake. There you are. Sorry. Right. Well.

Zipper remembered the rain in Paris. Tea would be brilliant, she said.

Ambrose escorted the magazine team to the street. While everyone waited for taxis and compared notes for their next presentation, Zipper conjured a case of performance nerves and told the team she'd catch up. Ambrose never went back to the office.

They spent the rest of the morning and the better part of the afternoon in a tiny café near Seven Dials. The next day a grinning Ambrose turned up at D&C at noon, wearing a shambled version of the clothes he had worn the day before.

Ambrose Zephyr later claimed that Zipper was the only woman he had ever been honest with. Not that he had ever misled anyone (perhaps a mild fib here and there), but with Zipper there would be no showing off, no blurring of unfortunate detail, no exaggeration for effect. In the face of all reason she was interested in him as he was. Not as he wished he was.

From that morning across the boardroom table, or earlier—depending on the storyteller— on a narrow street in Paris, Ambrose and Zipper were almost effortless.

They were married beside an anonymous willow near a statue of Peter Pan.

It was a small, drenched affair. All parents attended, as uncomfortable as newly met in-laws can be, but managing to find common ground in grumbles about the weather, the venue, the damned informality of it all. A blown light bulb from the recently acquired and completely bare Victorian terrace was broken under foot.

The following week a notice ran in the social pages of the Sunday editions:

ZEPHYR/ASHKENAZI. Saturday last, at Kensington Gardens. Ambrose Zephyr (Esq) and Zappora Ashkenazi (Ms), attended by Katerina Mankowitz (Ms) of Bayswater and Frederick Wilkes (Esq) of Her Majesty's Foreign Office. The bride, who will retain her maiden name, wore a vintage ensemble in off-white, tailored by Umtata's of Old Jewry. The couple is currently honeymooning on the continent. Their long-term plans were not available at press time.

Why you? Why anyone? responded the doctor.

I'm afraid not. Nothing to be done.

Unlikely, but perhaps.

Could be, but doubtful.

How long? Thirty days. Give or take.

Faculties may dull a bit. Blurred eyesight, ringing ears, numbed fingertips. That sort of thing. Happens rather quickly as far as we can tell.

Yes, the doctor offered, unfair would be a very good word about now.

Ambrose Zephyr's father toiled as a wordsmith for one of the more popular broadsheets of the day. Not long after writing his son's wedding notice, he had taken an early retirement. Enough reading about it, he told his wife.

Mr Zephyr died five days later. His heart had stopped as he walked to the corner shop for milk and the day's papers. There was no good reason, said the coroner.

Ambrose's mother called her son at the offices

of D&C. When Ambrose rang off, he threw his collection of antique type blocks across the room. They shattered the window separating him from the creative department. He sat there, surrounded by bits of glass and stared at by the younger talents in the office, for most of the morning.

In the months that followed, Mrs Zephyr took to calling her son at all hours, moaning about this ache or that pain. She began complaining about her tea, convinced someone had changed the mixture after two hundred years and how dare the bastards. She whined about the Queen.

On the good days Ambrose would offer, as pleasantly as he could, to take his mother to the National Gallery. Too crowded, she said. What's on the telly? Not *that* tea.

One Sunday afternoon, Ambrose stopped by for a visit. He found his mother sitting on the floor in her kitchen, surrounded by a week's worth of newspapers, whimpering at the mess around her.

I can't remember his face, she said.

A neighbour called Ambrose the next day to say his mother had passed quietly in her sleep. That evening, for the first time since he was old enough to read, Ambrose Zephyr did not look at a newspaper. There were other things happening in the world.

—

Ambrose Zephyr sat dumb and frozen on his front step. He may have seen something like the elderly man from number twelve carrying his tiny dog around the park. Or number eighteen returning from work, her children bouncing on the pavement and brandishing their day's art. Or the neighbour-hood stray rousing from its spot on the window ledge and strolling defiantly towards the birds.

Ambrose and Zipper made something like love that night. It was rough, frantic, tearful, quick.

Ambrose rolled away and went downstairs without saying a word. Zipper lay perfectly still, staring at the ceiling. Tears trickled into her ears. She thought she could hear her husband shaking in the dark.

Ambrose Zephyr began life a loved if overshad-
owed baby. Mrs Zephyr's labour started while
she was listening to the radio: the King was dead
and his daughter, now a young and sad Queen,
was returning from Kenya. Mr Zephyr was
delayed at the office—a new Queen did not come
along every day—and could not meet his son
until the special edition had started coming off
the presses.

———

Not so many years later, on a Saturday evening, Mr Zephyr took young Ambrose to the newspaper's offices. He showed his son the collection of retired wood and lead typefaces on display in the lobby. Young Ambrose liked the way the small type blocks felt large and heavy in his hand. He liked the tidy way each type was organized—one letter, one cubby—in a large flat wooden drawer. At the same time, he was angry that Z lived in such a small space compared to A. It isn't fair, he said with a dark scowl.

His father tut-tutted. Such is the manner of alphabets, he said. Some types are luckier than others. A may have more space in the drawer, but Z is no less important, particularly when it comes to words like zebra.

Or Zephyr, said Ambrose, straightening his small back.

Or Zanzibar, said his father. A place very far away.

A place with *two* z's?

Indeed. And two a's.

I think I would like that place, said Ambrose.

Mrs Zephyr worked as a junior art appraiser for a

large and prestigious auction house. The art she usually appraised was neither. When her son was eight or perhaps nine she took him on his first visit to the National Gallery. To see the proper stuff, she said.

She explained all that they saw: who the artist was, where the painting had come from, how old or new it was, who the people on the canvases were. Ambrose found some of the paintings boring, particularly those with snobby children in satin suits and silly collars. He liked the paintings that featured a lot of blood. Or people dying. This preference he kept from his mother.

Ambrose also noticed quite a few paintings of naked women. Lying on beds, wrestling with naked men, holding haloed babies, admiring themselves in mirrors. Ambrose wondered whether artists ever got erections as they painted these women. This question he also kept from his mother.

When Mrs Zephyr started talking about the *school* of this or the *ism* of that, Ambrose stopped listening. To him what he saw was what it was. Some paintings made him wonder, some made him giggle, some made him squirm. The Dutch Master with his floppy clown hat and thin beard and bright eyes, the chubby girls with their chubby dogs, the giant sunflowers drooping out of their pot like alien plant people with one bulging green eye.

. . . painted by a troubled young man, Mrs Zephyr was saying, . . . cut off part of his own ear . . .

Ambrose went back to looking. What he saw didn't need his mother going on about symbols and meanings and madness and genius, he thought. She knew a lot, but she didn't know when to stop complicating things. The sunflowers were like none he had ever seen, ear or no ear, troubles or not.

Ambrose Zephyr liked what he liked and didn't like what he didn't like.

It was as simple as that.

=

Zipper woke to what felt like something heavy being dragged from under her, mingled with the sound of her husband's whispers.

Must go now . . . leave today . . . no time . . . no waiting . . . arrangements . . . places to be . . . a list . . . A is for . . .

Ambrose was naked. Sweat dripped off him as he rummaged under the bed. The large suitcase snagged on the bedsprings. He pulled it free and in the same motion threw it on the bed.

Austria? . . . no . . . B for Belize? . . . no . . .
people to see . . . things must be done . . . make a
list . . . have a plan . . . go now . . . C is for . . .

It was a square and handsome case: oxblood
leather, reinforced corners, brass hinges. A thick
handle. A man's handle. It looked like it had never
been used for anything other than storage.

━━

As a boy, Ambrose Zephyr was considered by the neighbours to be well mannered, agreeable and quiet. *Average* was a word often used. That is, they said, aside from the travel brochures. And the alphabets.

He spent days alone in his room, compiling addresses for every embassy, mission and consulate in London. He wrote letters, in his best hand, to each ambassador or commissioner or consul explaining that he was planning to visit

their country in the very near future and would Sir
or Madam be so kind as to possibly forward any
and all information concerning their fine country
at the earliest possible convenience yours very
sincerely Master Ambrose Zephyr Esq. He worked
for hours perfecting the proper amount of swoosh
to his Z's.

On one wall of his room he had taped a large
map (which the Prime Minister's office had forwarded after Ambrose had enquired about the
nations of the Commonwealth and was there, Mr
Prime Minister, Sir, a particular reason why each
was shaded pink). Ambrose stuck redheaded pins
in the places that replied with the glossiest literature. Within a few weeks, Switzerland became a
small red hedgehog popping from the top of an
Italian boot.

When he wasn't corresponding with digni-
taries, Ambrose Zephyr was drawing. A's through
Z's. In the hundreds. Twenty-six at a time, plus
punctuation, numerals and ampersands.

Some of his alphabets were illustrated with
less popular members of the animal world: *A is for
anaconda, B is for booby, C is for codfish*. Some
depicted the world on his map: *D is for a Beach in*

the Dutch Antilles, E is for the Windy Coast of Elba, F is for Palm Trees in Florida. Some combined the two themes: *G is for Geckos in the German Woods, H is for Hellenic Capybaras in a Taverna, I is for Italian Bats in the Vatican Belfry.* When his father asked why A wasn't apple or B wasn't bird or C wasn't cat, young Ambrose explained that things didn't always have to be the way you'd expect.

Everybody does apples and birds and cats, he said, and it's boring to do what everybody else does and I'm not much good at drawing cats anyway I can never get the feet right.

A list of what? said Zipper.

. . . Calcutta . . . sorry? whispered Ambrose.
List? Yes. What?

Come back to bed.

Places . . . things . . .

What things?

Places . . . A is for . . .

Zipper pulled the duvet and her knees to her
chin and watched her husband empty the suitcase. Scores of brochures, advertisements, maps,

booklets, supplements, catalogues and flyers spilled onto the bed. Together with hundreds of drawings: some childish and faded, others by a more accomplished hand. All of them letters. A through Z. Everything formed a small mountain on the bed and spilled onto the floor.

Where? said Zipper.

Things, said Ambrose.

Like?

Places. A to Z equals twenty-six. A month equals thirty. The doctor said as much. Or is it twenty-nine? What year is this? Twenty-eight? A month, give or take.

I know what the doctor said. Are you all right?

Fine.

Then come back to bed.

What would you do?

What?

DO. What. Would. You. Do.

About what?

Time, time, time. Thirty days. No time. Weren't you listening?

Don't ask me that.

———

Tea came and went as Zipper reviewed her husband's list. *Places . . . Things. 1) A is for a Portrait in Amsterdam. . . .* There was no mention of putting affairs in order, no alternative remedies, no sprinkling of ashes under an anonymous willow in Kensington Gardens. Zipper's mind spun. This was not her Ambrose, she thought at first. But then, apparently, it was.

Paris being so far down the list and what happened after Zanzibar and why was X blank and how and what with and what if and are you mad and should we and shouldn't we and how could you and don't do this don't *be* this don't go without me don't go at all were thoughts Zipper fought to keep down.

Instead, she frowned and suggested that Andalusia might be nicer this time of year.

Habitually (in blind panic, she would later admit), Zipper edited. She pencilled a stroke through Valparaiso, a place she had never heard of, and in the margin wrote *Venice*.

The love they made that morning was tender, lingering and generous. She before he.

After, they talked of the Bridge of Sighs.

A.

The ferry from Harwich crossed a rough and cold
sea. The passage did not agree with Zipper and she
spent most of it below decks. Ambrose, waved off
for useless hovering, spent most of it at the railing
watching the lights along the European shore
grow brighter on the horizon. They ate lunch the
next day in a café at the edge of a pretty square
in Amsterdam.

Ambrose was dressed in his linen travel number: hastily pressed, pocket-squared. Zipper in a

white cotton blouse and black trousers cut in a capri style. Ambrose had always admired the way her back moved in that outfit. Her shoes were comfortable. Red.

Amidst sips of coffee and suggested itineraries, Zipper remembered a conversation.

Lovely, she said.

Sorry. What? Ambrose said.

The Velázquez.

Sorry? Yes.

They had been married most of a year. Having coaxed Ambrose into taking her on one of his usually solitary visits to the National Gallery, Zipper had done some reading beforehand.

Venus at Her Mirror, Zipper said.

The Rockeby Venus, said Ambrose.

The model was somebody's mistress?

The king of Spain. Philip, I think.

Had a thing for black taffeta sheets.

The king?

The mistress. And didn't a suffragette attack her with a knife?

The mistress?

The painting. Are you listening?

Right. Yes.

It's the sheets, Zipper said. They highlight the form. Her form. And Velázquez painted her hazy reflection in the mirror on purpose. Forces the eye to the form. Sorry, *her* form. Critics said the reflection looked unfinished. The optics were wrong. We should be seeing her torso reflected in the mirror. How am I doing?

Sorry. Yes. Lovely.

What, precisely, is so lovely?

Her. This. The Velázquez.

Why?

Because it is.

That's it?

I think so. Yes.

You're impossible, Zipper said. All I know is what I've read. All I'd like to know is what *you* know. What *you* think.

About what?

About *why*, damn it. Why the sheets and the optics and the mistress and the unfinished reflection? Why love it so much? Why her?

It is what it is, said Ambrose. Lovely.

You're exhausting.

Fine. If you insist, it reminds me of you.

Really. My backside is not nearly so lovely.

I wasn't looking at her backside.

Really.

I was looking at her front. The slope of the neck. Curve of the breasts, the smooth stomach. The gentle hollow around the navel. Her face.

You're imagining things.

Isn't that the point?

They thought better of visiting the Rijksmuseum together.

Zipper said she wasn't sure how she would spend the day. Ambrose did his best to reassure. There was, he said, no need to worry. They kissed and Ambrose set off to find a portrait he had seen before. But long ago and from very far away.

A younger Ambrose arrived behind his time, having spent most of the previous day in the pub with Freddie Wilkes.

It was the oldest lecture theatre on campus: a cavernous circular space with graceful plasterwork, smelling of mould and varnish and nervous sweat. The few windows it had were small, painted forever shut, and set high behind tiers of hard benches worn by a century or two of first-term buttocks.

Ambrose found a seat in the back rows and consulted his schedule. *The Place of the Portrait.* Below him the professor paced the dais, a small man gesturing with a long pointer at his latest slide: a Rembrandt, late in the artist's career. The reproduction was poor. The slide was scratched from years of projection, the contrast blown, the detail flattened to blobs.

It was a group portrait. *The Company of Captain Frans Banning Cocq and Lieutenant Willem van Ruytenburch,* announced the professor. Painted in 1642. You may, if you must, call it *The Night Watch*.

Captain Cocq's company—by the professor's pointed count—consisted of thirty-five adults, two children, one chicken and one dog, as well as various lances, spears, pikes, walking canes, drums, flags and muskets.

The professor rambled at length about dynamic magnetism and profound insight and asymmetric composition. NOTE IF YOU WILL, he kept yelling . . . the significance of this . . . symbolism of that . . . transcendence of genre . . . portrait of genius . . .

Ambrose raised his thick head and stared at the projection. Not once had the professor mentioned a shadowed half-face, hardly visible behind the painted crowd, peeking back at Ambrose with a pair of bright and smiling eyes.

In a grand and old department store Zipper wandered from floor to floor. Here a blouse held to her chest and re-hung on its rack; there the silk of a scarf, fingered and left folded. She sampled a lipstick that matched, precisely, the colour of her shoes. Assistants asked if madame required help. Zipper felt her eyes water and managed no thank you. She left the store without buying anything.

She came across a small bookshop in a tilted narrow building. A sign in the window advertised Gently Read Literature, Items for Composition and Correspondence Within. Zipper shuffled around the shop, finally settling on a small leather journal, rounded at the corners. An envelope for keeping reminders and receipts and bits of things was bound inside the back cover, a thick elastic band held all in place. The proprietor was still counting change as Zipper ran out of the shop.

She struggled to catch her breath, needed to sit down, went cold, thought she was going to vomit. She found a bench overlooking a canal and sat on her hands to hide the tremors. She stared at a passing tourist barge, her eyes filling with panic as those on board practised ducking under foot-bridges yet to come.

The shaking stopped as suddenly as it had begun. Zipper had nothing to wipe her eyes. Flustered, she used the sleeve of her blouse. She stood, unsure of her knees, and headed off to meet her husband at the train station.

Ambrose Zephyr reviewed the departures board, confirmed the overnight train would be leaving on time and made his way to the platform to meet his wife. If someone were no wiser, he might have looked as content as a man on holiday.

Zipper watched her husband approach. Relieved at his relaxed way, she closed her journal. A souvenir postcard—a garish reproduction of a group portrait by Rembrandt—peeked from the envelope inside the cover. Ambrose paid no attention. He was too busy telling his story.

. . . bigger than I expected. Enormous. More like a company of giants . . . There he was, behind the watchmen, the children, the chicken, the dog, the lances and spears and pikes and canes, the drums, the flags, the muskets . . . the master himself, peeking over a shoulder with those laughing eyes, I swear they winked . . .

Ambrose flailed and paced like an awkward conductor.

. . . and sweep and swirl and banners and action and such a good Rembrandt and luscious and bold and warm and thick with amazing outfits . . . the lieutenant in yellow of all things . . .

Ambrose caught his breath.

. . . and the genius?

Zipper ventured a guess. His use of light?

Work for hire, said Ambrose. Commissioned and paid for by the Captain et al. Hah! *There's* your genius. There's the art.

Zipper smiled. Until then, she had always assumed the Rembrandt was what it was.

On the night train to Berlin, Ambrose slept as well as anyone sitting upright on a train might. Zipper sat clutching the journal until her hands went clammy. She tried opening it a few times. A thousand words flew through her head but she couldn't manage to land any on the page.

After a while she gave up and watched the dark grey countryside speed past her reflection in the window.

B.

They sat at an outdoor table on the Unter den Linden. The sky was clear, blue, welcoming. The lime trees showed an early-spring green and offered comfortable shade.

Nearby stood a brooding Brandenburg Gate, all heavy stone and column. Tourists and locals and friends and lovers were enjoying the morning, strolling through the gate as if it wasn't there.

Zipper Ashkenazi's legs stretched from under

her, her shoes off. She watched a street entertainer prepare for the day's performance: unfolding a music stand, tuning a battered violin. She had passed a poor night, but on this morning and in this place she was content.

Ambrose stewed. He knew he needed to be here. He knew he needed to get past this. He knew it would make Zipper happy. But still he fussed and squirmed in search of a comfortable place in his chair. He kept an eye on the gate and scowled.

He claimed he was only thinking of his uncle, but Zipper knew there was more to it than that.

At one time or another, Ambrose had spoken of his Uncle Jack. How he had taught an annoyingly inquisitive nephew the subtleties of life. The first gentleman I ever met, Ambrose would say.

Every Remembrance Sunday, Jack came up to the city, wearing the same threadbare jacket and regimental tie he had worn the year before. His shoes always shone, he smelt freshly shaved, he stood whenever Mrs Zephyr entered or left the room. He had an unsure smile that matched his limp.

One particular November young Ambrose asked his uncle about the war. What had he done? Where had he been?

All over, said Jack. France, Holland, Berlin.

That's right. Germany.

Wasn't very nice.

People weren't very nice either.

Didn't like us, I suppose. They didn't like a lot of people.

They did. People they'd no business killing.

Friends? A few.

No. I didn't help my friends. I was away.

A few years later at his uncle's funeral, Ambrose read about someone named Sylvia. She had died when an air raid blew up her house near Spitalfields. Jack had left her a note, apologizing for not being there. For not keeping her safe.

Zipper knew that, with odd exception, Ambrose held a modern view of the world. He kept himself informed well enough, knew there was neither black nor white, believed what the BBC told him. Yet when she reminisced about her younger location-shoot days in Germany, she could watch his view become as black and blind as ash. With an unnerving Berlin at its centre.

In its greyness. The weather always threatening, the streets always wet. The architecture all cold stone: large and hard and lacking in windows.

With its inhabitants. Sour and stiff with permanently furrowed expressions. They spoke a jarring language: phlegmy, incapable of expressions of love. No one smiled. Laughter was faked. There never seemed to be any children.

With its music. Unlistenable. Funereal. Loud.

And its ghosts. Prowling, wearing uniforms, black, brown, grey. Lurking in doorways, dropping bombs on houses, burning Zipper's books. Watching and waiting to steal her away.

That was then, Zipper said. Jack was then.

She pulled Ambrose to his feet and they set off to walk the city she knew.

They made their way through the Reichstag. Once an asylum run by madmen, now through its centre an atrium of glass and mirror poured sky into the building and warmed Ambrose's upturned face.

They visited the zoo, where people had once eaten the animals left behind. On this day it was full of children, laughing at the monkeys, waving at the pandas, having their photographs taken by tired parents.

Along more than one boulevard Ambrose and Zipper jostled past crowded coffee bars and neon dance clubs and persistent gypsy beggars; bored fashion models and charged young lovers and old people with old dogs; graffiti artists and boisterous hawkers and women for sale and men who smiled like cartoon spies and made Ambrose chuckle.

They walked, perhaps a little lost, along Oranienburgerstrasse and through an ancient neighbourhood. They asked directions from a young man with a long and unkempt beard. He mumbled through his whiskers and pointed vaguely down the street. Zipper thanked him in the only Yiddish she could recall. The man grinned and shuffled Ambrose and Zipper along their way.

As dusk came, they returned to the avenue under the lime trees. The street performer was calling for last requests. Ambrose watched a woman in tailored red trousers and a black turtleneck approach the violinist. She whispered in his ear. The performer bowed and played the opening notes of the woman's request. She turned to her companion, a reluctant gentleman with greying hair, and offered her hand. The couple danced to a waltz composed by a German whose name Ambrose could not recall.

This is now, Zipper said, as she picked up a small stone and slid it in her pocket. The sky grew dark and the stars came out.

Ambrose smiled and asked if she had said something. If she was safe. If she was happy.

C.

As the high-speed train crossed into France, its vending machines served Ambrose Zephyr a breakfast of stale croissant and muddy coffee. He checked his watch, took a measure of the fields whizzing past the window, and announced to his wife that an improved lunch would, with luck, be served in Chartres.

Zipper declined breakfast for the apparent reasons. In silence she fretted over maths: days spent, days remaining, days to come. Couldn't we just stay in one place, she thought. *C rhymes with P.* Which stood for Paris. Too many days away.

She tried thinking of clever ways to rearrange the alphabet. Her brain refused the work. Instead she imagined a proper meal and a change of clothes; a nap in a quiet spot near the river, a view of the cathedral. At the least, food or fresh underwear or rest would pass the time while Ambrose attended church.

He was fond of repeatedly telling the story of his best day in advertising. A day, so the story began, when Ambrose Zephyr informed a client that they didn't need any advertising.

The client was a little church in the midst of London. For a hundred years or more, it had served its congregation plainly and true. But times—as are their custom—had changed. The parish had retired to the country and filled itself with a more distracted demographic. Those who worshipped at all were doing so in a score of different ways. The little church had fallen on competitive days.

A young priest was newly arrived in the parish and, in the way of the young and the new, saw an opportunity to make his mark. To put the arses, he whispered to Ambrose at their first meeting, back in the pews.

Ambrose was vague on church business. As a boy, he had attended Sunday lessons perhaps once or twice that he could recall. He was cinematically familiar with a few biblical stories. But he knew well the first law of his profession: walk in thy client's shoes. A tour of the little church was decided upon.

It stood, small and quiet and tucked away at the end of a noisy lane, surrounded by office blocks of glass and steel and looming business. Inside, three pews sat on either side of the aisle. Each pew held a sprig of fresh flowers. Changed every other day, said the priest with much pride. Whatever the market had in bloom. On this day the nave smelled of lavender.

A simple cross was placed on the altar, itself a plain wooden desk. A round window tucked among the rafters above the altar provided as much sunlight as could find its way between the office towers.

Someone had painted a pastel blue sky on the ceiling. Here and there a cloud. Angels, cherubim, beams of light were nowhere to be found. Around the walls were twelve tiny stained glass windows. Those, boasted the priest, were new.

Ambrose expected the windows to hold the usual scenes, rendered in heavy glass with thick colours and serious overtones. Instead they were as graceful as locket portraits. One depicted a young mother with a pushchair. In another a team of small boys played football. Here was a wedding party. There a lovers' kiss. An old man walking in a park with his dog, a tearful goodbye, a welcome home. The windows were the stations of a life, but the life was anyone's.

Ambrose spent a long time with the young priest's windows, quietly moving around the nave and saying nothing. Finally the priest cleared his throat and broached the subject of professional opinion. Where do we begin? he asked.

A party, answered Ambrose.

A party?

With a bar. Music, all kinds. Food, all kinds. Games for the children. Fun.

A *party*?

Any day but Sunday.

———

Ambrose's story always ended with the dashing of a young priest's hopes. Television time and electronic billboards and colour supplements and celebrity endorsements were not the thing required.

Sandwiches were the thing, Ambrose said. Together with a place where one can rest, gaze up at a blue sky with a few gentle clouds and take a breath. This place, Ambrose declared as he tapped his finger on the seat of a pew, is where the arses will go. Here is all the advertising you need.

A charming story, those who had heard it too often would say, but hardly believable.

Lunch, as promised, was improved. The waiter appeared with dipped madeleines. As madame prefers, he said. Zipper blushed at the discreet nods between her husband and the maître d' as Ambrose left the café. Nibbling at the chocolate, she watched her husband turn in the direction of the cathedral.

Zipper found a ladies' atelier and slipped into a new outfit of black blouse, red silk scarf and white calf-length skirt. She remembered the restorative effects of French clothes. At a flower shop she bought a small bouquet of spring blooms. She walked down a steep cobbled lane and chose a quiet spot by the river with a clear view of the cathedral.

She opened her journal and thought of writing. *E is for Eiffel's tower, standing in Paris. L is for London and home. Z is for Zipper. T is for terrified. H is hopeless.*

The journal remained blank. Shadows lengthened as Zipper made her way up the lane to the cathedral. *L*, she thought, *is for lost*.

The day's crowds had thinned and Ambrose was easy to find. He stood near the middle of the nave, at the centre of a labyrinth inlaid in the stone floor seven hundred years earlier. A few pilgrims traced the labyrinth's penitent paths. Zipper was unnerved by how cold, how dark, how threatening the huge space was.

All around Ambrose were the cathedral's famous windows. Windows that poured blue light into the black and frigid gothic space; that told stories and offered answers and provided comfort; that beckoned locals and pilgrims and tourists, the committed and the curious. And had been doing so long before television and billboards and supplements and celebrity.

Zipper hovered near the door, memorizing the view of her husband gazing around the cathedral whilst old women circled him on their knees. He spun this way and that, not knowing where to look next. He caught sight of Zipper and smiled.

Truly, thought Zipper. It had been one of his best days in advertising.

Nearing midnight, the hum of Zipper Ashkenazi's mobile raised a sweat in the small of her back.

On the line: the publisher of the country's third most-read fashion magazine. A sour-candy woman named Pru. A yeller in the workplace, a screamer on the phone.

WHERE ARE YOU?

The sound of Pru's voice turned Ambrose away from watching Normandy scroll past the train. He checked his watch and cringed sympathetically to his wife.

In France, replied Zipper.

THE ISSUE IS CLOSING. Photo needs another page. Your page? BLANK. *Fave Books of Fab People.* Really, who bloody cares . . . WHERE?

I meant to call.

WORLDS ARE CRASHING, ZIP. Subs down. Ads cancelled. Printer wants for payment. Have you resigned or something?

I should have called.

HOW BLOODY RIGHT YOU ARE. I'm tired of keeping this rag afloat. Sick or something?

I needed some time.

BE MY BLOODY GUEST. Meanwhile, what am I supposed to do?

Give photo the page. I wish I'd called. Honestly. Sorry.

NOT HALF AS BLOODY SORRY, Zip, NOT HALF.

Something came up.

SOMETHING LIKE LEAVING? If you jump I bloody swear . . .

I need a month. Give or take.

NOW IS NOT the time. Ring when you get

back. THE BLOODY SEC—

Zipper closed the phone.

Ambrose borrowed his wife's phone and placed a call to D&C. Someone would be there. Greta was always there.

Grets? Ambrose.

France.

I know. Sorry.

Nothing. Something came up.

Sorry, no. I'm not leaving. Not exactly.

It's more personal. I'll explain later.

Yes, I should have called.

The client will be fine. Storyboards done, shoot booked, talent hired, wardrobe enroute, print ads on my desk.

Yes, I'm sure. Wrote them myself.

The pitch? You do the pitch.

Can't. Sorry. It should be you anyway. It's your agency, your client. I'm just the help.

The client does not hate you.

He does *not* hate Germans.

Get the account lads to lend a hand. Threaten the sack. They'll understand that.

I'm okay. Thanks.

How Long? A month. Maybe less. I'll let you know.

You'll do fine in the meantime.

I'll call if I can.

D.

On their fourth day from home, Ambrose and Zipper sat in comfortable beach chairs watching the English Channel. It was a bright afternoon, the sun was high, the offshore breeze chilled a day more winter than spring. But for the time gone by and the time of year, they could have been any honeymooning couple.

Despite her squinting and her husband's pointing, Zipper could not see England. Just there, Ambrose kept insisting, jabbing his finger northward. Zipper could see the row of vacant bathing tents stretching along the beach, gaily striped for the coming season. A small girl in blue gumboots playing with a large dog at the water's edge, a calm sea beyond. A few working boats idled in the middle distance; a few heavy ships ploughed the lanes farther out. But there was no far shore in her sight. Past the ships, said Ambrose. At the horizon. *Just there.*

Zipper gave up and lay back in her chair, annoyed. She knew the story. The Curious Talents of Ambrose Zephyr, or, The Business of Seeing Things Just There. To a disinterested listener, it might have been another tired story of the imaginings of children. To Zipper it was a story a concerned parent might quietly slip to his new daughter-in-law, just before he and the missus waved their happy children off to a wedding weekend in Deauville.

According to Mr Zephyr's story, at the age of eleven, perhaps twelve, Ambrose announced to his parents that he possessed a talent. The announcement occurred during the family's annual motoring holiday. They were on the Cornish coast.

I can see better than anything, young Ambrose said.

Any *one*, said his father.

Better than animals.

That is something, said his mother.

Better than binoculars.

You don't say, said Mr Zephyr.

I do say.

And how did you come by this talent? asked Mrs Zephyr.

Ambrose shrugged.

Indeed, said his father.

Ambrose's face began to glow.

He was standing on the last cliff of England, squinting as boys do, and seeing America. A soft blue lump, right at the horizon. Just there, Ambrose insisted, jabbing his finger westward. The Manhattan skyline emerged through the low ocean mist. His parents apologized for not being able to quite make out the details. They blamed the time of day and the angle of the sun.

Two summers later. On a tour through north-ern Europe Ambrose asked his mother to stop the car before each border crossing: could he walk the last few metres and stand on the frontier? At one such stop, recalled Mr Zephyr, his son's left foot stood in Belgium, the right in Luxembourg. Ambrose then peered along the line (invisible to the senior Zephyrs) as it crossed the road.

On the same holiday Ambrose also announced he could see the difference between one country's soil and another's. The difference (and the talent to see it) was never defined. There was, young Ambrose said, just . . . something. Denmark was . . . browner, he offered his perplexed parents.

And the air too. From one country to the next, Ambrose could detect a change in the smell of things. Sometimes cleaner, sometimes mustier. France smelt like apples, Germany like freshly cut grass, Holland like wet socks. Ambrose declared he could smell it the moment he stepped over each border. Hopping in and out of Luxembourg, he explained: flowers . . . dogs . . . flowers . . . dogs . . . flowers . . . dogs.

As Zipper and her new in-laws stood on the platform waiting for the groom to return with the cross-Channel tickets, Mr Zephyr's hushed story continued. His son's curious and increasingly annoying talent extended beyond the here-and-now. He could see the past. Events great and significant, faces grand and notorious, battles won and lost. The further back in time the better, apparently. With the proper amount of squint, explained the boy, he could see what had happened or who had walked on the ground where he stood. Ten, a hundred, a thousand years ago.

Young Ambrose offered proof: the time he had emerged from the underground near the Tower of London and there was the Duke of Norfolk's piked and dripping head, as if the Virgin Queen herself had pruned it the day before. Or the summer he saw William the Conqueror wading through the sunbathers on the Hastings shore. Or the party of Druids he watched at Stonehenge while Mr and Mrs Zephyr read the visitor pamphlets. They were just a work crew, Ambrose assured his parents. Squaring a few lintel stones.

The end of the story came when Mr Zephyr mentioned that he and the missus had once spent a lovely picnic afternoon watching their boy gaze across a flat and empty field in Flanders. He just stood there, said Mr Zephyr. For hours. And I have no doubt, he added with a wink, the boy was in mud to his knees. Ah, here's your train.

Ambrose Zephyr gave up. Can't seem to see it either, he said. He lay back in his chair. After a moment or two of watching a few clouds pass overhead, he told his wife what he remembered.

The bloody queues. Bathing tents, ices, chairs, towels, the loo. Stretched the length of the beach. We changed in our room. Ran half-naked through the lobby. It took us hours to find a vacant bit of sand. Nasty dogs and noisy children everywhere. The tents were a different colour that year. Were they green? I remember it was too cold to swim. The Channel was rough. First weekend of the season. Windy. Not even the local boats were out. You hated the sand. Yes you did. Insisted on wearing those horrible blue trainers. From the ankle up you were breathtaking. A fantastic bikini, red I think. Fine, black. I drank too much calvados. You read three books and mentioned what my father had said on the platform. You asked—in that voice you have—if I could see any soldiers on the beach. I said very funny and told you they had landed farther along the coast. Which made you laugh . . .

Ambrose Zephyr's voice trailed off. A moment later he spasmed himself awake.

Tired, he said, then drifted away again.

When she was certain her husband was well asleep, Zipper walked along the Corniche. She bought a postcard—an amateurish watercolour from some time ago. The bathing tents depicted were green, and judging by the crowds and the queues in the painting, it appeared the beginning of the season.

She returned along the water's edge. The girl in the blue boots had coaxed her dog from the water. Zipper watched them leave, then squinted out to sea.

There was England. Just at the horizon.

E.

The Windy Coast of . . . Zipper read, in a tone she reserved for certain circumstances. They were on a train bound for Paris, a flight to Pisa, a short hop to . . .

Elba, said Ambrose.

Just a thought, said Zipper. Why not stay in Paris? Get out of the airport for a while.

Napoleon wasn't keen on the place.

We could take a later flight.

But the views are spectacular.

They will be.

We'll be back to Paris in a few days, Ambrose said. And we always go to Paris. You're not tired of it?

Tired? Yes. Of Paris? No.

How's this then: *E is for Eiffel, a Tower in Paris*?

Zipper pretended to frown. Not quite the music of *The Windy Coast*, she said, but if you don't mind.

Get out of the airport for a while.

Whatever you think.

It was a tone Ambrose could never resist. Nor had ever much tried to.

Zipper awoke in a modest room on the top floor of a hotel—their hotel—tucked in a corner of Place Saint-Sulpice. A band of sunlight found its way between the mismatched towers of the church across the square, through the window and on over the bed. It came to rest across Zipper's face. She slid farther under the duvet, warm and safe.

Home, she thought. Another five minutes. Then she remembered where she was. Where Ambrose was. Off on his stroll.

———

Whether Ambrose remembered it or not was never the point. The fact remained: they *had* met, and it *was* the first time, on the Rue des Rosiers.

A younger Ambrose Zephyr is midway through his usual walk. Deep in the Marais, a spring downpour forces him into the doorway of an antiquarian bookshop. He huddles, his trench coat dripping on his shoes, and searches the sky for a break. He does not see the young woman coming through the door behind him.

A young Zipper Ashkenazi—on a break from working a fashion shoot—purchases a second-edition *gastronomique* published many years before. The book is in only fair condition and she barters well. A good souvenir, she thinks, of a first trip to Paris. The small volume slips into her coat pocket and she opens the shop door.

Zipper does not see the young man's face as the bell above the door chimes an exit. Ambrose, fretting about his shoes, does not hear the bell.

In the politest French she can manage, Zipper asks the young man's back to excuse her. A startled Ambrose turns and stares at the young woman. Zipper waits, then begins opening her umbrella. Ambrose continues staring, oblivious to weather, shoes, umbrella.

The rain continues.

The staring becomes annoying.

After some time, Zipper breaks the young man's gaze and glances at his feet. Ambrose rediscovers his manners. He steps into the street and allows the woman by. He apologizes in the politest English he can manage. He would have removed his hat, had he owned one.

The rain pours and Ambrose stands watching the young woman disappear under her umbrella. As Zipper steps to avoid a puddle, she glances back at the young man and looks away.

He smiles, having caught her out. She vanishes around a corner and chuckles at the thought of the young Englishman's ruined shoes and drowned hair. A hat, she thinks, might have gone well with the trench and the weather.

Something had changed. The air seemed off. The sunlight through the window felt cold. Zipper thought it might be the cobwebs of a too heavy sleep. She glanced at the bedside clock, padded to the ensuite and ran a bath. By now her husband would be passing Notre-Dame, stepping on the *point zero* marker as he went.

His *flânerie*, Ambrose called it. It was habitual, rarely altered in either route or duration. Friends called it his cliché, mentioning the beaten path, suggesting other sites and different sounds. Ambrose would politely nod his head and wander where he wanted. They have their Paris, he would tell Zipper. I have mine.

She slipped inch by goosebumped inch into the steaming water. Her toes wiggled at the other end of the tub. Zipper closed her eyes as the heat went to her bones, releasing wave after raw wave of terror. She tried imagining something else, but all she could see was their time. Their Paris . . .

The narrow street off the Boulevard Saint-Germain with its family *boulangerie* and two-table cafés and produce stalls. Where they had always bought a workman's lunch and a bottle of *vin de pays*. Where Ambrose would sneak a foul cigarette while she selected a pâté . . .

The Bastille roundabout. Where he would narrow his gaze and point out peasants laying siege to the prison. Where she had mastered the grace of walking in heels amidst the helter-skelter traffic . . .

Zipper's shoulders heaved, she gulped for air, fought for calm. She looked down at her body and thought of his hands.

In Place des Vosges. His hands on her. In the dark beneath Victor Hugo's window, her hands on him. Breathless mouths, wordless tongues, losing themselves. Under the plane trees in the middle of the night . . .

She buried her face in her hands. *You cannot have it*, she screamed through her fingers.

The antiquarian bookshop. Soon it would belong to other lovers, selfishly claimed as *their* Paris . . .

The *bouquinistes* near the Pont Neuf. He would be there . . .

Zipper pulled herself from the water, hurried to dress, ran for her life.

He would be there by now.

Zipper rushed along the quai towards the Pont Neuf, checked her watch. She was late. Yet she smiled. She knew where he'd be and it wasn't far away and she could slow down.

A *bouquiniste*'s stall caught her eye. It was decorated with the bric-a-brac of the printing trades: agate rulers, bindery clamps, typesetters' trays. A collection of old type blocks.

One particularly worn wooden cube felt soft and good in her hand.

Zipper found Ambrose at the downstream end of Île de la Cité. Lying on the cobbled breakwall that sloped at a comfortable angle into the Seine. He was, as usual, admiring the view along the river to the Eiffel Tower, peeking above the rooftops, far in the distance. Zipper sat beside him.

You smell like cigarettes, she said. How was the walk?

Ambrose lied. Lovely, he said. Zipper caught sight of his slowly trembling hands, the subtle curling and uncurling of fingers.

How was your lie-in? he said. Feel better?

Zipper lied.

As is the habit of lovers in Paris, they spent the rest of the day on the island in the Seine. They ate a workman's lunch, drank all the wine, waved to the *bateau mouche*.

At some point Ambrose lay his head in his wife's lap and stared through the trees to the sky. He said he thought it might rain. Zipper laughed.

Admit it, she said. It *was* you with the soggy shoes. Ambrose smiled.

What remained of the day passed quietly. Without a cloud in sight.

I bought you something, Zipper said. For missing Elba.

They were in a taxi enroute to the airport. She put the wooden type block in his palm and closed his stiff fingers around it. No peeking, she said.

He knew the character by touch. Uppercase, a bold sans serif from a headline tray. He felt the sharp zig and zag of the letterform. The smooth face of the block, the worn and rounded edges. Feels large and heavy for something so small, he said.

I bought you something too. Ambrose handed her a fat and tired edition of *Les Misérables*.

Zipper glanced through the rear window of the taxi. A tower in Paris, tiny and far away, flashed through the skyline and was gone. The taxi merged onto the *périphérique*.

F.

Late afternoon stretched across the Piazza della Signoria. A marble David—muscular, walleyed, tall for his age—ignored the sightseers crowded about his base. A few with cameras backed away from the horde, cautiously measuring their strides, trying to fit boy king and mugging companions in the viewfinder.

In a quiet corner of a café at the opposite end of the square, Ambrose Zephyr ordered wine. Two glasses. *Rapido*, he snapped.

Zipper was surprised at her husband's tone. She gave him a look he chose to ignore.

They sank low in their chairs. It had not been the day Ambrose had in mind. It had all been too much, too many.

Those who knew Ambrose would later say they were not much surprised by F. After all, they offered, hadn't his mother introduced him—*and at such a young age*—to the great art of Florence? Wasn't he proud—*annoyingly so*—of the university away-term he had spent flirting his way through the city? Did he not know its architects, its Medicis, its masters? By name *and* date, they said.

An old man moved past their table. He was a picture of the casual Italian gentleman: polished shoes, cufflinks and cravat, practical sunglasses. He carried a walking stick, tapping it lightly on the cobblestones as he moved along.

The stick missed Ambrose and Zipper's table. There was a minor collision; a drop or two of spilled wine, a stumble. The Italian gentleman apologized as his hand searched for the edge of the table. Ambrose swore under his breath.

Zipper glared at her husband a second time, applying more disgust, less surprise. Ambrose slumped deeper into his chair and sulked at the crowd across the piazza.

No harm done, Zipper said to the Italian gentleman. He turned his body in the direction of her voice and smiled.

Zipper found a third chair. The old gentleman asked if he might rest. Just for a moment . . . the joints, you see.

You smell like my wife, he said. Zipper was embarrassed by her suddenly blushed cheeks.

When we would walk. In our evenings along the river, she wore that fragrance. A wise and clever woman, my wife. This I know, she would say: A man can see a hundred women, lust for a thousand more, but it is one scent that will open his eyes and turn him to love. And he will never thank the angels for making him blow his nose that morning.

The sightseers under the marble boy king grew more boisterous.

These crowds, said the Italian gentleman. They take many photographs. Such a sad thing. Such a long way to come to take bad pictures of one's friends.

He shrugged. This city is too much for them. he said. Too many paintings, too many churches, too many Davids. Too many other people taking pictures. Can you see the Duomo? someone will ask. I can see the back of your head, another will answer.

But enough, he blurted in Ambrose's direction. Life is too quick for such gloom. There are other things to see.

Ambrose scowled.

The old gentleman searched for Zipper's hand. Indulge me a bit of a game, he said. He took her hand and cupped it between his.

Signora's blouse, he announced after a moment, is as white as our marble. Crisp and tailored, like a man's. The cuffs are rolled, the collar is turned. Very casual. The buttons open just so and—forgive me, signora—there is perhaps a peek of black lace, a peek of something.

A smile inched across Ambrose's face. The gentleman continued.

She wears a silk scarf—reds and golds, I think. A flowing skirt, calf length. Red again, like Il Papa's cardinals. But it is late in the day—she has slid her sunglasses to the top of her head. A strand of hair hangs to the side of her face. She squints with the low sun. The feet of birds at the corners of her eyes. Have I missed anything?

Signora's shoes, offered Ambrose.

Aaaah, said the Italian gentleman, there you are. Now you wish to play my game. Very well.

They are . . . black. Yes. Flat. For too much rushing around. For too many people. For too much art. But I am guessing. Better, I think, for walking by the river?

Ambrose looked at his wife. Zipper noticed it was the first time his eyes had brightened all day.

A third glass was summoned and a toast to marble kings was drunk. Ambrose apologized for his behaviour. Not my best day, he said. The Italian gentleman said there was no harm done. Ambrose asked him about his wife.

The old gentleman produced a small photograph and handed it to Ambrose. I have many, he said. They never seem to be where I leave them.

Ambrose smiled. He passed the photograph to Zipper.

She expected an old and faded portrait of a young and beautiful woman. Instead, the face that smiled stiffly from the photo was worn, fleshy, a little pale. But the eyes were clear, the hair well styled. An expensive scarf was tied loosely around the old woman's neck.

The face in the photograph had been embossed. Raised creases and furrows traced the features: scarf, hair, eyes. The shy smile.

I think she might be like your own signora, the Italian gentleman said. Something to see?

She was, said Ambrose. Is.

The Italian gentleman finished his wine and stood as best he could. He kissed Zipper's hand, begging forgiveness for leaving so abruptly.

I promised to meet someone by the river, he said, and tapped his walking stick across the piazza. As he passed the marble boy king, he pulled his pocket square with a flourish and quietly blew his nose.

===

The Mediterranean was passing far below them, Zipper Ashkenazi nudged her husband. You were talking, she said.

Sorry . . . dozed off . . . what? What did I say?

You kept asking why.

Why what?

I don't know. You were asleep.

Must have been dreaming.

Of?

A woman in the distance, approaching. She wades carefree through the desert sand. She looks back towards the sun. She is barefoot, her sandals clutched by the heels, dangling in one hand. Her other hand holds the hem of her white cotton robe. Each step trails a fine stream of sand, caught in the hot wind and blown towards the Nile. The sun backlights her figure through the cotton, catches a glint of silver and ebony on her bracelets. Her walk in the desert has left her flushed and bronzed. Her hair is dark and fine.

A camel appears from nowhere, blocking the view. Everything swirls into the art on a package of cigarettes.

A boy lies on his bedroom floor. He is twelve, perhaps thirteen years old. He is drawing, with painstaking accuracy, the art from a pack of Camels. The arabesque curves of the serifs on the A. The ellipsed E. Three palm trees, two pyramids, one camel with its skinny legs. The pyramids tucked under the camel's sagging belly. The boy is careful, colouring the camel's visible eye a brilliant blue. He even includes the elegant ampersand between the words *Turkish* and *Domestic*.

The camel turns his head and grins.

Why so sad, Master Zephyr?

The boy frowns.

Death? Yes yes, death hovers near us all. And it is sad that it makes us sad. But I know a story.

There once was a camel whose days begin in the shade of a palm on a nameless wadi, somewhere to the east of here. In the Sinai.

By the age of ten, the camel is a veteran of the trading routes from Alexandria to Tripoli. At twenty he walks the rich Aswan run, kneeling politely as nervous Japanese women climb aboard to have their portraits taken. At thirty he is done working, his knees worn thin. At forty, his days as a camel come to a peaceful end. Eyeing younger things in the Birqash market.

He is gutted and skinned. For seven days he feeds his owner, his owner's family, his owner's cousins, his owner's neighbours. His hide is sold for a good and fair price in the bazaar, to a maker of furniture who knows a good many buttocks would sit on such a fine and worthy leather.

Was there anything before his days as a camel, you ask? Yes yes, Master Zephyr. The camel was a man. As you will be. Successful, well fed, loved by a clever and honest and beautiful woman. Happy they lived. Simply as husband and wife. Without extravagance, just off the high road between Suez and Aqaba.

The man misses his wife every day. Even now, as a camel in your drawing, as a comfortable chair under a large rump. But he sees her every day. He watches her sleep.

Why, you ask? There is no why, Master Zephyr. It is just a story. Life goes on. Death goes on. Love goes on. It is all as simple as that. Years from now, even you will return. Perhaps as the ochre that colours an artist's brush. Or a kindly stray cat in a small park in London. And you will love the birds you chase.

And then the camel winked, said Ambrose, and disappeared in a puff of sand.

Zipper blinked away a tear. He hadn't meant to make her cry.

G.

The small bedouin woman sat on her haunches beneath the pyramids.

Her robes were black and billowed in the wind. She smoked a dark cigarette and played with a small Polaroid camera: holding it to the sunshine, tracing circles in front of her face, mimicking a self-photograph, watching for the soft image to emerge from its slot. She cooed and chirped and sang to herself. As a child might. Her grinning revealed the gaps of a few missing teeth.

She kept her place, apart from the mob of touts with their curative river water and stuffed crocodiles and plastic scarabs. Tourists scurried and counted out their dollars and pounds and yen and avoided her altogether.

Zipper noticed the woman, as Ambrose was otherwise occupied. He stood to the shade side of the cornerstone and leaned in to sight the edge of the Great Pyramid of Khufu. He closed his eyes to slits, gauging the angle of the corner, the smoothness of finishing stones, the tiny army of labourers far above. Naked and sweating and laying the final course.

Zipper left her husband and jostled away from the crowds. She found a quiet spot and sat in the hot sand. She watched the bedouin woman. Zipper wondered who or what was in the woman's photographs.

The woman stopped her play, beckoned Zipper. Come come, she said. Sit sit. There is nothing to be afraid of.

Ambrose leaned his face against the stone. He ran his hands across the rough surface, following a groove here, fingering a worn edge, clearing the grit from a notch there. Checking for true.

Hush hush, said the woman.

Your singing is beautiful, Zipper said.

And you are afraid.

Zipper's heart thumped in her ears. She felt her hands go cold.

I should get back, she said. My husband . . .

I know what you see, the old woman said. What frightens you. But what you see you must not fear.

Zipper's eyes welled up.

Everything will be well, the woman said. For you. For your husband.

Zipper wiped her face and forced a smile.

The sign admonished visitors: To Climb Or Scale Or Deface The Sacred Tombs Is Highly Forbidden In Order To Protect Their Fragile And Historical Nature.

Ambrose Zephyr likely thought otherwise. Nothing so enormous and so immortal could be that precarious.

Or that tempting.

———

Yes yes. Hold his hand. He will not be away so long. Not so long.

As she spoke, the bedouin woman turned to watch a man struggling to climb the pyramid.

Zipper followed the woman's gaze to find her husband standing on the cornerstone of the first course of the Great Pyramid. Ambrose was hunched over, hands braced on his knees, wheezing and coughing.

The photograph is amateurish: the horizon tilting wildly, the subjects fuzzy and almost out of frame, a blurred black fingertip across one corner. In the photograph a man stands atop a great stone block, stiff and uncomfortable, beaming and posing as best he can. Like a schoolboy Lawrence, awkward but having gotten away with something.

He is pale in the dusky sun. His linen suit is scuffed and wrinkled and has become too large. Below him, a woman stands shy and reluctant. She is flushed, gently tanned, but appears lost.

H.

Somewhere between the Giza plateau and Cairo their taxi ran out of petrol. The subsequent bus rattled and inched along with the city's traffic. There were no seats and no handholds. There was something that sounded like no brakes.

When Ambrose Zephyr and his wife arrived at the airport, a sudden sandstorm had closed the runways, briefly but effectively.

Connections, and Haifa, were missed.

I.

It would have been clear to those queuing for the flight, had they noticed, that the Englishman was having difficulty.

Ambrose Zephyr's face was drained white. He smelt foul, soiled, rotten in his own sweat. He stretched and curled and twisted his hands, rubbed his joints, cringed when he stood, shivered in the airport heat. Every few minutes his eyes bulged in their dark sockets. Like those of a person afraid of something he could hear or smell but not see.

He snapped at his wife after she had asked him, again, if there was anything she could do.

I am fine, Ambrose croaked.

Is there anything you need? Zipper forced the question through her teeth.

I need to be left alone.

Zipper wanted to throw something at him.

Enough, he said.

Hit him.

Stop *fussing*, he said.

Stop him. Stop it. Go home.

Ambrose seemed to recover as the queue moved to board the flight to Istanbul.

They sat in the last row: Ambrose, Zipper and an enormous young man who said that he was flying to visit his sister she is a nice dancer in a hotel viewing the Bosporus saving money for hospitality school so she may return to our family's taverna back home nice to meet you English couple on holiday I am presuming I study my English very much and you should come to our taverna someday such a nice couple you are though sir you do not look so well perhaps it is the flying maybe do you smell something?

Where was I yes my sister the belly dancer she will help me and our father who is being most lonely since our mother left to be with her sister who is my aunt and raises many goats and makes their cheese best in all the Mediterranean yes now the card yes here it is the hotel where there is a view and my sister dances come if you are feeling well perhaps a *hamam* could help sir yes Turkish bath very good for all ailments can bring the dead back to life for madame as well I very highly recommend but remember please the hotel where my sister dances and sees the Bosporus if you get a chance my sister really is most good at the dancing perhaps a little heavy in the hips she should lose some weight but then who shouldn't ha ha there I think we are here and landed you nice English couple have a nice day it is a pleasure to be flying with you now remember you come and visit my family's taverna someday best coffee in all the Mediterranean truly even better than Istanbul perhaps we will see each other again remember a Turkish bath will do you no harm try the bath near the Blue Mosque very old very safe I know it well sorry let me slide over a little so you can get by apologies yes it is small in here I am perhaps too big for such a little airplane ha ha here let me move my so sorry can you get your leg over there okay sorry just a bit further maybe if I inhale a bit.

Walking to the taxi rank, Ambrose told Zipper that he had once imagined a view across the Bosporus. Or had seen it in a movie. He couldn't recall which.

Perhaps, said Zipper, a proper Turkish bath will clear your head. At the least the smell.

As boys of thirteen or fourteen are prone to do, Ambrose Zephyr received his first lesson regarding the intrigues of the near East, and sex, from a woman.

The woman in question was not Polly or Penny or Patsy what-was-her-name who had lived a few doors down. Prunella or Poppy or Priscilla was the gangly one. Breastless, with braces that cut his lip during a stolen kiss in his parents' garden.

No. The woman in question worked for the wrong side but longed to work for the right side. She was willing and well able to use her nakedness under clinging bedsheets. She was born on the steppes of Russia, nimble with a code machine and a gun, breasted, blond, and in possession of a suite overlooking the Bosporus.

Her name was Tatiana, said Ambrose as he and Zipper got out of the taxi in front of the oldest bathhouse in the city.

Of course it was, said Zipper.

And Bond meets her in the hotel room, said Ambrose.

The one with the view?

Right. She's wearing nothing but a silk ribbon around her neck. Completely naked, and our man in a dinner jacket. Imagine that.

Imagine that.

Zipper thought of a polite and curious boy of thirteen or fourteen years, sitting alone in a cinema. Possibly a matinee near Piccadilly Circus. His eyes bugging at the views of Istanbul.

Zipper emerged from the women's side of the baths to find her husband attempting to brush the wrinkles and smell from his suit. His hair was slicked flat to his head, his face was flushed and shaved, his smile was broad. A child freshly plucked from the Sunday tub. Zipper's expression was black, her face drained of everything but anger.

How was your bath? Ambrose asked.

Excruciating, said Zipper.

Large attendant?

Amazonian.

Small towel?

Humiliating.

Steam?

I've had enough.

Luffah glove?

You need to deal with this.

Massage?

That is not it.

Oil? Liniments? Palm fronds?

THAT IS NOT THE POINT.

Zipper stared at her husband in disbelief. They were still standing in front of the Velázquez Venus.

I mean yes, that is a point. Just not *the* point.

Sorry, said Ambrose.

Stop apologizing.

Sorry.

The point is you never say anything. I haven't a clue what you think about anything important.

Sorry.

Stop it. Stop being so damned . . . absent.

Ambrose shrugged.

Don't you care about anything? I mean really have an opinion. Beyond *it's lovely?*

Fine, said Ambrose. If you must know. I think the Velázquez is remarkable because it doesn't matter to me that she was an actress or that the sheets are black. I think abstract expressionism is crap. I think Brussels sprouts are crap. I think I could paint but I don't have the nerve. I think I am an unbelievably lucky man who is married to a woman who I think looks a little like the Rokeby Venus and I think if I open my mouth to say something I think is important I think she will discover she's married a fool.

You are many things my love. A fool is not one of them. You're imagining things.

I am keeping things to myself. Having an opinion doesn't require sharing it with everybody.

It requires sharing it with me. Because *I* get to know what you think. *I* get to know you better than anyone else.

You do. Always have, always will, full stop. Let it go.

One more thing.

What?

You're wrong.

Am I?

Luck had nothing to do with us.

Outside the baths, Ambrose's scrubbed smile disappeared. THEN WHAT IS THE POINT?, he said, smoothing another crease in his suit. Deal with what? What would you have me do?

Care. Worry. Say something. Aren't you afraid?

Yes.

So?

So what? So there it is. Here I am. There's nothing to deal with. If there were I would do it. But there isn't and I am terrified and this isn't happening to you.

You selfish, silent, shitty bastard. This *is* happening to me.

Really? In less than a month, you'll still be alive.

Really. I can hardly wait. Lying in on Sundays? At last. A decent cup of tea? Brilliant. No more squinting, no more visions, no more imagination, no more silence? I can hardly fucking wait.

———

In a lane near the Blue Mosque, around the corner from the oldest bathhouse in the city, curious pedestrians might have noticed a rumpled Englishman embracing a sobbing woman as if she might fly apart. She struggled to free herself, he held tighter. He whispered, she lashed out. He kissed her wet eyes, she turned her face away.

After a moment or two, the woman said she was fine. The Englishman handed her a thin bauble, a *boncuk*. He told her that Turkish mothers pin the blue glass trinket to their children's clothes. To keep them safe.

The curious might have watched for a few more moments and then moved along and thought nothing more of it.

That evening Ambrose and Zipper found a bench in a corner of the gardens of Topkapi Palace, where grand and terrible sultans had once lived. Ambrose claimed the sultans had attended to the needs of their harems in this garden. After they had emerged from their baths, he said. Zipper said that sounded like something only a man would think up.

In the sultan's garden, Zipper and Ambrose stole as much love as they dared. A few buttons undone. Straps moved gently aside. The slip of a warm hand. The smell of bath oil and perfumed soap. Luffahed skin, sensitive to the touch. They whispered to each other not to worry.

The evening deepened and the lights on the Asian side grew more numerous. Zipper asked where the *boncuk* had come from. Ambrose said he had bought it while waiting for his lover to emerge from her bath.

They sat for a while longer and wondered whether the nice hotel dancer would ever get back to the taverna and whether she was as good as her brother had advertised.

In my opinion, said Ambrose, the best in all the Mediterranean.

The next morning near sunrise, London called nine times in as many minutes. None were answered.

Four calls came from Zipper's office, two from the offices of D&C. No messages left. One call just kept yelling *pick up, pick up, pick up, pick up*. One was from the Foreign Office: *In town. Drinks?* The ninth call left a message: *Sir's shirts are ready and may be picked up at his leisure as it were.*

Ambrose stood at the hotel window, looking at the Bosporus through the dawn haze. He wavered slightly, leaning his forehead against the pane to catch his balance. It was time to go home, Zipper announced, knowing her husband would never admit so on his own.

Ambrose turned and managed a sad smile. Home then?

Home then.

They slept that night in their own bed in the narrow Victorian terrace in Kensington.

J, and the shirts, could wait.

K.

Ambrose Zephyr stood shaving in his bathroom.

His wife hovered in the doorway, watching her husband's hands. A subtle tremor, more noticeable in the right. The razor hand. Ambrose leaned into the fogged mirror and pulled a slow stroke. His hands steadied. The knot in Zipper's stomach eased.

We can't keep avoiding them, Zipper said as her husband finished his neck and began on his chin.

I'd rather not be today's topic, said Ambrose.

Friends wouldn't do that.

Zipper stood beside her husband and rested her head against his shoulder. Ambrose looked at her reflection in the mirror. What he could make out appeared hollow. As if she wasn't quite there.

Everyone does it, said Ambrose. One minute you are who you are. The next it's strange looks and wringing hands and poor Ambrose is there anything we can do Ambrose let's all dance on eggshells Ambrose. Suddenly it's all that you are. All you will be.

Ambrose held out his razor hand and watched the tremor shake a few drops of water to the floor. This, he said, is not me.

He looked back at the mirror. They, he said, are not us.

When the Mankowitzes lived at twenty-six and the Ashkenazis lived at thirty, the girls would meet in front of twenty-eight. Neighbours said that *with that pair*, that Katerina Mankowitz and Zappora Ashkenazi, there was always much to decide. What to do about boys. What to do about Katerina's beastly little sister. What to do about their hair, their shoes, their skin. Zappora called her best friend Kitts.

When Kitts found a job as a photographer's assistant, she put a word in with her employer regarding a friend looking for work.

When Kitts thought she was pregnant, Zappora found a discreet clinic. As it turned out Kitts was late. The friends celebrated at the local. Zappora bought a round for the house.

When Zipper announced she had met someone, Kitts approved. As long as he can be trusted, she said. It was Kitts who found the wedding dress.

When Kitts left her most recent lover, Zipper made up the spare room. She used some of Kitts's photography to decorate. Kitts would never say as much, but what hung on the walls was worth thousands. Moody black-and-whites of backlane characters in rough countries were much in demand by the world's collectors.

Pick up, pick up, pick up, pick up. PICK UP.

Zipper answered the phone.

Kitts said she was on her way.

Ambrose opened his front door and found Kitts glowering at him. She was, as always, tall and haggard. Like a woman just returned from working in a place with no running water. She called Ambrose a bastard and hugged him. Longer and warmer than usual.

Lovely to see you too, said Ambrose as Kitts went inside. He sat on his front step and lit a cigarette left over from Paris.

In her kitchen, through two pots of tea, Zipper came apart. She started laughing like a schoolgirl. L is for List, she said. W is for Was It Something I Did? D is for Something I Didn't Do? S is for Something I Should Have Done?

She showed Kitts the journal, fanning the pages like a conjuror. She pulled odd items from the journal's envelope. Souvenirs, Zipper said. What a grand bloody tour it's been.

Other bits and baubles materialized from Zipper's pockets. Everything formed a small mound on the table.

A postcard featuring a muddy reproduction of an enormous Rembrandt.

A is for a Portrait in Amsterdam, said Zipper.

A small and smooth stone, grey and warm.

Barbaric Berlin.

A flattened lavender bloom, barely fragrant.

Advertising in Chartres.

Another postcard, this time offering a jolly watercoloured *Bienvenue à Deauville*.

A honeymoon by the sea, Zipper said.

A fat and worn copy of *Les Misérables*, an embossed photograph of an Italian woman in an elegant scarf, an unflattering Polaroid snap of Ambrose and Zipper by the Pyramids. A child's blue glass bauble.

Our Paris, laughed Zipper. Florence, Giza, Istanbul. Did I mention we missed Haifa?

Zipper picked up the journal. Page after blank page.

And what will I have when he's gone? Nothing. No growing ancient together, no retiring to the *pied-à-terre*, no children, no grandchildren come to that. No more. No life. Nothing. Blank.

But you never wanted children, Kitts said.

I never wanted this. I is for I Don't Know What to Do.

Kitts sat in the eye of her friend's storm, nodded, shook her head, held tight, wiped Zipper's dripping face, put the kettle on, wept, buttressed, agreed. Listened.

When the worst had passed, Kitts did what she had done since the childhood meetings in front of twenty-eight. She said something smart at the precise moment when there was nothing to say.

He's right, the bastard. Live what's left. Live it as large as you both can. That's what he wants. *That's* what you want.

Zipper threw her journal on the table.

But the words. How do I start? Where do I end?

The words will come, said Kitts. They always do.

Wilkes and Zephyr met at university.

They took a loose interest in the other's academics: Ambrose sneaking his friend into a life-drawing class to prove that artists did not get erections; Freddie instructing his friend on the proper balance between single malts and thesis writing.

After graduating, they shared a shoebox flat in a hard part of London and lied on each other's cv. They began referring to each other by last name only. It sounded good, they'd explain. Something professionals might do.

When it appeared likely they were destined to drive cabs, Wilkes passed his foreign service examinations and Zephyr landed a junior position as a copywriter. Which, much later in their lives, they would characterize as ironic.

Between distant postings and demanding clientele, the friends rarely saw each other. They never reminisced when they did. They kept every piece of wish-you-were-here correspondence and look-what-I-created souvenir each had sent the other.

No one, least of all Zipper, could explain why they had remained friends for so long and at such distance. Or why they had even become friends in the first place.

Drinks? always meant the Savoy bar.

All Ambrose would later say about his evening with Freddie was how good it had been to see an old friend. They spent the time talking mostly of each other's work, said Ambrose. State secrets, slagged clients, that sort of thing.

What likely occurred was that after enough kirs and enough whiskeys, Ambrose reluctantly described the circumstances. There would have been long silences, pinched glances, calls for same again please.

After some time the friends would have found their Gallipoli courage and looked each other in the face. There would have been tears in their eyes. Stoic ones, but tears nonetheless.

Damn, Freddie likely said, turning away for a moment.

Ambrose probably apologized.

The friends would have pulled themselves together. Freddie, as always, would then have said something clever and wise.

You need to edit. Enough with A through Zed. Toss the list. You'll end up hating half the places you go anyway. Think of Zipper. Stop dragging the woman about. Wasn't she the one who said it was time to come home?

At the end of the evening, the friends would have stood on the street waiting for taxis. They would have embraced, as old friends do when parting. If you need anything, Freddie no doubt said.

Right then.

Right.

Taxis would have appeared.

Neither friend would have said goodbye. They never had before.

J.

Ambrose Zephyr would sometimes remark that a better man was one supplied with an intelligent woman, the ability to tango and an able tailor.

For those who knew Ambrose, *an able tailor* became the explanation for why Ambrose Zephyr had stroked out Jaipur on his list and pencilled in Old Jewry.

Mr Umtata sailed from home a younger man, stowed away in the hold of a runt freighter. When the authorities realized he was gone, he wasn't missed. Good riddance, they said. Another kaffir away.

On the day the freighter docked in London, Germany was invading its neighbours. A week later Mr Umtata found work in the army. Nothing at the sharp end of course, they said. You understand. Still doing your bit as it were.

He learned a trade. Mind the break at the cuff, Major would say. A bit snug across the shoulder. Give those buttons a polish, there's a good fellow. Mr Umtata's war raged through the officers' mess. When it ended Major and his buttons went home to the country and Mr Umtata went to Cheapside.

He took up piecework in a ladies and gents shop. Alterations To All Garments Our Specialty The Smartest Styles Within Bespoke Orders Upon Request Satisfaction Assured For All Closed Sundays. He enjoyed the ladies' work particularly.

He learned how to dance. To understand how the clothes move, he told his employer. Mr Umtata was a small man whose teeth were too big for his mouth, but his partners did not mind. He was always impeccably dressed, he smelled heavenly and he could move. Like Astaire himself, they said.

After twenty years Mr Umtata purchased the shop. It was a narrow concern, too dark in summer, too hot in winter, and could neither boast nor hold the selection common among the Savile shops. But Mr Umtata's handwork was slow and sure, his service humble, his discretion reliable. Observation and counsel were parcelled out as he saw fit. Upon request.

They met the morning a younger Ambrose Zephyr produced his first television commercial: thirty seconds for the finest cleanser the mod '70s housewife could ever wish to own.

The concept involved a red-haired actress, grinning in a mod '70s housewife manner, on her knees scrubbing the average English street—a tip to the product's mod '70s scouring power. What the woman's hot pants tipped to was left to interpretation. Old Jewry stood in as average street.

The commercial was to be filmed from an extreme angle and Ambrose had split the seat out of his trousers checking the first setup of the day. An assistant from the agency shoved him through Umtata's door for repairs. The tailor's first advice: a proper fit through the buttocks.

When asked by Ambrose what he thought of the activity in the street, Mr Umtata replied that it all appeared interesting but sir may want to reconsider the hot pants.

Ambrose became as regular a customer as wages and wear would allow. Jackets now and then, shirts by the gross, flirtations with bellbottomed trousers (against contrary advice). At the rear of the shop, in a wooden box marked Active, Mr Umtata kept a file card with particulars: *Zephyr, A. Dresses left, favours right shoulder, prefers contrasting linings. Poor colour sense. Requires some direction. See also Ashkenazi, Z (Mrs).* It was the only card filed under Z.

Ambrose brought Zipper to Old Jewry to meet Mr Umtata, as a young suitor intent on impressing might. Do you approve? asked Ambrose.

Indeed sir, said Mr Umtata. I believe the expression is yin to your yang. And if I may be so bold sir. Does the lady dance?

Mr Umtata cut, lined and hand-stitched the suit Ambrose was married in—double breasted, trousers in the full and classic style, startling yellow tie. At his final fitting, with Zipper observing, Ambrose suggested a matching yellow carnation for the lapel. Zipper rolled her eyes. Mr Umtata frowned in silence.

I think it makes a statement, don't you? said Ambrose.

Indeed sir, said Mr Umtata.

Just the thing for the big day.

Quite.

Bit much?

As you say sir.

Mr Umtata also fit and altered Zipper's dress (an off-white vintage number, one previous owner, purchased in Portobello Road). With my compliments missus, Mr Umtata said as he snipped the last thread and stood aside to allow Zipper a full look in the mirror.

The lady does indeed dance, said Zipper as she swished.

Mr Umtata and Zipper then toasted her impending marriage with a deep and expert dip. To ensure proper movement, said Mr Umtata through a toothy smile.

On the day, the newlyweds looked like famous people, despite the downpour in Kensington Gardens. Zipper's bouquet was a handful of small white rosebuds. Complemented by a small white rosebud in Ambrose's lapel. Mr Umtata was unable to attend. Saturday was a brisk day at the shop in Old Jewry. He sent regrets.

Years later the wedding suit still fit. The linen number, however, was in urgent need of attention. And there was the matter of shirts being ready.

At the rear of the shop, Mr Umtata uttered a stream of sighs. Ambrose asked if anything could be done. Zipper mentioned time was pressing. Mr Umtata then suggested sir might strip to his boxers. Missus might want to take a seat.

In silence the tailor of Old Jewry worked his needles and threads and scissors and irons. Ambrose searched for somewhere to put his hands. Zipper watched her husband's white skin, stretched thin over bone.

We've been abroad, said Ambrose.

Indeed sir, said Mr Umtata through the pins between his teeth.

Rather suddenly.

Indeed.

Travelled light.

So it would seem sir.

Sorry for the rush.

As am I sir, said Mr Umtata, hiding the last seam, his eyes fixed on Zipper's wet eyes.

A fresh shirt was unwrapped. Ambrose strained out a smile as he dressed.

A miracle, Umtata. As always.

As you say sir.

A bit loose across the shoulders though.

Indeed sir. Shall we check the fit?

With that Mr Umtata took Ambrose Zephyr in his arms. Allow me the lead sir, he whispered. The men dipped. Deeply, expertly.

Zipper Ashkenazi laughed out loud. For the first time in days.

L.

The sun began to rise as Ambrose Zephyr sat on his front step. It was, still, his best time of the day.

He watched number twelve with his tiny dog. The elderly man frowned: he had forgotten his hat. Number eighteen, naked this morning and trusting that no one was awake at such an hour, gathered the morning paper from her doorstep. The neighbourhood stray, ignored, eyed the birds in the park across the way.

The night fog burned off. For Zipper Ashkenazi, standing at her front window wearing one of her husband's new shirts, it looked to be a rare morning. A fine one, for the time of year.

Ambrose sipped his coffee, certain his wife was catching just five minutes more. He waved to number eighteen and sheepishly smiled an apology for having seen more than he should have. The elderly man went home to get his hat.

Zipper waited until the sun came through the front window, then made a cup of tea. She joined her husband on the front step.

I need to deal with the office, Ambrose said.

Zipper watched the neighbourhood stray.

Loose ends, that sort of thing.

Zipper examined the dregs in her cup.

I should have called, she said.

Near Leicester Square stood the offices of Dravot, Carnehan. A few streets away stood the offices of the third most-read fashion magazine in the country. Zipper and Ambrose had managed to work in the same part of the city, but neither one could remember when they had managed lunch together. Or ridden the underground as a couple off to work. Isn't it funny, thought Zipper, to be doing that now. They decided D&C would be first and best dealt with.

Few heads turned as Ambrose and Zipper walked through the creative department to his office. Everyone is too fresh, thought Zipper. Too busy. Too young.

Greta sat in Ambrose's chair, looking out the windows and fidgeting with his collection of type blocks. Without turning around she said how odd it all felt. D&C had gotten the account.

I'll just clear up a few things, said Ambrose.

More annoying than odd, actually, said Greta.

I won't be long.

Big meeting next week. Strategy.

Most of it you can toss.

Tactics. New staff.

The plants are fake. They'll last.

Global campaign. Much work to do.

Just a few things.

The billing will be huge . . .

Greta's voice trailed out through the window.

Ambrose picked over his desk. A photograph of himself at a location shoot: longer hair, horrid bellbottomed trousers, a red-haired actress nearby. A newspaper style manual. A pocket atlas, leather-bound with ribbon marker. A few travel brochures from the sixties: *Ski Zermatt This Year, Beautiful St. Moritz, Now Is the Time for Geneva.* A moody black-and-white photograph of Zipper. Taken in a rough country in a younger time.

You can keep the type, said Ambrose. My gift.

Greta turned away from the window. Tears flowed down her cheeks and dripped from her chin.

Bloody annoying, she said.

Yes it is, said Ambrose.

I hate this. I want to go home.

I hear Berlin is lovely this time of year.

Ambrose smiled and kissed Greta warmly on both cheeks. He pocketed the photograph of Zipper and left.

Pru was yelling at Milan or Paris or New York or her assistant when Zipper appeared at her door. Pru threw her earpiece across the room, glanced at Ambrose as if he wasn't there and began yelling at Zipper.

I quit, said Zipper. Her life had unravelled. It

didn't need Pru picking at the threads. She wished *quit* had come out sounding angrier.

YOU WILL NEVER WRITE AGAIN, Pru said as quietly as her disposition could manage. I WILL SEE TO IT.

Perhaps you will, said Zipper.

MNOPQRSTU.

It took most of the day for Ambrose and Zipper to reach Hyde Park. Here and there Ambrose's gait had slowed to the shuffle of an old man. Crowded pavements and clogged traffic had taken their own toll.

Through Kensington Gardens the pace improved. In other times, on better strolls, Ambrose would say he could see the King out for his morning ride: mounted on a dapple grey, overdressed in lace and buckles, the court blundering behind him like a bad comedy sketch.

They stopped to rest at the edge of the Round Pond. Canvas deckchairs had been put out for the season. Ambrose looked across the water and the swans and into nothing.

What would you have done, Zipper asked.

I would have sat on a beach in Mumbai, said Ambrose, and had my hair cut. For extra rupees the barber would have told my fortune. *Sahib will be leading a surprising life.* You would have worn a sari the colour of aubergine.

New York. I'd been there once. On business? No. You were there. For the spring shows. Did you take me along? Or was it business? Funny how I can't recall. It was much farther away than I remembered.

O. O . . . is Osaka. I bow to the department store hostesses, they cover their smiles when they hear my Japanese. You and I are at the theatre. *Bunraku* I think they call it here. A tragic tale. Montagues and Capulets, judging by the acting. You cry during the final act. P. Pago Pago. Paddington. Perth? I learn a new language, Queensland gone walkabout. We waltzed, didn't we? The beach . . .

———

There was an odd half-smile on Ambrose's face. He looked away.

Keep going, said Zipper. Please keep going.

What?

R. You were about to say R.

. . . Rio . . . the beach. Ipanema. They have professional foot washers imagine that I can see Africa from the beach and you are not so young or tall but very tanned and quite lovely and there's Shanghai sea of tai chi women scowling at me a tiny string ensemble of five-year-olds playing something in a minor Barber's *Adagio* sad for such little hands . . .

Don't stop, said Zipper.

I can't.

T?

Can't remember. Timbuktu?

Don't worry. U then.

Ambrose looked at his wife as if he didn't know her. The King, he said, is not much of a horseman.

Oh God.

Ambrose and Zipper did not move until dark. The panic was slow to ease.

The moon rose above the treetops and they walked the rest of the way home. As they turned into their road, Ambrose said he remembered.

V.

We were staying in a *pensione* near the Piazza San Marco. I woke up too early. It was difficult putting on the linen number in the dark, but I didn't want to wake you. I borrowed a blanket from the hotel and walked across the piazza.

Everything was mist and fog. It was raining, softly, off and on. The air felt cold for the time of year. It was too early for the cafés to open.

I found a chair and pulled it to a better spot near the lagoon. The gondolas were still tied to their posts, bobbing like toy boats. I wrapped myself in the blanket and soaked in the hazy view across the lagoon. In all the years we talked about Venice and pictured Venice and dreamed of Venice, did we ever once imagine it might smell?

I was sleeping when you found me. You said you had worried. I'm fine, I said. How could I not be? I've kept a promise.

You smiled and said yes, finally, I had.

The waiters were unstacking chairs, wiping tables, opening umbrellas. The piazza began filling with tourists bundled against the chill, griping about the weather, trying to fit the Campanile in the viewfinder.

You and I left the edge of the lagoon and went off in search of breakfast. We found the Bridge of Sighs, lost our way to the Erberia, and decided we weren't hungry anyway. We were wet and cold and our clothes reeked of dead fish and it couldn't have mattered less.

Zipper said that was how she remembered it as well.

Z.

I'll be along in a minute, Ambrose said. Zipper went upstairs and crawled on top of the duvet. She stared at the ceiling.

What felt like hours later Ambrose appeared at the bedroom door. Zipper helped him into bed, wrapped him in an extra blanket to stop the shivering, curled herself around him. She was drifting in and out of sleep when the air in the Victorian terrace turned suddenly thick. The silence startled her awake.

——

Zipper cried quietly for a long while before ringing Kitts and Freddie. They would know what to do, whom to call.

She kissed her husband's eyes and went downstairs.

On the kitchen table she found her well-thumbed edition of *Wuthering Heights*, a ragged slip of paper tucked in the first few pages. *Chapter One. 1801—I have just returned from a visit . . .*

On the paper, Zanzibar had been scribbled over. In the margin was written *Zipper*. With the proper amount of swoosh to the Z, and in a remarkably steady hand.

———

A few evenings later, Zipper Ashkenazi sat on her doorstep under a threatening sky. She wore a borrowed linen jacket, too large across the shoulders, but warm enough against a stiff spring breeze. Beside her stood the leather suitcase from under the bed.

She watched number twelve carry his tiny dog around the park. Number eighteen hurried along the pavement, a few minutes behind her time. The neighbourhood stray strolled towards the birds.

When the elderly man passed by, he paused. He put down the dog and turning smartly towards Zipper, took off his hat and bowed. The dog stood unsettled at his master's feet, trying to ignore the neighbourhood stray. The man replaced his hat, collected his dog and walked slowly home.

Number eighteen kept walking past her waiting children and stopped a step or two below Zipper. The woman's smile was shy. After a moment she found something to say. She told Zipper that she had always enjoyed her column in the fashion magazine. It was the first thing she read every month. You always have an interesting story to tell, she said.

There was another pause. Yes, well, the woman said finally. Tea, she suggested, might be nice. Perhaps . . . sometime . . . when you're ready then.

Zipper thanked the woman for her kindness. Tea would be brilliant. Soon. The woman's children waved their art, and off she went.

Zipper sat for a while longer, watching the empty park. It began to rain. She opened the journal that had come from the bookshop in Amsterdam. With slow and gentle care, Zipper emptied the contents of the envelope into

Ambrose's suitcase. From a pocket of her jacket she pulled a type block. Boldface, sans serif. She paused, then put the worn wooden cube back where it belonged.

She turned to the journal's first page, wiped her hand down its blank face, thought for a moment, and began to write.

This story is unlikely.

ACKNOWLEDGEMENTS

For gracious friendship, confederacy, and editorial wisdom nonpareil: Martha Kanya-Forstner.

For representation in the face of all reason: Suzanne Brandreth, Dean Cooke. In London: Will Francis. In Zurich: Sebastien Ritscher. In Milan: Marco Vigevani, Claire Sabatie Garat.

My Doubleday family: Maya Mavjee, Kristin Cochrane, Scott Sellers, Martha Leonard, Amy Black, Lara Hinchberger, Nicholas Massey-Garrison. The sales and marketing cousins: fearless, generous, and able bodies all. And new and wise American friends: Christine Pride, Bill Thomas.

For extraordinary craft in the making of books: Kelly Hill, Carla Kean, Christine Innes, Stephanie Fysh, Shaun Oakey.

For patience, enthusiasm, and Ambrose's suitcase: Hannah Richardson, Sanger Richardson.

And for saying yes: Rebecca Richardson, without whom the above would have never read a word.

CSR, 10.06

CS Richardson is a novitiate novelist and accomplished book designer. He has worked in publishing for over twenty years and is a multiple recipient of the Alcuin Award (Canada's highest honour for excellence in book design). His design work has been exhibited at both the Frankfurt and Leipzig Book Fairs. *The End of the Alphabet* has been sold in ten countries. He is currently at work on his second novel.

A NOTE ABOUT THE TYPE

The End of the Alphabet has been set in Filosofia, a typeface designed in 1996 by Zuzana Licko. The face is a modern interpretation of the classic Bodoni, allowing for applications that Bodoni's extreme contrasts cannot address, namely good readability in smaller text sizes.

ESCAPE AND RETURN
MEMORIES OF NAZI GERMANY

To Marshal
with my best wishes
Fritz Ottenheimer

FRITZ OTTENHEIMER

ESCAPE AND RETURN
MEMORIES OF NAZI GERMANY

Second Edition
Published by Fritz Ottenheimer
Copyright ©2000 Fritz Ottenheimer
All rights reserved.

Cover and Book Design: Craig Seder
ISBN: 0-9704277-0-0
(previously published by Cathedral Publishing, ISBN: 1-887969-11-x)

Library of Congress Control Number: 99-41302

Printed in the United States by:
Morris Publishing
3212 East Highway 30
Kearney, NE 68847
1-800-650-7888

CONTENTS

	Foreword	ix
	Prologue	xi
1	When Life was Good	1
2	Hitler Takes Over	4
3	The Austrian Anschluss	19
4	Kristallnacht	26
5	The Only Way Out	41
6	A Learning Experience	52
7	Basic Training	57
8	My Return to Europe	63
9	Peace at Last	75
10	Sifting Through the Rubble	105
11	Rebuilding My Life	122
12	Remembering and Repairing	156
	Epilogue	159
	References and Updates	163
	About the Author	167

In gratitude to my parents.
In memory of Aunt Martha, Uncle Leon, and Gigi.
In love to Goldie, our children and grandchildren.
With respect for the few Germans who had the courage
to do what was right.

*The entire world is but a narrow bridge, and the most important
thing is not to be afraid.*
—R. Nachman of Bratzlav

Acknowledgments

I want to thank several people for their contributions to this book: My wife, Goldie, for her encouragement and support. Tony Del Prete for his editing and Linda Wilson for her clerical work. Craig Seder of Cathedral Publishing for layout and design.

FOREWORD

World War Two was, as author Studs Terkel aptly dubbed it, "The Good War." Unlike the two wars that followed, the Korean War and the Vietnam War, it was a popular war—Americans knew whom, why, and what they were fighting for. The war saved Europe from fascism, made women more independent of men, educated the country with the GI Bill, created a wealth of technological inventions, made America the number one nation in the world and produced, as Tom Brokaw would say, "The Greatest Generation." However, it was responsible for much destruction, pestilence, and chaos. It also gave the world Hitler, The Atomic Bomb and the Holocaust.

Escape and Return is an autobiographical work that not only tells about the horrors of the Holocaust but puts them into the perspective of history. Ottenheimer begins by describing what he calls "The Good Life" in Germany before Hitler. He relates the effect of Hitler on Germany after he came to power, the unification of Germany and Austria (something which is downplayed in most documentaries), life in German concentration camps before 1939 and his escape from Germany to the United States. He describes the basic training that he received in the US Army and his return to Germany just prior to the end of the war. Finally he relates the effects the past has had upon his life. The work is chock-full of anecdotes and stories and is told as only one who has lived through it can tell it.

Specifically, Ottenheimer gives a first-hand account of how his father and others in his hometown helped several hundred Jews escape to freedom. He relates the beginning of the German Final Solution (the liquidation of the Jews). After escaping Germany, Mr. Ottenheimer and his family came to America, where he attended Public School 73 in New York City. He encountered the problems of discrimination inherited by all immigrants. Upon graduation from high school, he joined the Army in October 1944, took his basic training in Florida where, among other things, he had to give up his individuality by eating pork and anything else they gave him or face near starvation. After basic training he was sent to Europe, where he worked with displaced people left after the surrender. He saw the last days of the war and the havoc of the prison camps. It is here that he asked himself "How could it happen?"

The author missed the Holocaust but saw the results. This is where the book is at its best. Here he relates his personal experiences; when he interviewed many Germans he found, like so many others before him, that most claimed that they were never *real* Nazis. They only joined the party for social events and to drink beer—they thought of it as fun.

Now retired, Mr. Ottenheimer has made eight return trips to his native land, where a longer German version of his work was published in 1996. This autobiographical work is interesting, riveting, and exciting. It is Mr. Ottenheimer's true story about his odyssey and well worth reading because it tells the way it was some sixty years ago. While it never really answers the troubling questions that still bother Ottenheimer today, it keeps alive the story for others to contemplate and remember, with a hope that the world will learn from the past and that this will never happen again. This is history the way it should be written and told by someone who was there.

Donald M. Goldstein, Ph.D.
Professor
Graduate School of Public and International Affairs
University of Pittsburgh

Prologue

How could it happen? This is the unrelenting question about the Holocaust—about hatred and violence, about greed and indifference.

Social psychologists may know a part of the answer. They studied an incident in 1964 of a woman being repeatedly attacked and finally stabbed to death on a street in Queens, New York with 38 neighbors watching and doing nothing to help her. When they questioned the witnesses, they found that each one had looked to see what the other neighbors were doing. When they realized that no one else was taking action, they chose not to 'get involved.' There were no leaders, only followers.

There were millions of witnesses to Nazi persecution of Jews in Germany, too. Where were the moral leaders, the role models, who could have done something? The professionals, the educated people, were the ones that the ordinary people might have looked to for guidance. But they were busy trying to get into positions from which their Jewish colleagues had been fired. Many others found it advantageous to do Hitler's work. University graduates became SS leaders, engineers designed gas chambers and crematories; physicians experimented on, tortured, and murdered children in the name of medical science; renowned jurists wrote and enforced Hitler's laws; top church leaders enunciated divine approval for Hitler's policies; and teachers and professors made it all seem right. Then there still remains the question of how Hitler was able to find thousands of enthusiastic murderers, not only in Germany but in the conquered nations as well.

Some authors claim that Nazism and the Holocaust were distinctly German phenomena. I wish it were so. Then we would simply have to watch that one country in the future. But recent examples of ethnic hatred and genocide in various countries and the world's indifference toward them show that the potential for such atrocities exists everywhere.

How could it happen? Before we can answer that question, we must be aware of *what* happened in Germany during Hitler's rule. I hope that my memoirs will make a modest contribution to that education.

1 WHEN LIFE WAS GOOD

I was born in Germany; so were my parents, my grandparents, my ancestors as far back as I can trace them. One of the early Ottenheimers must have come from the town of Ottenheim, but I can't follow our family tree back that far. I would guess that my family's roots were solidly planted in southern Germany before the Mayflower brought the early European settlers to America.

I have no specific knowledge about my early ancestors other than they were Jews. Since Jews were not permitted to join craft guilds or to own land, chances are they were peddlers or laborers. At various times they were probably exploited, evicted, persecuted. At best they were tolerated.

The ideals of liberty, equality, and justice were spawned in the American and French Revolutions and carried across Europe by Napoleon's troops in the early 1800s. The society of Western and Central Europe changed dramatically and with it, the status of the Jews. As a consequence, all four of my grandparents received a decent public education, owned their own homes, and considered themselves German: absolutely, unconditionally, patriotically German.

There was a time when Jews were wandering all over Europe, not by choice, but because they were not permitted to settle down anywhere for any length of time. When a few villages gave permission for Jews to establish permanent residence there—typically because the population had been decimated by the plague—all the Jews in the surrounding areas rushed in to take advantage of the opportunity. These villages suddenly acquired a large Jewish population and were therefore referred to as "*Judendörfer*," meaning Jew villages. That is why a century ago, about the time when my parents were born, fully one-half of the population of both Rexingen and Gailingen was Jewish.[1]

My mother was born in Gailingen and my father in Rexingen. They used to tell me that the conversational language of both Christians and Jews in both places consisted of the local dialect of German with a lot of Hebrew words woven in. Surprisingly, this is still the language of some old people in both places today, although there is not a single Jew living in Gailingen or Rexingen any more. Most of the Christians in both places eked out a living on small, unproductive family farms and sank deeper into debt with every passing year. The Jews traditionally were peddlers. So, what could they peddle in a rural setting? They peddled cows. They became cattle dealers in Gailingen and Rexingen.

Rexingen is located on a mountain in the Black Forest. A number of Jews owned some land and farmed it. The Jewish cattle dealers would leave home early Monday morning on the mail bus and make the rounds of a lot of small, unproductive family farms in the Black Forest. With little to show for their effort, the men would head back to Rexingen on Friday before the start of Sabbath. Everyone went to synagogue on Saturday morning. My father, who was not a cattle dealer, used to complain that while the cantor prayed with all his heart on the altar, the cattle dealers got together in the rear of the synagogue to talk about the cows they sold or failed to sell during the week. At harvest time, many Jews stayed in the village to help their neighbors harvest the crop. Most of the year, everybody lived together in harmony, raised a few vegetables, baked some bread, and made just enough money to stay alive.

Gailingen is located near the Swiss border, which made a significant difference. On Monday mornings, the Jewish cattle dealers took a train to the thriving dairy farms of Switzerland, the farms that supplied milk for Swiss cheese and Swiss chocolate. When these cattle dealers came home for Sabbath, they generally brought back quite a bit of money. Every few years, there would be a poor harvest in Gailingen, and some of the indebted farmers would have to sell their homes. The Jews could now afford to buy them. In the early part of the century, the Jews of Gailingen owned the best homes in town as well as several stores, a hospital, a large home for the aged, a synagogue with a full-time rabbi—and one of their number was elected mayor. Many of the younger Jews (actually, only the boys) went to college, became professionals and moved to larger towns. But in spite of the economic disparity between Jews and Christians, relations were generally peaceful and polite.

A number of my relatives volunteered for service in the German army during World War I. In fact, I was named after one of them, my father's cousin, Fritz, who died for his beloved fatherland before his 18th birthday. My father was a sergeant in the German infantry during World War I. Shortly before the end of the war, while he was on patrol, a bullet passed through both of his arms, shattering his right elbow. He was discharged in 1919 with a stiff right arm and a few medals for bravery, medals he deposited in a trash can in 1939 following his return from Dachau concentration camp.

The author's father, fighting for the Fatherland, 1917

2 HITLER TAKES OVER

History documents that Germany lost World War I. The Treaty of Versailles was framed by the vindictive elements among the Western Allies, overriding U.S. President Wilson's attempts at reconciliation. The objectives were understandable: to prevent a resurgence of German military power and to rebuild, at Germany's expense, everything the Germans had destroyed. It is ironic that the very same Treaty of Versailles is frequently blamed for Hitler's rise to power a mere fourteen years later, resulting in a resurgence of German military power and the near destruction of most European countries.

Grandfather Metzger became a millionaire of sorts after World War I. He found it necessary to sell the family house in mid-1922. Thanks to post-war inflation, he received several million Marks for the house, all in cold cash, neatly bundled. But German inflation continued at a horrendous rate, and my grandfather's "fortune" became worthless. A U.S. dollar, which traded for 4.20 Marks before the war, became equivalent to 4,200,000,000 Marks by November 1923. In effect, my grandparents' house had been sold for less than one cent! Millions of Germans lost their life savings in this way. Ten years later, my sister and I would play with a suitcase full of paper money, an amusing plaything donated by our grandfather.

Germany recovered from the inflation by issuing a new currency. There was even a period of economic prosperity after 1924, but the world-wide crash of 1929 brought Germany back to her knees. Germany had a history of autocracy and tight police control prior to 1914. Major aspects of daily life had been subject to strict discipline, either self-imposed or under bureaucratic regulations. But now, all rules were being openly violated. Street battles were common. The work ethic, which was practically a religion in Germany, was scuttled by an unemployment rate in excess of 25 percent.

Many Germans were ready to follow Adolf Hitler and his Nazi party in 1933. A people that had prided themselves on law and order, industry and discipline, found themselves in a state of chaos. Their government, which unjustly was given the blame for losing World War I, was incapable of preventing or solving major problems. The Weimar Republic was grossly divided. Parties and factions — even those of similar ideology — were unable or unwilling to cooperate. Economic burdens imposed on Germany by the Treaty of Versailles or by world-wide crises exceeded the capabilities of the government, particularly since the general population had never really gained confidence in democracy.

Nazism and Communism were active at opposite ends of the political spectrum. Both offered a totalitarian approach to law, order, prosperity. But Communism was seen as a foreign ideology which tended to frighten rather than reassure the populist masses. Hitler was different. He had a Prussian-style leadership personality (which appealed to the Prussians) but was not Prussian in speech or background (which endeared him to the others). He intended to wipe out the ineffective parliamentary government and establish the longed-for superiority of Germany among the nations. He offered a not-so-new scapegoat of international Judaism (either Communist or Capitalist, take your choice) to explain Germany's problems, implying a simple solution. His strong personality and his oversimplified, angry way of reacting to the conditions fit in perfectly with the people's feelings of frustration, helplessness, fear, disgust. He promised a return to order, pride, prosperity, and control. Hitler's early followers were mainly the dregs of society. Their methods, actual and proposed, were belligerent and crude. This was conveniently ignored by the general public, who were interested only in the ends, not the means, or who thought that, once in power, Hitler would "settle down."

The only ones who recognized the danger, who might have been able to oppose Hitler and his gang, were the leaders of the opposition parties. But they were hopelessly divided. Organized labor and religious organizations found it to their advantage to go along, though reluctantly, with the wave of nationalism. Industrial and military leaders thought they could use and control Hitler in pursuit of their own ambitions, and many top academicians and professionals flocked to Nazism as a way of gaining promotions or other advantages. Each of these groups contributed significantly to the strength and prestige of the Nazi movement. The Communists fought the Nazi party openly, often in response to Nazi attacks, causing those who feared Communism to side with Hitler. Finally, there were many, so many, who simply did not care.

Hitler was ruthless and may have been insane, but he was not stupid. He was a skillful orator, a forceful organizer, a determined leader. There were no others of comparable effectiveness to oppose him, either in Germany or in other nations. The time had come to avenge the "stab in the back" of Versailles and to defeat all the hostile forces, internal and external, real or perceived.

Adolf Hitler became the leader of Germany on January 30, 1933. He did not seize power by military coup. He had tried that in 1923 but failed. He decided to use the system in order to kill the system. In an election in 1932, Hitler received about one-third of the popular vote. Even though this was far short of a majority, the Nazi party had received more votes than any one of the 36 other parties. A power struggle ensued, and Hitler emerged as chancellor.

Hitler demanded and was granted emergency powers. That was the end of the Weimar Republic. Hitler used the emergency powers to eradicate all democratic constraints and to concentrate all authority in his own hands. Newspapers, radio stations, courts, police, schools, military forces everything was soon under Hitler's control. Opposition parties were declared illegal, and opposition leaders were arrested and sent to newly built concentration camps. The Nazi party was now able to rescind any existing regulations and to enact new laws that would legalize even the most immoral acts. Laws are normally made and enforced to protect good citizens from criminals. In Germany, laws were now made and carried out by criminals and their opportunistic followers. There followed the bloodiest chapter in the bloody history of mankind: Nazi Germany.

My parents, Klara (Metzger) and Ludwig Ottenheimer, were mar-

Klara and Ludwig Ottenheimer, parents of the author, 1921

ried in 1921 and settled down in the beautiful little town of Constance (German spelling is Konstanz). It is located in Southwestern Germany, right on the border of Switzerland. My sister, Ilse, was born in 1922. I came along in 1925. I do not claim to remember this, but I was told that I was born with the umbilical cord wrapped around my neck and sporting a rather bluish complexion. I survived my first medical crisis without any noticeable effects, except that my mother was very protective toward me for the rest of her life. I had no way of knowing how precarious my young life would become.

Our family had a men's wear store in the center of Constance. It was not a thriving enterprise, but there was a loyal following of customers who appreciated better than average quality and integrity. We were not wealthy. We did not own a car or a house, but we lived comfortably at a time when many others were struggling to keep afloat.

We had many friends in Constance. Most of my parents' friends and most of my schoolmates were Christians. We were believing, practicing Jews. We complied with dietary laws and went to synagogue and religious school every week. But social activities were not conducted along religious lines. Occasionally, my parents were even invited to attend the military ball of the local garrison. My after-school games were generally with Christian boys during my early childhood. It was simply a matter of numbers: There were fewer than 500 Jews in a total population of 35,000. In Germany as a whole, a population of 65 million included only one-half million Jews.

I was eight years old when Hitler came to power. Eight-year-olds do not normally get too excited about changes in a nation's leadership, but even I was painfully aware of Hitler's arrival. I could see parades and hear speeches nearly every day. Swastika flags were hanging out of thousands of windows. Every German radio station presented fanatical tirades all day, praising the new regime, playing military music, condemning the Jews and other "enemies" of Germany, and extolling the glory of dying for the fatherland. Non-German radio stations were *verboten*. Anyone caught listening to a foreign station was taken away by the secret police, the Gestapo and never seen again. Many Germans took advantage of this opportunity to settle old grudges by denouncing neighbors. Children were instructed by their Nazi youth leaders to expose the "enemies of the people" who listened to foreign stations. We heard reports of children denouncing their own parents and becoming orphans.

I heard a radio commentator educating his audience one day about the Jews: that Jews are devious, corrupt and unscrupulous; that Jews are a dirty, smelly, foreign race; that Jews are conspiring to destroy Germany.

I turned to face my parents. "We're Jews, aren't we?"

"Yes, of course!" they replied.

"Well, is that man talking about us?"

"Don't listen to that idiot," my father said. "He's one of those Nazis."

"But aren't a lot of other people listening to him?"

"I'm afraid so. But they won't believe those horrible lies." My parents went on to explain that German people were honest, decent, educated people. That they would not follow that crazy Hitler and his gang very long. They would get rid of him. Evidently my parents underestimated the power of nationalism and propaganda, of greed and fear.

Local Nazi newspapers were more specific and more unscrupulous than radio stations in maligning Jews. Honorable doctors and lawyers, including the highly respected Dr. Moos,[2] were falsely accused by name of having committed moral or criminal offenses in the past or of being incompetent or dishonest. It was impossible for a Jew to win a libel suit in a Nazi court. In the 1930s nearly every German had a Jewish friend or at least a Jewish acquaintance that was respected. In spite of this, the Germans learned to hate and fear the Jews, Judaism, and the "other Jews" they didn't know. The propaganda explained to the German citizenry that a good Jewish acquaintance was an anomaly, that the "other" Jews were the enemy. One national newspaper, the *Stuermer*, was a vicious collection of anti-Jewish caricatures, editorials and horror stories from front to back. According to the *Stuermer* and many widely circulated propaganda pamphlets, every Jew, no matter how decent he *seemed* to be, had his mind set on raping, robbing, betraying, and exploiting the gullible German people. I was a student in the St. Stephan Elementary School and didn't want to hear anything about the nasty politics. "Why can't they leave us alone?" was my naive question. The whole thing was incomprehensible to me.

Apparently, the politics were incomprehensible to my fellow students too. They were saturated with hateful speeches: In Race Study class, on the radio, in newspapers. Everywhere they were incited against the Jews -- to fear them, to shun them, to despise them. In spite of that, we remained friends. In Hitler youth meetings they learned new songs that declared: 'The Jew must get out!' But then they came home and played with us Jewish kids.

Propaganda pamphlets were used as textbooks in public schools. A new course, Race Study, had been added to the curriculum in order to enlighten the German children about the need to keep their "Aryan race" pure and about the dangers posed by inferior races particularly the Jews. Children were prime targets of the Nazi propaganda machine. Membership in the Hitler Youth Movement was practically mandatory. Boys learned to be good Nazis and brave soldiers, while girls were taught to be good Nazis and proper Aryan wives and mothers. I remember hearing a group of boys rehearsing a Hitler Youth song that declared that when Jewish blood squirts from the knife, everything is going well. Fortunately, Jewish boys and girls were not required—not permitted—to join Hitler Youth or to attend Race Study classes.

Soon, the disturbing propaganda became reality. My father went to our store one morning, as he had always done, about two months after Hitler had come to power. He saw sound trucks cruising through Constance on this day. "Don't buy from Jewish stores," the people were warned. "Buy only from Germans!" When my father arrived at the store, he saw a uniformed S.A. guard standing in front of the door.

My father turned around, went back home, and returned a few minutes later carrying a little bag. This time he passed by the storm trooper and unlocked the door. He took the shirts, socks and ties out of the shop window and spread out his World War I medals in their place. He then stepped outside, stood next to the storm trooper, and rolled up his right shirt sleeve, exposing his war injury. He did not have to wait very long. A number of people who knew my father's military record stepped up to the storm trooper and explained that Ludwig Ottenheimer was a good German, a disabled war veteran, who had done more than just his duty for his country. "Surely you would not deny him the right to make an honest living!" The storm trooper was not interested in their logic and tried to ignore them. But more and more people arrived, and their voices grew louder. The storm trooper finally recognized the futility of his task and left the scene. A number of people visited our store on that day to tell my father how strongly they objected to their government's actions.

The boycott of Jewish stores was not successful in Constance; as a matter of fact, business picked up for a few days. However, the Nazi propaganda campaign was to succeed where the boycott failed. Nazi propaganda was massive and blatant, but extremely well organized. Dr. Goebbels had the official title of Propaganda Minister in Hitler's cabinet, so there was nothing subtle or confidential about his work. Hitler recognized the importance of propaganda and made full use of it.

We had a neighbor, Mr. Berger, who occasionally did some work for us as a handyman. Our families got along well with each other. I remember playing with their little girl when we were both six or seven years old. My father was surprised to see a Nazi party emblem on Mr. Berger's lapel a few months after the Nazi takeover.

"I see you have joined the party," my father observed. "Would you mind telling me why?"

"Not at all," replied Mr. Berger. "You know, our new government is trying to get the country straightened out, so we have to support our leader and do our share. Besides," he added, "I picked up a few new jobs since I joined the party."

"Tell me, Mr. Berger, how do you feel about what the party is doing to the Jewish people?"

Mr. Berger looked uncomfortable. "Ah, yes," he finally replied. "It's too bad that the good have to suffer along with the bad." It was a statement we were to hear many times in those days. This time, my father continued the conversation.

"Which ones are we?" He asked. "The good Jews or the bad Jews?"

"You must be joking!" Mr. Berger laughed. "Of course, you and your family are our friends! We love you!" My father did not stop.

"You know most of the Jews of Constance. Which ones are the bad ones that we have to suffer along with?"

Mr. Berger thought for a few seconds. "They are all good, honest people," he finally admitted.

"Well then, who are the bad Jews?" my father asked.

Mr. Berger was angry now. "That's a stupid question," he shouted. "All you have to do is pick up a newspaper or turn on the radio and you'll find out who they are!" Then he added, "Where there's smoke, there's fire!"

Papa's half-sister, Aunt Emma, and her husband Jonas had a modest bakery in Constance. They were peaceful, unpretentious people. Their whole life was wrapped up in their bakery and their beloved daughter. Therese was much more cosmopolitan than her parents. She did a lot of reading about history and science, and she had definite tastes in art and music. Her parents admired her quietly without trying to comprehend the subjects she was interested in.

I loved to visit the bakery. Sometimes they would allow me to wait on customers. Their place was always filled with the most delicious aromas, so sweet and airy I could taste them from the street corner. They had a big, soft, cuddly cat that always purred and frequently gave birth to kittens. On two occasions, I brought a kitten home and my mother made me bring it right back. But at the bakery, I could play with the cat and kittens as long as I pleased.

Aunt Emma had a weak heart, and Uncle Jonas had the after-effects of head injury and shell shock he endured as a German soldier in World War I. A competing baker, who was a zealous Nazi and had the full backing of the Nazi party, demanded to "aryanize" the bakery, i.e., to buy it for a fraction of what it was worth. Uncle Jonas resisted but collapsed under the strain and died in September 1933. Aunt Emma carried on the struggle for almost three years, then died of a heart attack. Meanwhile, Therese married Ernst, a young Jewish baker, who had been hired from another town to help Aunt Emma. Therese and Ernst were able to hold on to the business for a couple of years until they could immigrate to America.

During the 1930s, the Nazi government issued a series of new laws whose purpose was to harass, isolate and impoverish the Jews. We were no longer permitted to attend movies, concerts, sporting events, swimming pools, hotels or restaurants. Even park benches along the shore of Lake Constance bore stickers prohibiting Jews from sitting on them. All Jews who worked for the government were fired—judges, teachers, postal workers, laborers   regardless of merit or seniority. Jewish doctors and lawyers were not permitted to serve non-Jewish clients, nor were non-Jewish professionals allowed to have Jewish clients any more. Books written by Jews, as well as other "subversive" books (such as anti-war books) were removed from libraries and stores and publicly burned. Possession of one of these books would be grounds for severe punishment. During all this time, the German people were being sternly warned not to associate with Jews in any way. Our customers gradually responded to these threats, and my parents had to give up their little store. It was a sad day for the family. So much of our lives had been tied up in that store.

My father now went to work for the tie manufacturer who used to sell us ties for our store. Papa would travel by train over a large part of southern Germany, carrying two suitcases full of swatches from store to store, taking orders for neckties. He would come home on weekends. It was a strenuous job that did not pay well. More importantly, it seemed only a matter of time until he would lose even this modest way of earning a living. There was only one solution: We had to get out of Germany.

Leaving Germany would seem to have been an easy matter. After all, Hitler wanted to get us out. The problem was to find a country that would let us get in. We were fortunate to have several relatives in the United States. My father wrote a desperate letter to my mother's brother, my Uncle Sieg, describing the urgency of our situation, but being careful not to write anything critical of the Nazi regime. Every letter sent to or from another country was opened and read by a German censor. Uncle Sieg's answer was not enthusiastic. "The United States is in a state of depression. Even healthy men who speak English as their native language have trouble finding a job. What chance would you have with your stiff arm and inability to speak English? Your chances are much better in Germany!" After another exchange of letters, Uncle Sieg agreed to sponsor my sister, but not any others. We now turned to my father's cousin, Aunt Flora (Kahn), who agreed to sponsor us.

United States immigration regulations required a sponsor to issue an affidavit listing his or her property and income and offering all this as security to assure that the immigrant would not become a burden to US society. Even after this was done, the applicant still had to wait several years for his "number to come up." The number of immigrants admitted to the United States per year was rigidly limited by national quotas. Aunt Flora's affidavit was submitted in 1936, and we started to wait and hope.

We were getting more and more isolated from our Christian friends and concurrently drawing closer to the other Jewish families of Constance. Our former friends frequently assured us of their affection for us, but also pointed out that further contact with us would be dangerous. We understood their concerns. My sister and I were still going to public school. Our teachers avoided making pro-Nazi remarks in our presence. When they were required to read Nazi propaganda to the students, they did so with a noticeable lack of enthusiasm. One of Ilse's teachers, Miss Kirn, openly voiced her disagreement with Nazi policies. Her entry into Ilse's album was: "*Allen Gewalten zum Trutz sich erhalten*," which translates roughly as "In defiance of all powers survive!"

Aunt Flora

Our schoolmates never lost their decency. One by one, they were ordered by their parents to stay away from us, and we tended to withdraw into our own shell. Some hung on to the bitter end. None of them became insulting or hostile towards Ilse or me, which was amazing in view of the tremendous amount of vicious propaganda with which they were inundated. Most of our school assemblies now consisted of standing in the gymnasium for an hour, listening to a speech by Hitler via loudspeaker. Invariably the speech would be angry, filled with hatred for Jews. I "stole the show" one time by fainting in the middle of the tirade.

I must point out that Constance was one of the least hateful towns in Germany, possibly due to two reasons. First was the proximity of Switzerland. All residents at first, and non-Jews for many more years, were permitted to go to Switzerland every day to buy groceries which were of better value than those obtainable in Germany. Many of these commuters would use the opportunity to read Swiss newspapers, which were generally critical of Nazi policies. This enabled them to recognize Goebbels' lies in their own newspapers. The second reason for the relative kindness in Constance was the high degree of assimilation of Jews in society and the exceptional extent of Jewish involvement in civic activities, sports and humanitarian causes. Before Hitler appeared on the scene, the Jews and Christians of Constance interacted freely in the volunteer fire department, the volunteer ambulance corps (organized primarily by a Jewish doctor), on weekend soccer teams and hiking clubs, in coffee houses and choirs. Jewish doctors and lawyers were reputed to be particularly considerate, even if fees could only be paid with potatoes or chickens or not at all.

Unfortunately, a core group of Nazi fanatics and opportunists placed in positions of responsibility carried out all federal edicts with enthusiasm; but there was very little spontaneous Nazi activity among the general populace of Constance. This was in sharp contrast to conditions in many nearby communities and most towns in other parts of Germany. We heard many reports of Jewish children having to quit school because they were frequently beaten by their schoolmates and constantly ridiculed by their teachers. In many towns, Jews were attacked by gangs when they left their homes, or even if they stayed at home. Some 300 of these people had moved to Constance during the late 1930s in order to escape their tormentors. But the relatively benign atmosphere of Constance led to a tragic consequence: It kept Jewish inhabitants from fleeing to neighboring Switzerland. Their escape would have been an easy matter during the early Nazi years, provided they were willing to leave their belongings behind. But they waited, hoping for better times.

One of the few overt anti-Semites in Constance was a man who was born Jewish and converted to Christianity. He evidently tried to prove the sincerity of his conversion by using every opportunity to make disparaging remarks about his former religion and its practitioners. When he decided to hire a new sales person for his shoe store, the want ad closed with the statement: "Jews need not apply." He was happy to see the Nazis come to power, until he found out that he himself was considered Jewish under Nazi laws. He discovered to his dismay that Nazi persecution of the Jews was organized on "racial," not religious, grounds. He now had to pass through another conversion, from hate monger to victim.

In the early years after Hitler came to power, it was still possible to travel to another country as a temporary visitor. Our family took many walks to two Swiss towns that were within easy walking distance of our home. All that was needed at the checkpoint was a friendly nod to the border police as we passed by. We particularly enjoyed the friendly atmosphere and freedom of speech, but also the beautiful scenery and the delicious cheeses, chocolates, and pastries of Switzerland. After a couple of years, our passports were canceled.

I remember with great pleasure the summer vacations I spent with the Wertheims, our relatives in France. Uncle Léon was a wholesale shoe salesman; Aunt Martha, my mother's younger sister, was a housewife; and Gilberte (we called her Gigi) was a vivacious bundle of cheerfulness, a year younger than I. She had dark curly hair and flashing dark eyes. In my pre-teen fantasy, I saw her as my future wife. She apparently had other plans. When my mother asked her what she wanted to be when she grew up, she exclaimed that she would be a dentist. On being told that this would require many years of education, she reconsidered: she would marry a dentist in that case. I remember spending many joyful hours in Colmar, and I still recall the taste of fresh figs from a tree in my uncle's backyard. Aunt Martha was deeply concerned about our safety after 1933. Conversely, it was comforting for my mother to know that her sister's family was living safely in France. It was one less thing to worry about. How wrong we were.

On November 1, 1936, at about 4 a.m., vandals broke into our beautiful synagogue, piled up prayer books and Torah scrolls in the middle of the sanctuary, poured gasoline over them and set them on fire. A Christian neighbor noticed the fire and notified the volunteer fire department, who rushed in and extinguished the fire immediately. The building was saved by the quick response, but seven Torah scrolls had been damaged or destroyed by the fire. They were buried in a formal funeral service in accordance with Jewish practice. My grandfather conversed with one of the police detectives that investigated the fire. The officer was quite frank (off the record). "We know pretty well who was responsible for this," he admitted.

Uncle Léon and Aunt Martha

"But we are not allowed to do anything about it." Surprisingly, the insurance company paid for complete restoration and replacements, even for special provisions to make the building "burglar-proof." The reopening celebration in July 1937 seemed to express the hope that things were going to improve from then on. How wrong we were again.

Our rabbi and his family immigrated to Palestine in 1935. I remember him only as an elderly, dignified gentleman who gave a scholarly discourse every Saturday morning during synagogue services. As a boy, my religious contacts were with Mr. Bravmann, our cantor, who also taught Sunday school. Although not formally ordained, Mr. Bravmann now became acting rabbi in addition to his other duties. He was highly respected among congregants of all ages.

My Bar Mitzvah ceremony was celebrated in the newly renovated synagogue in March 1938, following my 13th birthday. Bar Mitzvah marks the coming of age of a Jewish boy (Bat Mitzvah for a girl), the attainment of religious maturity in the congregation. Mr. Bravmann had high confidence in my ability and picked a long, difficult Torah passage for me to chant. We worked together for several months. I had a nervous rehearsal on the evening before my Bar Mitzvah. I stumbled through the passage, stuttered, mispronounced several words, stopped a few times, and missed some of the high notes. Mr. Bravmann listened calmly, never correcting me. "That was fine," he assured me. "You'll do very well tomorrow!" Much to my surprise, his prediction came true.

Mr. Bravmann and his family were able to immigrate to the United States a short time later. If he were alive today, he would be happy to know that I still remember the essence of the sermon he gave for my Bar Mitzvah. He pointed out that whenever God called on our patri- arch Abraham for some task, the latter always responded willingly with the word "*hineini*" here I am. Mr. Bravmann predicted that I would react similarly in the future whenever a need was expressed to me by God or by man. I have tried to live up to that expectation, especially since my parents taught the same lesson by their daily ac- tions and attitudes.

3 THE AUSTRIAN ANSCHLUSS

Hitler solved Germany's unemployment problem by preparing for the next war, while staunchly professing to be striving for peace. Everyone was put to work (many at minimal wages) building arms factories and infrastructure. Other countries were slow to recognize the danger they were facing. Then they started building up their defenses. Early in 1938, Hitler announced his intention of absorbing Austria into Germany. There were many loud protests, but nobody was willing to risk a war. Germany had become the strongest military power in Europe. The German army marched into Austria in March. The Germans were received not with bullets and bombs, but with flowers and Swastika flags. It seemed that many Austrians liked the idea of belonging to the dynamic new Germany.

Shortly after the *Anschluss* (annexation), a number of Jewish families from Austria showed up in Constance. Since Jews were no longer permitted to stay at hotels, the congregational leadership asked various local Jewish families to take the Austrians into their homes for the night. The family that stayed at our apartment was very grateful for our hospitality. Following one of my mother's special dinners, our visitors told us of their experiences after the German takeover. Austrian (not German) gangs marched through the streets of their town (Vienna) and broke into Jewish stores and homes. They stole or broke anything of value. In many homes, the mobs pulled the Jewish residents out onto the street and beat them. Where was the Austrian police while this was happening? They were standing right there, watching the action, doing nothing to interfere. The people who were staying at our home had lost everything they owned except for the clothes they were wearing.

We were shocked to hear these reports. We had lived under Hitler for five years by this time, but we had never experienced anything approaching that level of violence in our town. Why had these people come to Constance? They knew that Constance was a border town, and they hoped that somehow they could find a way to escape to Switzerland. It turned out that they picked the right town. While the Rhine River and Lake Constance generally form the boundary between Germany and Switzerland, the old part of Constance, where we lived, is located south of the Rhine River. The boundary between the two countries in this area is a little creek, appropriately named "*Grenzbach*" (border creek), but locally known, equally appropriately, as "*Saubach*" (pig creek).

On the morning after their arrival, following breakfast, my father took our guests for a ten-minute walk from our house to an area of fields and gardens. They tried to look like a family out for an early-morning walk, as they watched the border guard pass by on their periodic patrol. Then my father pointed to a little creek and said: "That's the border. The other side is Switzerland. Good luck!" The Austrians stepped into four inches of water . Their next step was on Swiss soil. They waved back to my father.

The escapees walked away from the Border Creek and must have headed for the nearest telephone. Starting two or three days later, a steady stream of Austrian Jews, mostly from Vienna, arrived almost daily at our home. I was 13 years old at the time, a small-town boy. It was exciting and, at the same time, frightening to meet all these desperate people who were putting their lives into our hands. My father had lost his job by this time and was able to devote his full time to this operation. Aside from the task of walking our guests to the border, there was a great deal of cleaning, washing and cooking to be done, and my mother no longer had the benefit of household help. Many of the refugees brought suitcases, trunks or bundles of belongings. Obviously, it would have looked a bit suspicious if the Austrians had walked toward the border carrying a suitcase. They would leave their belongings with us, write us a letter from Switzerland, and then my father would mail their baggage to their new address. My sister and I also helped with shopping, washing dishes, and trying to cheer up these very discouraged, fearful people. Occasionally, we would have to walk one of our guests to the post office, a dentist's or attorney's office, or a drug store.

We had to be very careful not to violate any regulation. Any Jew who broke a law, no matter how trivial, was severely punished. Moreover, his offense would be publicized in the next day's newspaper, along with some editorial comment such as: "Jew Smith and the others of his corrupt race will have to learn that they can no longer willfully abuse the hospitality of our great country. Our Fuehrer will not tolerate the devious ways of these filthy parasites." Naturally, there was no chance of appeal or rebuttal.

There was a Nazi law that limited the amount of money a person could take out of the country (10 marks, or about $2.50 US). A refugee who had managed to keep a larger amount of money had several options: He could hide the money on his person or in his luggage; we discouraged this because it might get him and us into serious trouble; he could send it to a relative or friend in Austria; he could share it with destitute fellow refugees; he could give us money to cover our expenses. Everything worked out quite well on a voluntary basis.

There was another law we had to comply with. This one had been on the books since before the Hitler regime: Anyone having overnight guests had to register them with the police, unless they were members of the family. Whenever our guests arrived, we asked them to fill out little forms, which my sister or I would run down to the police station in the evening. About once a week, a uniformed traffic policeman would drop in unannounced, usually between 10 and 11 p.m., for a spot check. He would compare our guests' identification cards against the forms that had been turned in that evening. Everything always checked out, and the policeman was always very polite.

There was good reason why everything always checked out. A few of our guests told us on their arrival that the Gestapo was looking for them. Obviously, we could not register them. My father would immediately take them down to the creek. I remember one of these, a prominent Christian journalist who had written anti-Nazi articles in a Vienna newspaper prior to the takeover by Germany. He later became a professor at a Swiss university.

Sometimes a week would go by without any new arrivals. At other times, twenty Austrians would arrive on a single day. On those nights, people would be sleeping on sofas, on easy chairs, and on the floor. It was on one of these nights that the police check was performed, not by the usual traffic policeman, but by a plain-clothes man, a criminal police inspector. My mother, who was always having grim forebodings, nearly collapsed when he introduced himself. Mama turned him over to my father in the living room.

The conversation started out with the realization that my father and the police inspector had both served in the 142nd infantry regiment during World War I. While they had not known each other before, they now had many people and events to reminisce about. And talk they did while my mother was getting increasingly nervous, wondering what this man was up to. He finally seemed to be getting to the point. "Mr. Ottenheimer," he stated, "I know why these people are here, and I also know what you do for them." My mother's blood pressure probably jumped up 50 percent. The inspector continued, "Why not let me help you? Keep on registering your guests every evening, as you have been doing. I'll take care of getting them across the border." He then specified three requirements: Each person can take only the amount of cash permitted by the law. Refugees cannot take any baggage along. A payment will be required for each person.

My father interrupted, "The first two requirements are no problem. We have already imposed them. But the payment...you must understand that most of these people are very poor. How much would they have to pay?"

"Ten marks per person," the inspector replied. Now my parents were really confused. A thousand marks they could have understood as a bribe of a public official. But just 10 marks didn't make sense. My parents called our guests of the evening into the room. After a brief discussion, they all agreed to go ahead with the arrangements, probably because they thought it might be unhealthy to reject the inspector's offer.

On the following morning, all our guests stood in front of the building, and at seven a.m. sharp, five taxicabs pulled up. Our guests got in, and the cabs drove away. About 20 minutes later, we received a phone call from one of the Austrians: All went well. When they arrived at the border checkpoint, each of the cab drivers showed a police document to the border guard. The drivers were waved on into Switzerland, where they discharged their passengers. We now realized what the 10 marks per person was for: cab fare.

A stream of Austrian refugees continued to flow through our home via cab until August 1938. At that time the Swiss government decided to close its border. (Even after August 1938, Switzerland granted passage *through* the country to anyone who had a visa for immigrating to another country. But the other countries kept their gates shut.) All refugees caught crossing the border after that were arrested by the Swiss police, escorted back to the border and turned over to the Gestapo. Their next destination was Dachau concentration camp. But even the "fortunate" refugees who entered Switzerland prior to the deadline did not enjoy a happy life. Unless they had Swiss friends or relatives who could support them, they would have to move into camps erected for this purpose by the government. We received many letters from our Austrian friends in Switzerland. Some expressed their joy at being permitted to move on to rejoin other relatives in France or Belgium. Of course, they had no way of knowing that this would lead to their destruction. Following Germany's conquest of these countries, Jewish refugees residing there were the first to be deported to death camps. Switzerland was one of the very few countries in Europe to be spared the horror of Nazi attack or domination.

We often wondered about the police inspector's reasons for helping the Austrian refugees. Was this his way of avoiding an embarrassing accumulation of refugees in the Constance area? They were not really accumulating. We kept them moving. Did the Nazi government smuggle their spies into Switzerland along with the refugees? Hardly. German spies were able to walk or drive across the border by themselves without difficulty. Dr. Erich Bloch, a former Jewish resident of Constance, wrote a fascinating book chronicling the history of the Jews of Constance during the 19th and 20th centuries.[3] The author mentioned three police inspectors, all veterans of the criminal police department, who were transferred involuntarily into the ranks of the Gestapo. On numerous occasions they warned individual Jews and other victims of Nazi persecution of impending danger. One of the officers, probably the one who helped us, was known to have been involved in smuggling many Austrian Jews into Switzerland.

Two other inspectors were involved in a dramatic incident: A Jewish prisoner of Dachau concentration camp had somehow escaped from a work detail outside the camp enclosure. Somehow he stole or was given a set of clothes and was able to dispose of his prison uniform. And somehow he made his way to Constance, which he knew was a border town.

The escapee knew nothing about the geography of Constance, and he was not acquainted with any of its inhabitants. He decided to check into a small hotel and to make the necessary inquiries from there. That's when his luck ran out. He did not have any identification papers, and his alibi as to their absence failed to convince the hotel clerk, who notified the criminal police department. Two police inspectors were sent to the hotel to investigate.

The police inspectors identified themselves to the escapee and proceeded to question him. The escapee realized at once that he would not be able to talk his way out of this situation and made a full confession. In the presence of several hotel guests, the inspectors arrested him formally, escorted him downstairs and ordered him to enter the side car of their motorcycle. They drove him away to an area of fields and gardens and invited him to cross over a little creek into Switzerland.

After the end of World War II, all former members of the Gestapo were investigated for war crimes. Even if no evidence of specific crimes was found, they were dishonored and discharged from police service without pension. The three inspectors mentioned above shared this fate, because they had been involuntarily transferred into the Gestapo. But then a number of people who had been helped by them came forward and testified on their behalf. The Dachau escapee was one of them. The three inspectors now had all their rights restored to them and were honored publicly for their courage.

The three inspectors were in no way typical of the German people. They were very rare exceptions, three men who were willing to risk not only their careers but also their lives, even the lives of their families, to do what they considered to be the right thing. It is they and others like them, rather than our overpaid sports heroes, who deserve to receive our acclaim and respect. In our present world with our present values, this is not likely to happen.

I often think about my parents' role in helping between 200 and 300 Austrians to escape into Switzerland. There was never any doubt in their minds that they were doing the right thing, although some of the Jews of Constance warned us that we were endangering the whole community by our actions. Many of the Austrians who were helped by us have died by now, as have my parents. But their grandchildren may be living happily today in various parts of the world, completely unaware of the role played in their lives by a couple of strangers in an accident of history.

There was one specific young family I think of quite often. They had lived a normal, happy life in Vienna. One day, their Austrian neighbors robbed them and beat them (because they were Jews). They still had their most precious possession, a five year old daughter. So they fled for their lives to Constance, where their little girl suddenly came down with polio and died. They left their beloved daughter in a lonely grave in a strange town in a strange country that hated them (because they were Jews) and escaped into another strange land that didn't want them. If they are alive today, they must still be asking themselves the eternal questions, the unanswerable questions: Why? Why did this happen to us? What horrible crime did we commit unknowingly to deserve this punishment? And they were the lucky ones, the survivors.

4 Kristallnacht

The disability pension my father received on account of his war injury was now our only regular source of income. It was a small amount, not even enough to pay our monthly rent. Fortunately, another source of money appeared at this time.

My Uncle Isi and Aunt Celia Ottenheimer, who lived in Rexingen, had received permission to immigrate to the United States. They sold the family house and paid for the passage , but they were not permitted to take the remaining money out of the country. The money was transferred to my parents as a loan. It kept us going for about a year. My grandmother Fanny, the mother of my father and Uncle Isi, had lived with my uncle and aunt for many years. She could not accompany them to the United States, however, because her number had not come up yet. So she moved in with us.

Grandmother Fanny was an extraordinary woman. Anytime I saw her, she was always working: cooking, baking, cleaning or knitting. Her husband, my grandfather, passed away when my father was not quite 12 years old, leaving Grandmother to raise three children through many difficult years. (Two older children were on their own.) She developed a calmness and a stoic faith in providence that not even a screaming disaster could penetrate. My mother was the exact opposite: She worried about the most remote possibilities and grieved about everybody's misfortunes. Rather than being reassured by her mother-in-law's calmness, she was irritated by what she perceived of as apathy. But a polite neutrality was maintained between the two women.

Grandfather Metzger, our Opa, was my idol. He was warm and spirited with a gentle sense of humor and a quiet self-assurance. His wife, our Oma, died of heart failure in 1933. Opa now lived at the Hotel Bahnhof in Frauenfeld, Switzerland, during the week, buying and selling cows. On Fridays, he would head for our home and stay until Sunday or Monday. Ilse and I always gave him a big welcome perhaps because he always brought us delicious Swiss candy bars. Opa got along very well with the Swiss peasants. He spoke their dialect and smoked their *Stumpen*, a crude local version of cigars. And, like the Swiss, he had an earthy, honest, modest way of viewing life. As Nazi regulations became more obstructive, Opa's visits to Constance became less frequent and finally stopped. He was now a permanent resident of Switzerland, with frequent visits to his other daughter's family in France.

Gigi with her Opa, 1939

Ilse left us. Shortly after the start of the Austrian action, my sister received her visa for immigration to the United States. She was exactly 16 years old, a very sheltered 16 years. Ilse was an excellent student, much better than I. Her education did not include English. Evidently, there were no English teachers in the Constance public schools. It was hard for her to leave her family and friends. There would be relatives in America, but she knew them by name only. Ilse took a train to our relatives in France. From there, Uncle Léon accompanied her to LeHavre, where she boarded the S.S. Manhattan to New York City. Ilse was now on her own.

A few months later, we were instructed to report to the U.S. Consulate in Stuttgart for our final interview. We understood this to be only a formality. Our number had come up, our time had come at last! My parents did not want to spend one extra day in Germany, so we moved into a single, furnished room while our furniture, dishes, clothes, and linens were being crated for shipment. The trip to Stuttgart was no problem. We stayed overnight with my aunt and uncle who lived there. About a week after our return to Constance, we received a note from the consulate that our application for immigration had been reviewed and was rejected. The note did not state a reason or indicate any possible remedy.

We knew a man in Constance who could speak English. We asked him to phone the consulate and ask for the missing information. He was told that we were turned down because of my father's war injury. The consul felt that Aunt Flora's affidavit was not adequate to assure that our family would not become a public burden. A supplemental affidavit would be required.

My father sent telegrams to our various relatives in the United States. Uncle Sieg was now apparently more aware of the dangers we were facing in Germany. He immediately submitted the necessary documents. We were notified that we would have to wait once more while the new documents were being processed. That would not take long. We put our crates into storage and waited in our furnished room, my parents, my grandmother, and I.

Our family living room, which doubled as a bedroom, was fairly large, but naturally there was no privacy. We also had bathroom and kitchen usage, shared with the landlady and the other tenants. The apartment was located around the corner from the synagogue, which had become the social center for the Jewish community since other facilities were no longer available to us.

The landlady, Mrs. Hauser, was a fat, jovial woman who was forever misplacing her dentures. She enjoyed redecorating her home by moving furniture around. She would place her rear end against a chest or wardrobe and apply a series of bumps in the proper direction. Mrs. Hauser had an inexhaustible supply of humorous anecdotes that always left her laughing at the end. One of these stories was about the time she swallowed her denture. She consulted a physician, who recommended that she eat lots of sauerkraut and keep her eyes open. The treatment was successful, and her teeth were recovered on the next day.

Mrs. Hauser was a really good Christian woman without the slightest interest in politics and without a single hostile thought in her mind. She had two beautiful cats that became my best friends. This was a real treat for me, because my mother never allowed me to have any pets, except for two gold fish that were not the least bit cuddly and did not live very long. Now, two cats. Wow!

Mrs. Hauser had two other tenants in her big apartment. I only remember one of them. LaValenta. That was her stage name. She used to be a cabaret dancer. One of her better known acts consisted of a dance in a lion's cage, and she was proud to show us the photographs and the scars derived from that experience. She was no longer dancing, but she was still a beautiful woman. She rented the room next to ours. Sometimes we could hear her arguing with her boyfriend, an S.S. man. She told us that the only thing they ever disagreed about was Hitler's treatment of the Jews. It seems that LaValenta had had some good Jewish friends in her cabaret days.

One of my daily chores was to get the mail from the mailbox downstairs and to distribute it to the various apartment dwellers. On one particular day, I knocked on LaValenta's door to deliver her mail. She called out, "Yes!" In her mind, "Yes" meant "Yes, who is it?" In my mind, "Yes" meant "Yes, come in!" I opened the door and saw a basin of water standing on the floor, with LaValenta standing in the basin and wearing absolutely nothing. We stared at each other for what may have been one second or ten seconds. Then I dropped the mail on the floor and ran out. If she was at all perturbed by this incident, she never let on.

LaValenta, the dancer

I missed my friends from the old neighborhood. They had previously stopped playing games with me after school, but we had still been able to have fun walking to and from school together. We would play and clown around all the way, take turns kicking an apple, jump over a puddle, pick a few hazelnuts when we passed the church, play tag. Hans would stop to pet a dog. When we got to Kurt's house, Kurt would keep going to walk me home, then I would walk him back to his house, he would walk me back again, etc. That was all over now. Sometimes we would exchange a few words at school, that was all.

I gained a new friend, a Jewish boy named Leo. His parents had come to Constance from Poland and spoke Yiddish, but Leo spoke the Constance dialect of German like the rest of us. Leo's father was a tailor. One of the rooms in their apartment was used as a workshop. Leo and I could not enjoy ritual walks to school because he lived at the opposite end of town, near the Rhine River. But our friendship grew closer as our ties with our respective neighborhood friends weakened.

On the morning of November 10, 1938, I was awakened by the sound of an explosion. It must have been the gas station across the street, I thought. I jumped out of bed and ran to the window. Everything looked normal at the gas station, but I could see a flickering red glow in the sky. I ran to the stairwell and looked out the window to the backyard. I stared in shock: Where our beautiful synagogue used to stand, there was now only a wall of flames! I ran back to our room and got dressed after reporting the tragic news to my parents and grandmother. My father ordered me to stay in the house. Mrs. Hauser went out to make some inquiries and reported back to us. Yes, the synagogue had been blown up. But there was more shocking news: All the Jewish men in Constance had been arrested by the Gestapo early that morning. All except my father, that is! Was the world going crazy? And why wasn't my father picked up? Maybe they looked for him at the old address, or maybe they did not arrest him because of his war record. We prayed and waited in our room.

My father decided to shave after lunch. Suddenly, there was a loud knock on the door. Two Gestapo agents had come to arrest my father. "Can I finish shaving first?" he asked. "No. Wipe off your face and get moving!" The three walked away quietly.

We did not realize until evening that the events of that day were repeated in towns and villages all over Germany. It was to be referred to later as "*Kristallnacht*," or the night of broken glass. It started on the previous day, November 9. A young Jew, 17 years old, had murdered a German official in Paris, France. This was apparently the sort of thing Hitler had been waiting for as a pretext for taking the next step against all the German Jews. During the night of November 9, practically all synagogues in Germany were destroyed, and gangs marched through the streets breaking windows and property in Jewish stores and Jewish homes. On the following day, some 30,000 Jewish men, age 16 and up, were arrested by Gestapo agents and sent to concentration camps. Fortunately for me, I was 13 at the time.

Aside from the destruction of the synagogue, not one window was broken in Constance during the night of broken glass. Constance was a rare exception, perhaps because the people were less hateful than in other towns, or perhaps because orders had been given to "go easy" in towns where Swiss visitors and journalists would witness the events. Probably, it was a combination of the two.

German newspapers and radio stations reported on November 11 that the events of *Kristallnacht* were the German people's spontaneous reaction to the "Jewish crime" and that a number of Jews were taken into "protective custody" for their own safety. I doubt that Hitler expected anyone to believe this "explanation." The Nazi government extended their transparent hypocrisy by claiming that the Jews themselves were to blame for *Kristallnacht*. Every Jew had to pay a "fine" of 25 percent of his property. All damaged buildings other than synagogues had to be restored to their original condition at the expense of the Jews, and any insurance compensation had to be turned over to the government. Jews were now excluded from all business activity, and Jewish children were no longer permitted to attend public schools or universities.

For the longest time we did not know where my father had been sent. We heard that all the arrested men had been taken to Gestapo headquarters and that some had been beaten. But they were no longer there. Were they still in Constance? Were they still alive? Nobody knew.

It occurred to me that my father — all of us — could have been in America by now, if only the consul had not turned us down.

Days, weeks passed by, weeks of fear and confusion. We managed as well as we could without my father. Late one night in December, there was a soft knock on our door. It was Papa. We could hardly recognize him, he was sick and had lost a lot of weight. But thank God he had come back home! Had they kept him for just one week longer, he would probably have succumbed.

Most of the other Jewish men were also released over a period of about six months. Some, especially the old and sick men, did not survive the ordeal. My uncle in Stuttgart was among the men who were arrested on *Kristallnacht*. He was fairly young and in good physical condition. After two months, my aunt received an official government notice informing her that if she would send 100 Marks to a specified address, the government would send her the ashes of her late husband.

Meanwhile in Gailingen, the Nazis had appointed their most fanatical party member as mayor. He and his henchmen made sure that every Christian home was decorated with a swastika flag. They organized weekly Nazi parades and Nazi meetings, and they produced a steady stream of vicious anti-Semitic propaganda. The boycott of Jewish stores and the provisions of the Nuremberg laws were enforced with enthusiasm in Gailingen. Rocks came crashing through some Jewish windows long before *Kristallnacht*, and Jews could expect to be insulted and harassed any time they left their homes. Jewish children were beaten up regularly on their way home from school, and prominent Jewish residents were arrested for no particular reason and kept overnight "for questioning."

On *Kristallnacht* in Gailingen, all of the Jewish people, including the oldest, the youngest and the disabled were marched or dragged through the village, ending up in front of the synagogue. They shivered on that cold November morning while the mayor subjected them to an abusive tirade, while many of their neighbors screamed and spat at them, and while a squad of storm troopers carried dynamite into the synagogue and carried out everything of value. The proceedings were interrupted by the explosion in the synagogue. The women and children were sent back to their homes, some of which had been plundered in the meantime. Most of the men were taken away by the Gestapo, beaten up and sent to Dachau concentration camp. There they were held in the same barracks as the men from Constance.

My father told us some details after he came back from Dachau. The main food item at Dachau was a greasy, smelly soup. Dr. Bohrer, the rabbi of Gailingen, urged all the men to eat the soup, explaining that the Jewish religion considered the preservation of life to be more important than compliance with dietary laws. He himself, however, refused to eat and died shortly after his arrival at Dachau. The survivors were allowed to return to Gailingen after a month or two.

When World War II started, the Jewish community of Gailingen, which at one time numbered 1,000, had shrunk to about 300. The unhappy 300 were deported to Camp Gurs in southern France in 1940. This included all the residents of the home for the aged, many of whom were senile, crippled or blind. Those who survived this ordeal were sent to Auschwitz in 1942 and immediately murdered. Thus ended the Jewish community of Gailingen.[4]

In Rexingen there was little noticeable effect at first from the change in national government. There was a growing amount of Nazi activity, and there were isolated anti-Semitic incidents; but the intensity was nowhere near that of Gailingen. Incidentally, there were no Jewish stores to boycott, no Jewish lawyers, doctors or civil servants to be fired. On *Kristallnacht*, a squad of storm troopers from the nearby town of Horb entered the synagogue, piled up all the prayer books and Torahs in the middle, poured gasoline over them and set them on fire. As soon as the storm troopers had run out of the building, the local volunteer fire department ran in through the back door and put out the fire, while a local police officer personally saved a Torah scroll. The men were questioned at length on the next day and severely reprimanded by party officials. But the synagogue of Rexingen still stands (one of very few left in Germany), although converted to a church after the war. All the Jewish men were arrested by the Horb Gestapo and sent to Dachau for one or two months. About 50 Jewish families, one-half of the remaining community, were permitted to immigrate to Palestine on the basis of their farming background. The others perished in death camps. The immigrants formed Shave Tzion, a large agricultural kibbutz (communal farm) on the Mediterranean coast. After World War II ended, a number of trips were arranged for former Rexinger Jews at the kibbutz to visit Rexingen and for the Christians of Rexingen to visit their former neighbors in Israel in continuation of old friendships.[5]

Dr. Erich Bloch's book about the Jews of Constance[6] contains an interesting description of the destruction of the synagogue on *Kristallnacht*. The S.S. commandant in Stuttgart issued orders to his unit in Constance, early evening of November 9, to burn down the synagogue. A concurrent order was directed to the police department not to interfere and to restrict fire fighting activity to nearby houses.

"Is Constance asleep?" was the next message from Stuttgart around midnight. They were waiting impatiently for word that their order had been carried out. But Constance was not asleep. The S.S. could not get into the synagogue thanks to the burglar-proof doors and locks that had been installed after the 1936 fire. They tried burning down the doors, then sent for a locksmith, all in vain. They finally broke down a door leading to one of the outer rooms and started a fire there, which produced only smoke and forced the S.S. men to run out for air. A neighbor noticed the smoke and notified the fire department. Several fire trucks rushed to the scene at about 3 a.m. but were intercepted by several S.S. men, who were getting very irate. Their leader shouted, "We don't need water. We need gasoline and oxygen masks!" The fire trucks returned to their stations, but some pro-Nazi firemen apparently returned with the requested items and showed the S.S. men how to open a ventilation opening in the roof. They poured gasoline through the opening, followed by several lit torches. Still, there was not much of a fire in the synagogue. In desperation, they called for an S.S. demolition squad in a nearby town to rush in. The squad arrived at 6 a.m. The street was now blocked off, the fire trucks were brought back for protection of neighboring houses and three

The synagogue in Constance before and after Kristallnacht.

explosive charges were set off. The walls of the synagogue collapsed, and the interior burst into flames.

A priest on his way to church was appalled to see the fire and the inert fire department. "Why aren't you putting out the fire?" he shouted. "That's a house of God that's burning!" An S.S. man struck him and yelled, "Keep moving, you black devil or we'll burn down your house of God, too!" By 10 a.m., only a smoldering pile was left of our beautiful synagogue and of any false hopes any Jews might still have had.

My father never talked much about his month at Dachau concentration camp. He was completely silent about it while we were still in Germany. He had to sign an oath of secrecy when he was released from Dachau, and he did not want to place the burden of secrecy on us. He did tell us about the strange circumstances of his arrest, however. The two Gestapo agents ordered him to get into their car. They drove him into town and stopped in front of a tobacco store. The agents now got out and ordered my father to stay in the car while both went into the store to buy cigarettes. This was obviously not standard procedure. Either the agents wanted my father to escape across the Swiss border (a 15-minute walk away), or they wanted him to make a run for it, giving them or hidden accomplices justification to shoot their prisoner while trying to escape. My father also considered the possibility that the border might be heavily guarded on this particular day and the likelihood of punitive action against the family if his escape were to succeed. He decided to sit still. After about five minutes, the Gestapo agents returned and drove him to headquarters without any further conversation.

I asked my father some thirty years later about his life at Dachau. It was constant harassment, he explained. It started with roll call at 6 a.m. in front of the barracks, which sometimes lasted for an hour if someone failed to respond to his name. They were then ordered to run across the area to the fence, where they might have to stand at attention for half an hour. They might then have to jog around the field for a while, then stand for another roll call. All this was done in sub-freezing weather, with the prisoners wearing only a striped cotton uniform. They were fed twice a day, each time a bowl of smelly, greasy soup, which my father thought was made by boiling hides and bones of animals in water, and a piece of moldy bread. After the first week, every prisoner was suffering from dysentery, and many men were dying. At this time, concentration camps had not yet been converted into killing plants. They served only as sadistic prison camps.

I believe that Hitler saw *Kristallnacht* as a test of public reaction, both within Germany and in other countries. When he saw that public reaction was no more than words, he understood the message he had received from the world: "They are your Jews. You can do with them whatever you want." It was the beginning of the Holocaust.

It was good to have papa back. But we were still concerned. There

Gus, our friend

was no word from the US consulate about our immigration papers. Every morning I would race down to the mailbox as soon as the mail was delivered, and my parents would meet me at the door. Nothing from the consulate. Why would it take them more than six months to process the new papers? But one day there was a note from Gus.

I was 10 years old the last time I saw Gus, but I still remember him clearly, especially when he played the piano at our home. Gus was a professional soldier in the German army, a first sergeant. His original home was far from Constance. That's probably why our home became a second home for him. He was a frequent house guest with us, and after dinner, we would move to our special room, and Gus would play the piano.

The piano was not in our family room. It was in the "good room," *das gute Zimmer* as it was called. It was reserved for special occasions. We kids were normally not allowed to enter the good room, perhaps to keep us from banging on the piano. But when Gus played the piano, the whole family would gather around him in the good room, and we would sing the beautiful German folk songs and Viennese operetta songs with him. I remember it very clearly and very fondly. I also had some good pillow fights with him, and I always listened attentively when he told us about occurrences in his daily life as a soldier. But Gus became the respectful listener, in turn, whenever my father related stories about his adventures as a sergeant in the German army during World War I. Gus was a good friend.

When Hitler came to power in 1933, many friendships were destroyed instantly. Not so our friendship with Gus. But Gus was becoming more and more depressed. He told us about arguments he had had with other soldiers and warnings he had received from his superior officers. We did not expect him to sacrifice his professional career for the sake of our friendship, and we told him so. Gus got very indignant: "No one is going to tell *me* who I can be friends with!" he shouted.

Gus came less frequently now, and one day his visits stopped completely. He did not communicate with us in any way. But we understood. It would have been too dangerous: Houses were watched, telephones were tapped, mail was censored.

In early 1939, while waiting in our one-room abode, the mail that morning included a letter from Uncle Léon, Aunt Martha and Gigi. As was the practice with all mail to or from a foreign country, a slit had been cut across the top of the envelope and resealed with adhesive tape that proclaimed in big letters: "Opened by censor." But there was also an unexpected enclosure in the envelope: A note from Gus. He was the censor. Gus had been transferred to this desk job as punishment for his friendship with us. In his note, he told us that he valued our friendship very highly, that he was sorry not to be able to see us any more, and that he was ashamed of what his government was doing to our people. It was obvious that Gus had read Aunt Martha's letter, because he closed his note with a wish that we would be able to leave soon and that we would have a happier life in the United States. We read the note about five times and then burned it.

We never heard from Gus any more. Many years later, my parents were told that he was returned to active duty after the war started, that he was transferred to the Russian front and was killed there.[7] In recent years, a number of Jewish ghetto and camp survivors have told of incidents where their lives were saved by the actions of some anonymous German soldiers. The question always occurs to me: Could one of them have been Gus? Unfortunately, I will never know.

In late April we received a letter from the US Consulate -- our application was approved; we could go. There was no time to lose. My father made all the formal arrangements, tickets for train and ship, release our crates for shipment, telegrams to relatives, forms to fill out, etc. My grandmother was going with us. She received her visa earlier but chose to wait for us. She was 87 years old, and she was undoubtedly calmer than any of us about starting a new life in a new land. We all felt like prisoners being released from jail, and I looked forward to the adventure of an unknown future. But we also felt the pain of parting from the only life, the only country, the only people we knew. We had always tried to live a decent, honest, caring life but we were now being insulted, throttled, pushed out because we were Jews.

It was a time of dire confusion. The pain of recent abuse and rejection by Nazi Germany created feelings that were in direct conflict with residual feelings of affection for the land of my happy childhood years. I wasn't worried about my future in the United States. Unlike my sister, I still enjoyed the protection of my loving family. They were my immediate environment, insulating me from the world around.

They would take care of me.

But it was difficult for my parents to retain any faith in themselves. What happened to their life's work, to their plans? Could the family survive in a strange country whose language we didn't even understand? It may not make sense, but Nazi propaganda was actually having an effect on us. We felt inferior, dirty, guilty—of what?

I was 14 years old when we left Constance in May 1939. It was hard for me to say good-bye to Leo, his sister and their parents. They, too, had relatives in America

Gigi with Fritz, on his way to the United States

who had applied for their immigration visa. But they were on the Polish quota, which meant that they would have to wait 10 to 12 years for their number to come up. Unfortunately, Hitler was not as patient as the U.S. Immigration and Naturalization Service.

It was more difficult than we expected to leave Mrs. Hauser, LaValenta and the two cats. In just a few months, we had grown very close to each other. We took a cab to the railroad station. There was no one to see us off when our train pulled out. It was a sad moment, but we were the lucky ones.

We stopped at Frauenfeld for a brief reunion with Opa. We were happy to learn from him that Uncle Sieg had provided an affidavit for him. Opa would be joining us in the United States in a few months. Maybe things would work out from now on. Our next stop was in Colmar, France. We stayed overnight with Aunt Martha, Uncle Léon and Gilberte. Gigi, at age 13, was still a sweet, fun-loving girl. We all had a very happy evening together in spite of any concerns about how we would manage in America. We were not at all worried about Aunt Martha's family. Neither we nor they had any way of knowing that their young lives would end in three years.

We left Colmar for LeHavre, where we boarded the S.S. Washington for our trip to New York City. It was exactly three-and-a-half months before the start of World War II. I had no idea of what lay ahead, chose not to think about what I was leaving behind. There was only today—and the vast ocean all around us.

5 THE ONLY WAY OUT

I loved to travel when I was a boy, no matter where I was going or by what means. Unfortunately, I was plagued by motion sickness. As soon as I smelled locomotive or car exhaust fumes, I would feel nauseous, and shortly after the vehicle started moving, I would have to reach for a bag or bucket or head for the toilet on a train. Still, I loved to travel. Much to my surprise, I did not have any discomfort at all during our long train ride from Constance to LeHavre or during any land travel any time afterwards. On the ship, crossing the Atlantic Ocean, I felt fine as long as I was on deck or lying down in our cabin. If I tried to go to the dining room, I would immediately feel sick. I suppose I lost a little weight during that week, subsisting on sandwiches and fruit that my parents and grandmother brought up to the deck for me.

I straightened out on the last day at sea, just in time for the ship's party. For the first time in my 14 years of life, I enjoyed a real steak dinner followed by champagne ice cream. My parents did not have the heart to point out that this was a violation of Jewish dietary (kosher) laws. Following the dinner, there was a lively sing-along session for everybody. It was my first introduction to America. The cheerful songs, the carefree American college students, the festive atmosphere it was a different world already so unreal, so happy. Everybody was on deck when we entered New York harbor on the following morning. Look, there is the Statue of Liberty and over there the skyscrapers. I wished that the ship could go faster.

At last the ship was tied up alongside the pier, and the passengers started to disembark. There was extensive paperwork. We were directed to a small group of refugees on one side of the hall. Something was wrong with our papers. We had to carry our hand baggage along as we boarded a small ship that took us to Ellis Island. We entered a large building. More paperwork, questions, discussions. No, this place was not really America, not exactly. What was it then? My grandmother was allowed to leave with her sponsors on the next day, but we would have to stay until everything was straightened out.[8]

All day long we were in a huge hall with a high ceiling. There were many chairs and a few tables in there, occupied by forty or fifty people, mostly from Germany. All the windows were barred. There was a beautiful view of the Statue of Liberty, located on the next island, seen through bars. Another window allowed us to see the New York sky-line through bars.

At mealtime, we passed through a door and a hallway to a big dining room. There were several lines of picnic tables and benches. We were served typical institutional food (meat loaf, stew, spaghetti) of good quality and generous quantity. We were told that this was ko-sher. On the way to and from the dining room, we were counted by a uniformed employee   a tall black man who always held a counting device in his hand and a friendly smile on his face. He was the first black person I had ever seen. He seemed very nice.

At night, we were directed through another door to the sleeping area. There was a room for men and boys and another for women and girls. There were many more bunk beds than the number of people staying there at the time. Connected to the big bedroom was a com-munal shower/wash room. Again, we were counted entering at night and returning to the central hall in the morning. Evidently this place was a jail   a pleasant, clean, polite jail.

My parents were frantic with fear: "Will they send us back to Ger-many?" I remember my mother asking. My father could only shrug. Our sponsors were informed of the problem on the day of our arrival. Now the bureaucratic wheels were turning, and all we could do was wait.

My sister, Ilse, and some of our other relatives came to greet us at the ship but were not allowed to meet us until we were safely stowed away on Ellis Island. The stress of the situation overpowered the joy of our reunion. What would happen to us?

I was more fatalistic than my parents. Besides, I was busy explor-ing our new surroundings. There was another German-Jewish boy, also age 14, among the residents of Ellis Island. We found a checker game board and started to play. After a few hours of this, I realized that the other boy was cheating. I looked around some more and found a Chinese boy who apparently was interested in playing checkers with me. There were minor problems: I could not speak Chinese, he could not speak German, and neither of us could speak English. And there were some obvious differences between the German and Chinese rules for playing checkers. We found out that nodding and shaking the head meant "yes" and "no," respectively, in both countries. In no time at all we agreed on an acceptable set of rules, and we became good friends.

Uncle Sieg showed up on the seventh day, along with his lawyer. I had never met Uncle Sieg before. He seemed to have some of his father's personality traits a quiet, sensible approach to problems and the same sense of humor as Opa. The attorney discussed our situation with an official, Uncle Sieg posted a $1,500 five-year bond, and we were free! It took no more than five minutes to pack our things. There was a short ferryboat ride to Manhattan. Uncle Sieg had some brief business to take care of in downtown New York. We all got into a taxicab and rode a few blocks. Uncle Sieg and the lawyer got out and asked us to wait for them in the cab. We were still stunned from the events of the day and the drastic change of surroundings.

Our cab driver left his vehicle and entered a store right in front of us. He returned a few minutes later and handed us a paper bag full of oranges. It was his welcoming gift to a family of strangers on their arrival in the United States. It was a kindness I would remember for the rest of my life.

Our next stop was the apartment of Uncle Isi and Aunt Celia, formerly from Rexingen. Grandmother had moved in with them again. Uncle Sieg had to leave immediately to get back to his business. We stayed with relatives for two or three days until our crates were delivered and unloaded at our apartment.

Unloading our belongings from their crates presented us with a bitter disappointment. It turned out that the crates had been stored outdoors all of these months. Several pieces of furniture were warped, some veneers were peeling off, and quite a bit of our clothing was mildewed. Mama had always been particularly proud of her hand-made tablecloths, embroidered pillow cases, knitted and crocheted items, some of which had been handed down from her grandparents. So many of these now had to be discarded. "It's too bad, but we have our health and our freedom, and we're back together with our Ilse. That's more important!"

When Ilse had arrived in the United States a year earlier, Uncle Sieg had advised her to stay in New York, because it would be easier for her to find a job there. She did find a "live-in" job right away, taking care of a family's children, even though she herself was only a child of 16. There was no way for her to continue her education. She got free room and board plus a very small salary, which she saved every month in order to get us started after our arrival. She rented an apartment for us in the Bronx. I remember it cost $35 per month, which seemed like a lot of money to us.

We were happy in our new home. It contained an electric refrigerator, a luxury we never enjoyed in Constance. We were not very happy to find out later that the apartment also contained mice, roaches and bed bugs, but we managed to control these after a while. We had a serious language problem, of course, but we had quite a lot of help from another family in the apartment building who had come from Germany earlier. The owners of a little grocery store on the ground floor of the same building spoke Yiddish, which is similar enough to German to permit mutual comprehension with some effort. We would not starve.

We were helped considerably at this time by our New York relatives. The Auerbachers, my father's sister, Aunt Sophie, her husband, Uncle Alfred, and their three daughters had immigrated five years before we did. They became our guides.

My parents were anxious to get me back to school as soon as possible. It was two weeks before the end of the school year when I showed up at Public School 73, Bronx. Being 14 years old, I should have been just completing the eighth grade. But I had missed the past seven months of school, and I could not speak English. Actually, I knew about a dozen words, such as hello, good-bye, thank you, you are welcome, yes and no as well as a few numbers. The principal decided to enroll me in 7A, the first term of seventh grade.

I was a complete misfit, older than the other children, unable to understand them or talk to them. They played ball games during recess that were completely unknown to me. There was a serious fashion problem, too. When I lived in Constance, boys of my age were expected to wear only short pants, summer and winter. If a boy wore long pants, everyone laughed at him: "What do you think you are a man?" When I showed up in shorts at P.S. 73, everyone laughed at me. Nobody wore shorts at P.S. 73 at any time in those days. A chorus of snickers followed me around all day, and nobody wanted to sit next to me.

Money was scarce for us, but I insisted that I needed to buy long pants and a few other "in" items. However, this did not assure me instant popularity or even acceptance. If a teacher asked me a question, I generally could not understand it, which resulted in a roomful of giggles; and if I did manage to comprehend, my answer came out in broken English, bringing loud laughter and imitation. Following one of these disasters, my history teacher surprised me by responding in German: "*Du bist ein Dummkopf*" (You are a dummy), she remarked.

My self-esteem was lower than the cuffs on my new pants. During recess, I sat on the edge of the school yard, next to the fence, hoping that no one would see me. I watched the boys throwing a ball and hitting it with a long stick, and I tried to figure out what the rules of the game might be. I also watched the girls skipping rope and playing hopscotch, as I had seen Ilse doing many times in Constance. The kids generally ignored me, which was fine with me. Before I knew it, two weeks had passed by and summer vacation had arrived.

My parents were determined never to ask our sponsors for help. A job was absolutely essential. My mother grasped the first opportunity that was available. She cleaned people's apartments, a different home every day. It was hard, tiring work during the hot, muggy summer days of New York City, and the pay was very poor. My father was unable to find any work. He took a subway train downtown every day to check with HIAS, the Hebrew Immigrant Aid Society. I went with him once. It took about half an hour to get there. We sat for about two hours until his name was called. We were told that there was nothing available. We rode back home. Fortunately, subway rides cost only a nickel each way. My father did all the shopping, cleaning, washing and cooking at home, with some help from me.

Yet we needed to learn to speak English. My father needed it in order to find a job, and I needed it in order to survive at school. We heard of free English lessons being offered, and we signed up right away. It was a government program, WPA, that created jobs for unemployed people, teachers in this case, during the Depression. It was a godsend for the teachers as well as for the students. I was pleased to discover that I could learn much faster and retain the knowledge much better than the adults did. My father found it particularly difficult because of a hearing problem, another liability from World War I. By the end of summer, I was able to understand, speak, read and write the bare essentials, still with a heavy German accent, of course.

Our English language instruction was not limited to the WPA course. We listened to the radio every day, and my father tried to read the *New York Times* from cover to cover every day. English did not come easily to us, and we would generally speak German. There was a radio station, WBNX, "the station that speaks your language." For an hour every day, we could enjoy German songs, dances, and commercials. There was a weekly newspaper, the "Aufbau," that was the voice of the German-Jewish refugees in America. It was an excellent publication whose staff included some of the top journalists of Germany evicted from their native country because of their religion.

Then there was the social center of German Jews in New York City, *the* Cafeteria. There must have been more than a hundred cafeterias in New York, and each of them undoubtedly had a name. But if you mentioned "the Cafeteria" to a German Jew, he knew exactly which one you meant. It was located in Washington Heights, the upper part of Manhattan, where a large number of German Jews made their new home in the United States. Hitler called his regime the Third Reich (empire); we referred to Washington Heights as the Fourth Reich. And the Cafeteria was right in the middle of the Fourth Reich.

Every evening, a number of German Jews would meet at the cafeteria to exchange information and rumors about friends and relatives, about happenings in the old country, about job opportunities. The cafeteria was a place for meeting, seeking advice, worrying, mourning, deliberating, and reminiscing. On Saturday nights, it was standing room only. That may sound like a boon for the owner, but it was not. It was a calamity. These were not rich people. They were porters, maids, Fuller Brush salesmen, unemployed men and women. They would buy a cup of coffee for five cents and nurse it for three hours. Any paying customers could see that all the seats in the place were taken and would look for another restaurant.

If only a philanthropic organization had taken over the cafeteria and maintained it as a community center for German-Jewish refugees! No need to hire social workers or entertainment directors. Just keep the coffee hot. Or, if a university had kept the cafeteria going, the conversations overheard every night would have provided material for a thousand Ph.D. theses in history, sociology, economics, and psychology. But no one took over the cafeteria, and after a couple of years, it closed its doors forever. There was no other institution to carry on its vital function.

Papa got very frustrated about his inability to find a job. There must be something he could do. He analyzed his own housework and noticed that he used a cake of kosher kitchen soap (made from coconut oil) and had to replace it frequently. He decided to sell kosher soap door to door. Everybody needs kosher soap, and they could buy several cakes at a time because it wouldn't spoil. He took an empty suitcase to the subway station, rode a subway train to the factory in Brooklyn, and returned home with the suitcase filled with kosher soap.

My father was eager to get started. His judgment must have been swayed by the percentages of the transaction: buy at two cents per cake and sell at five cents. What he now found out was how hard it was to sell 10 cakes of soap -- how many steps he had to climb, how many door bells he had to ring, how many doors were slammed in his face. Then there were the frugal housewives who argued that they could get three cakes of soap for a dime at the supermarket. Even if papa sold 100 cakes of soap, he would have only $3 profit to show for all that effort. His project was not a total failure, however. He gained sorely needed outside activity, a few days of hope, and we did not need to buy any more kosher soap for a long time.

It seemed that way in all of our daily struggles: a little bit of hope and a lot of work. There was a small produce store across the street from our house. The owners, two Greek brothers, placed baskets of fruits and vegetables on the sidewalk every morning and moved the residuals into the store in the evening. We always did our shopping on Saturday evening, that's when they lowered the price on produce that would not keep until Monday. Papa enjoyed negotiating with the men.

"We have nice, ripe peaches tonight. But a few have brown spots." Papa held one up. "How much?"

"You can have them for five cents a pound." I noticed that the tag on the box said 20 cents per pound.

"Okay. We have five pounds, please."

"Five pounds coming up." With that, he emptied the entire basket of peaches into several paper bags. It must have been 15 to 20 pounds. "That's 25 cents," he said. "Can you use some tomatoes?"

After we had gathered up what we needed for the coming week, the owner would collect the token amount of money from us and thank us profusely. We would carry all the bags across the street and up the steps to our apartment. Then the family would sit around the kitchen table for the next hour, removing the brown spots and pits from the peaches. When we were done, Papa would cook the peaches. While peaches were in season, we seemed to eat cooked peaches with practically every meal, but I never minded it. Those peaches tasted so much better than the ones we can get today.

Soon summer ended. I was not looking forward to school, even though my knowledge of English had improved. On the first day back at school, I returned to my seat at the fence during recess. I cringed when I saw a quiet boy, Carl, approaching. He asked me a question about one of the school subjects. I answered as well as I could. Carl did not laugh. He sat down next to me and asked me about Germany. He mentioned that his family came from Finland. On the following day, before I had a chance to retreat to my sanctuary, Carl asked me if I would like to play ball with him and his friends. "Uh, yes. Yes, I would!" It was a turning point in my life at P.S. 73. There would still be an occasional smirk when I "talked funny," but I was now accepted, more or less, by everybody.

My scholastic performance improved substantially after I found the courage to speak up. Mathematics was my best subject. I was far ahead of everybody. Much to everyone's surprise, I rose to the top of the class in English grammar, although I still had trouble carrying on a conversation. As a foreigner, I was able to learn the formalities of English grammar objectively, rather than intuitively, the way a native child does. I also learned to master the unruly rules of English spelling. There was a spelling contest in the class, boys versus girls, in which I turned out to be the final boy contestant. I lost out to two girl finalists when I left out an "r" in "marriage." But before that happened, I enjoyed the unusual experience of being cheered on by all the boys in the class. At midyear report card time, I was promoted from grade 7B to 8B, skipping 8A.

Conditions were deteriorating in Europe, but we received some good news. My grandfather was coming to America! Opa arrived in October 1939 on the last voyage of the Italian ocean liner "Rex." He was 76 years old, but he was still as alert, energetic and personable as ever. He would live with us in New York nine or ten months of each year and spend the summers in Ohio with his son's family (Uncle Sieg). It felt so good to have Opa back.

Papa finally got a job. Uncle Isi had been working as a porter in a movie theater. He heard of a similar job being available at another theater and told my father about it. Papa rushed to the theater immediately and was hired. The Prospect Theater was old and dirty, in a poor neighborhood. Papa's job was to sweep up the trash, to vacuum and mop various parts of the theater, and to clean up the restrooms. His hours were from midnight (after the last show) until 8 a.m. There were supposed to be two porters working together, but the other man was either absent or drunk about half of the time. The pay was very poor, but it was a steady job and would enable my mother to reduce her working hours a bit. My grandfather took over much of the cooking and cleaning for the family.

Papa was proud of his work. He was only a porter, but he was determined to be the best porter in New York. Papa changed work procedures, experimented with new cleaning chemicals, and gave us a detailed report every day about his progress. After his first month at the Prospect, Papa was able to quote "the boss" as admitting that he had never seen the place this clean before. After a few years, he transferred to a newer theater, the RKO Fordham. Papa's ambition never waned, although his wages hardly ever grew. It was his way of proving to the world that he was just as capable, just as honest as anyone else.

We were making the best of our new start in the United States. But soon there was more bad news from Europe: Germany attacked Poland on September 1, 1939. It was the start of World War II. Leaving Germany, legally or otherwise, became almost impossible now. Had the U.S. Consul kept us waiting just four months longer, we would have been trapped in Germany. We were lucky, so many others were not.

In the ensuing months, one by one, practically every country in Europe was attacked and conquered by the powerful German army. Of personal concern to us, following the fall of France in June 1940, Aunt Martha, Uncle Léon, and Gilberte were now living under Nazi occupation. We were horrified. Has evil become invincible? Is there no way to stop Hitler's onslaught? I remembered a Nazi song that we were taught in school and that Nazi gangs used to sing in Constance. It ended with the words: "We shall keep on marching, though everything were to shatter; for today Germany is ours, and tomorrow the whole world!"

Our condition had stabilized. Our lifestyle was certainly not luxurious, but we were managing nicely. Once in a while I waited outside a grocery store and offered to carry bags for women. Tips were skimpy. Nobody was rich. My parents did not want me to look for a job. My education was much more important to them. It was their investment in the future. When people found out that we came from Germany a year ago, they invariably asked: "How do you like this country?" We could now answer truthfully, "We like it very much!" Especially considering what our life would be like if we were still in Germany.

The time was approaching for me to pick a high school. I asked my teacher for advice. "What do you want to be when you grow up?" she asked. I did not have a good answer to that question. The teacher tried a different approach "What kind of business are your parents in?" "My father is a porter, my mother is a cleaning woman." She shifted gears once more: "What kind of activity do you like best? Do you like to sell things or fix things or help people or explain or argue or..." "I fixed an alarm clock last week and I made a telegraph set once," I recalled. "Maybe you'd like to be an engineer," she concluded. "You could try to get into the Bronx High School of Science."

I asked some of my friends if they knew what an engineer does. They did not know. I asked what they knew about the Bronx High School of Science. They laughed. "Only the best students from all over New York get into that school. Forget it!" I had already filled out an application form by that time, and before long, I was asked to take an entrance examination. There were twenty applicants from P.S. 73. Three students were accepted. Everybody was shocked to find out that I was one of the three. A thought occurred to me: Do they still think that I am a *Dummkopf*?

As their laughter echoed in my mind, I thought about my future and the opportunities ahead. I was regaining some degree of self-confidence, but the fate of my friends and relatives in Germany and France filled me with overwhelming anxiety. Nazi hatred of the Jews, which had given rise to the horrors of *Kristallnacht*, was now undoubtedly exacerbated by growing war hysteria. What would happen to our loved ones? They were at the mercy of their monstrous rulers, and we were unable to help them.

6 A Learning Experience

The Bronx High School of Science was the best public high school in the United States. Its main assets were a young, enthusiastic faculty and a small student body—boys only at the time—carefully selected for their scholastic interest and ability. No less than five Nobel Prize winners have been spawned at Science High. The teachers had a special talent for making each student feel important, capable, and interesting. The boys were highly motivated, competitive and, at the same time, appreciative of others' individuality. There was only one black boy in the school. He was elected president of the student council.

The school was located on 184th Street, necessitating a daily round trip by subway train from our house. It was a decrepit old building, reputedly condemned by the New York health department. The noise of building renovation work sometimes drowned out the teacher's voice, and I remember seeing a couple of mice running across the floor. But the science laboratories were completely equipped and immaculate.

My self-esteem rose considerably during the next four years, starting with my unexpected admission to Science High. It was easy to make friends there, possibly because there was a strong in-group feeling among its "elite" population. Since only two or three students were admitted from each elementary school, there were no established cliques, and everyone was looking for new friends. Extracurricular activities were booming.

It seemed that everybody liked me at Science High. How come? Couldn't they hear my foreign accent? I joined the Mathematics (Service) Squad, the French Club, and the Soccer Squad. In subsequent years, I added the Nature Club and the Chess Club and became editor of the school's first guide book. I loved school now, even subjects that I had previously disliked. Naturally, my grades rose.

One of my classmates introduced me to Hashomer Hatzair. He described it as just a bunch of kids who get together to have fun. On the surface, that was a good description—but there was much more.

It was a socialist-Zionist youth organization, well-managed by its own highly spirited members. I found myself immersed in Zionist culture - singing, dancing, and discussing far beyond anything I had ever experienced. I was embraced with love and enthusiasm by my new friends. Both of the leaders and more than half of the members were girls. They loved independent thinking; they hated artificiality. They were my first American girlfriends.

But all good things eventually end, and so it was when the United States was drawn into World War II by Japan's attack on Pearl Harbor, followed by Hitler's declaration of war against the United States. Considering Hitler's hatred for America, our involvement in the war seemed inevitable. I did not think this would happen, however, until after England and the Soviet Union had been eliminated. As it worked out, we still had two strong allies and several strategic staging areas in our campaign against Hitler, and we could count on the British Empire and China in our struggle with Japan. But now America had to build up its own military strength rapidly while keeping its allies alive with a steady flow of armaments.

We had become enemy aliens. Since Germany was at war with the United States, any German national was technically an enemy of the United States, unless proven otherwise. Hitler had deprived the Jews of German citizenship several years earlier—but as far as the American bureaucracy was concerned, we were followers rather than victims of Hitler. We had to report to the Kingsbridge Armory to get our Enemy Alien Registration Cards. Actually, it was just a formality, and nobody paid any attention to our new status. But it bothered us.

With the United States at war with Germany, mail service from occupied France was terminated. Occasionally, we received a brief, innocuous message from Aunt Martha, Uncle Léon and Gigi via International Red Cross, and we replied the same way. Their last message was dated May 17, 1942. After that, there was silence.

We had other relatives who lived in France: my cousin, Sylvain, and Sylvain's elderly parents, the Grumbachers; my mother's cousin, Louise Levy, and her son, Orest. They also disappeared from us, al-

Paula and Leo, 1938

though they were to survive the war.

We heard from my friend Leo, his sister Paula, and their mother. They had been sent to Camp Gurs in unoccupied France in October 1940. Conditions were terrible. Leo, Paula, and their mother were very hungry and cold. Could we help them? We sent several packages, then there was silence. We found out later that Leo, at age 16, had escaped from Camp Gurs and joined the French underground. Paula was allowed to enter Switzerland by children's transport. They both survived the war. Their father had somehow fled to England and died there in 1943. Their mother was deported to Auschwitz concentration camp, where she was killed. It was an early example of the sickening news that would unravel over the next several years.

The victories and defeats of World War II were an important part of our daily lives. Every morning we would listen to the news or read the newspaper to find out what happened in the various war arenas during the night. This was how children learned to read maps and to find the location of various countries.

Physically, the war had very little effect on us. Gasoline was rationed, but we did not own a car. The rationing of some foods (e.g., meat, butter and sugar) was only a minor inconvenience. What became increasingly important to me was the prospect of being drafted into the U.S. Army following graduation from high school. I probably had a better understanding than any of my schoolmates of the need to defeat Hitler. But I was very timid. I could not visualize myself as a participant in military service, in the violence of warfare. I looked forward to graduation with mixed feelings.

We all felt that we ought to do something for the war effort. I decided to join Civil Defense. Since I was less than 18 years old, I was only qualified to be a messenger. Our local headquarters was an empty store three blocks from home. I had two duties to perform: to put in as much time as possible at headquarters in case a runner was ever needed and to patrol our neighborhood with an air raid warden during air raid drills. Both tasks were quite pleasant. The other messengers in our area were very sociable, and there were several card and board games available at headquarters to pass the time away.

The air raid warden to whom I was assigned for drills was very interested in my experiences in Germany as well as the family's adjustment to U.S. conditions. He never ran out of questions. What was our reason for coming to the United States? Why had my father been imprisoned at Dachau? Had he committed a crime? Why did we give up our store? What kind of work did my parents do now? How did they feel about it? Did we want to return to Germany some day? Like most other Americans, he found it difficult to understand what was happening in Germany—or why.

Our life was a series of ups and downs, and as the war went so went our lives. My sister, Ilse, had joined the New World Club, a German-Jewish social organization. At one of their dances, she met a tall, serious young man, Henry Cohen. They were married in 1944. D-Day, the Allied invasion of Normandy and my high school graduation also both occurred in June 1944. My high school graduation was a significant event for the family. I was elected to membership in Arista, the scholastic honor society. My parents beamed with pride. I had grown fond of several teachers and many students, and it was hard to say good-bye to them. My knowledge of English had improved considerably during my high school years. Only an occasional upward inflection at the end of a sentence betrayed the fact that I had learned English as a second language. My accent was gone.

Shortly before graduation, I registered for the draft and also applied for admission to City College. This apparent contradiction turned out to be the proper procedure. The army medical examination classified me as 4-F, physically unfit, due to a pilonidal cyst. I had been aware for months of a lump of sorts existing on my rear end, but never considered it worth mentioning to my parents or the doctor. It was only a minor inconvenience—but now it would keep me out of the army. Somehow this did not please me. It seemed dishonest. I immediately arranged for surgical removal of the cyst. I was able to attend summer school at City College while recovering from the operation.

City College was a highly accredited university located in upper Manhattan. We had moved to upper Manhattan earlier, so I lived within easy commuting distance of school. Tuition was free for residents of New York City; otherwise we could not have afforded this luxury. The courses I took seemed very easy, thanks to the excellent preparation I got in high school. There was very little social activity at City College, since everybody commuted from home. I missed the camaraderie of high school.

My draft board ordered me to report for another medical examination in September, after my operation had healed completely. I was now in good physical condition. Since I was not an American citizen, I could not be forced to serve in the U.S. Army. I was asked if I would sign a waiver, which I agreed to do. I became a proud but frightened member of the U.S. Army.

7 Basic Training

I reported to the induction center at Fort Dix, New Jersey, on October 5, 1944. The inductees were subjected to orientation lectures, short haircuts, uniform issue, and vaccinations, followed by many hours of KP (kitchen duties). Fate intervened in my case. I caught a bad cold on the day before my induction into the army. Following the vaccinations, I went back to the infirmary rather than to KP. I waited for two hours, then received a small bottle of cough medicine. I had now lost my place in the normal routine. Instead of being sent to the mess hall, I was assigned to work at the infirmary for several days, cleaning medical supplies. A steady line of inductees passed through all day long to receive their blood tests and shots. I was intrigued to notice that every tenth or fifteenth man fainted or got light-headed when a drop of blood was extracted from his finger for a blood test. I did not have this kind of problem. Who knows, maybe I could hold my own in this strange world of army life.

We were given a general aptitude test (Army General Classification Test) and a physics aptitude test. A staff member then evaluated our test results and interviewed us. The evaluator was visibly impressed by my test results. I scored 151 on the general aptitude test; only 110 was needed to qualify for Officers Candidate School. I noticed that the evaluator wrote "Recommended for Physics Laboratory Assistant" on my chart.

On October 17, we boarded a train that departed to an unknown (to us) destination. Two days later, we left the train and walked through heavy rain to a big quonset building, where we were issued helmet liners and portable shovels. We were informed that we were at Camp Blanding, Florida, and that a hurricane was expected to arrive any moment. It got a little gusty after a while, but then the wind and the rain subsided. We were driven to our company area, our home for the next 15 weeks.

Life at Camp Blanding started off the way Fort Dix life ended: Our records were evaluated. This evaluator was not very thorough, though.

He opened the chart, glanced over it, closed it and said, "Next!"

"Would you mind telling me what's ahead for me?" I asked quickly. He looked at me for the first time.

"You are at Camp Blanding," he replied. "This is an Infantry Replacement Training Center. Didn't you know?"

"Yes," I answered. "But what about the recommendation on my chart?" He reopened the chart and looked at the specified spot. He smiled.

"If we went by these recommendations, we'd have to fight Hitler and Tojo with armies of Physics Laboratory Assistants!" He shook my hand sympathetically. "Good luck! You'll be a rifleman when you leave Camp Blanding." I was shocked: Me, a rifleman?!

We were marched into the post theater for a welcoming address by the commanding general. The camp band started the meeting with a rousing Sousa march. The general addressed the band first. "That wasn't bad, but it wasn't good enough. If you don't shape up, you'll ship out with the next crew." I could not tell whether the general was joking. I still do not know. It was the only time we ever saw the general or the band.

The real introduction to Camp Blanding came from the first sergeant of our training company on the following morning. He was a small man with a big voice. He indicated that his mission was to make our lives as miserable as possible. By the time our training period was over, he warned, we should have built up an intense hatred for him and for camp life. At this point, they would ship us up to the front lines. U.S. troops had just started to invade the Philippines, and a major German counter-attack, the Battle of the Bulge, had just been launched in France. We would have an opportunity to release our hatred toward the designated enemy.

Our training was very intensive. My civilian life had always been very sedentary, and I was barely able to keep up with all the required activities. I had never touched a gun before; but now, I earned a "Marksman" medal for the M-1 rifle and a "Sharp-shooter" medal for the carbine. By the end of the training period, I was able to do the required 50 push-ups and to complete the required 25-mile hike. There was another surprise: during basic training, I was always hungry. I was convinced that the quality and quantity of army food were deliberately kept low in order to starve us into an aggressive disposition. When I stepped on a scale after "graduation" from basic training, I found that I had gained 25 pounds.

With the exception of the first sergeant, I had the highest respect for our cadre. The noncommissioned officers (sergeants and corporals) were veterans of the Aleutian Island service. The officers (captains and lieutenants) were recent graduates of Officers Candidate School. They were all very conscientious. Sergeant Ryder was my favorite, once I got used to his vocabulary. He was quiet, serious, never got angry—but preceded every noun with the F-adjective.

As could be expected, everything did not always go well for everybody. Bayonet practice was our most strenuous exercise. With the bayonet mounted on the muzzle of our M-1 rifle, we had to run through an obstacle course of sorts, jabbing and slashing at target dummies that popped up along the way. The bayonet had to be dismounted after the exercise, but occasionally it would become stuck on the rifle and could not be dislodged. We would then look for a tree, drive the bayonet into the tree trunk, push the release button and pull the rifle away. On this particular day, Murray, a young man from New York, could not find a tree. He was forced to march back to the barracks with the bayonet still mounted on the rifle, much to the amusement of his buddies. He rushed into his barracks and decided to use his foot locker in lieu of a tree trunk. He planted his left foot on top of the trunk lid and drove the mounted bayonet with all his force—right through the foot. I yelled for someone to run to the first sergeant to call for the medics while I pulled out the bayonet and removed Murray's boot. In short order, the first sergeant, the platoon lieutenant and the captain (company commander) came in successively to question Murray. They evidently grasped what had happened but questioned his motives. Someone finally drove Murray to the infirmary. Murray was lucky. The bayonet had passed through between two bones, and he was able to limp along on all the remaining training activities. Otherwise, he would have been tried by court martial for draft evasion.

We had an exercise of advancing against a hypothetical enemy, using live ammunition. One of the men lagged behind the advancing line and fired his rifle just as another man stood up in front of him. The bullet passed through the steel helmet of the man in front. It entered the rear of the helmet through a half-inch hole, tore a hole in the helmet liner and in the wool knit cap the man was wearing, scratched his scalp imperceptibly and tore a hole about two inches wide where it passed out of the helmet. The owner of the helmet was the only trainee who was allowed to take his helmet home as a souvenir.

We had a man who vomited every time we went on a speed march. Another man fainted every time he went on a long march. Their x-rays did not show any visible physiological cause of their problems, so they had to keep running and walking, vomiting and fainting for 15 weeks.

My religious practices were more or less suspended while I was in basic training. I did not want to eat pork. But there were many days when we had Spam for breakfast, ham for lunch, and pork chops for dinner. Had I abstained, I would have starved. Weekly religious services for Jewish trainees were held on Friday nights. But Friday night was clean-up night in every company. Theoretically, we were authorized to miss clean-up every week in order to attend services. In actual fact, this would have resulted in weekly pogroms by those who would have been stuck doing our work. We decided to pray individually, privately, and quietly. Speaking of religion, I was amused at the time that a popular gift item "for your man in the service" was a pocket-size bible to be carried close to the heart. The bible was provided with a bullet-proof steel cover. It was a good example of the principle of redundancy.

Friday, December 15 started out like any other day. We lined up in formation after breakfast, ready to march to our first activity. Sgt. Ryder called me out of line, told me to change into my (f——) dress uniform and to meet him at the office in ten minutes. When I came back, he motioned for me to get into a Jeep with him, and we took off.

Ryder was always very stingy with words. After half an hour, I asked him where we were going. "Jacksonville," he replied. That was the extent of our conversation until we pulled up in front of the federal court house in Jacksonville. As I was being photographed and had to sign various documents, I became aware of the fact that I was about to become an American citizen. The return trip to camp was as quiet as the earlier ride. But I think there was a happy smile on my face.

I wrote a letter to my parents nearly every night during basic training and every three to four days during my subsequent army career. (My father saved all those letters, and they provided much of the material for this book.) Our training cycle was coming to an end. The 25-mile march was quite an experience. Fortunately, it took place at night. The Florida sun would be too hot, even in January. We carried a full field pack and our rifle. After five or six hours, I saw the man in front of me drifting across the road. He stumbled when he reached the far side of the road, woke up, and scrambled back into line. I recalled a sergeant's prediction: "You'll end up walking on bloody stumps—but you just keep walking." At last, we arrived at the company area. I dragged myself into the barracks, dropped the pack, rifle, ammo belt and canteen and collapsed on my bunk, instantly falling asleep. A cheerful voice announced: "Hot chocolate and doughnuts in the mess hall!" Sounded great—but I just couldn't get up.

February 3 was graduation day. I was now officially a rifleman. On February 4, I was on a train bound for a "delay en route" in New York City, with orders to report to Fort Mead, then to Miles Standish (near Boston) by February 14. Ten days at home passed by very quickly. Miles Standish was our port of embarkation to either European or Asian war zone. We were not told which would be our destination. We sat around for two weeks, then we boarded the S.S. Wakefield, a large troop transport. Prior to the war, this had been the S.S. Manhattan, the ship on which my sister Ilse had come to the United States. The ship departed on March 1. On March 3, we were told that we were headed for Europe.

I was going back to Germany, the country in which I was born, to fight against Germany, the country for which my father had fought only 30 years earlier. I had discussed the possibility with my buddies in basic training, but now that it was happening it seemed surreal. I felt I had better reasons for fighting against Germany than my buddies did. After all, Hitler and the Nazis had declared war against the Jews long before they did the United States.

8 My Return to Europe

The S.S. Wakefield traveled by itself, not in a convoy. It zigzagged across the Atlantic Ocean in eight days, changing course every few minutes, supposedly never giving a submarine enough time to zero in on us. I slept on a stretched canvas sheet, whose edges were laced to a rectangular pipe frame. As I recall, each bed was about six feet long by two feet wide and had to accommodate one man plus his duffel bag. The vertical space between canvases was about 15 inches—less than that if the man on top was heavy. Five or six beds were stacked on top of each other. Aisle space between stacks was minimal. The air was hot and musty.

They served two meals per day. One of these generally consisted of beans. Meals were eaten standing up at counters. In order to reach the dining area, we had to stand in line for two to three hours. There really was not much else to do all day. The problem was that about 15 minutes prior to our arrival in the dining area, we had to pass by the door that led to the boiler room. At this point, hot diesel fumes enveloped me and sometimes gave me instant sea sickness. I would then have to leave the line and run up to the open deck for fresh air. I am sure that during the eight days at sea, I lost most of the 25 pounds I had gained during basic training.

I did not know any of the men around me. On my arrival at Miles Standish, I had been arbitrarily picked to work in a sandwich-making detail. When my chore was completed, the barracks assigned to my training company was filled, so I was simply transferred to another unit from a different camp. I was very unhappy about that. But when I happened to meet one of my old fellow trainees after the war, he told me that our training company from Camp Blanding had been thrown into the heaviest fighting and that about two-thirds of the men were either killed or seriously wounded during their first week of action.

Our ship arrived in Glasgow, on the west coast of Scotland, on March 9, 1945. During the night we left the ship and boarded a train for Southampton. We crossed the English Channel to Le Havre, France, on a Polish ship. A freight train carried us to Verviers, Belgium, where we checked into the First Army replacement depot on March 14. On March 13, 1946, exactly a year later, I wrote a letter about these events:

A year ago today, I arrived on the European mainland. I remember it clearly. It was shortly after midnight when we left the ship that had carried us across the English Channel in a convoy. We moved in small groups. We had arrived at Le Havre on the afternoon of March 12, but troop movements took place only after dark. Everything we owned we carried on our shoulders. We moved through the ruins of Le Havre, which I had seen only six years earlier as a lively city.

About 1 a.m. we marched into the Red Cross building. Sleepy, heavily painted French women poured hot coffee into our metal canteen cups. We felt very important and heroic as liberators, were rather disappointed to note that the friendliness of the "liberated" seemed forced, obligatory. We had no conception on one hand of the misery these people had to endure during the Nazi occupation, on the other hand of the hardships of daily life that still remained after liberation. It was the same problem that still exists today: The oppressed expect their liberators to offer recognition of and compensation for all their suffering and deprivation; the liberators expect profound gratitude for their effort—not realizing that the survivors still have to struggle with the daily demands and frustrations of an arduous life.

We marched to the railroad station about 3 a.m. Of the beautiful, modern building I remembered from 1939, only the railroad tracks remained. A train of 30 or 40 box cars was waiting for us. They had a French inscription, "*40 hommes ou 8 chevaux*," i.e., 40 men or 8 horses. Thirty of us climbed into each car, hung up our packs above us, slid into our sleeping bags, lay down on the bare floor with our legs on top of someone else, and stayed in this position with some interruptions for two days. The train stopped occasionally to allow us to relieve ourselves and to pick up rations. A group of natives would always swarm around us in order to buy, beg, or trade for cigarette butts, coffee powder, crackers, or other food items. It was my first contact with the ubiquitous dealers and beggars of wartime Europe, who would trade their possessions, their bodies, their honor for a Lucky Strike. It was a condition that we would learn to tolerate—or exploit. And diplomats still speak of war in terms of honor and justice.

Facilities were comfortable and food was excellent at the replacement depot. It was like the last meal of a condemned man. Steak or chicken was served for dinner nearly every night. There was little danger of spoiling the guests since they would generally move on to a front-line outfit after a day or two.

I had made friends on the troop transport with J.L. Lee, a soldier from Flint, Michigan. We now enjoyed the luxuries of replacement depot and the sights of Verviers together. There was very little to see in Verviers. Four years of German occupation had impoverished the town and its people. March 18 was my birthday, and Lee had managed to dig up two big waffles with applesauce for me in lieu of a cake. Food was scarce in Verviers, but cigarettes were scarcer. This gave American soldiers a powerful exchange medium.

How come we were still at the replacement depot four days after our arrival? An infantry unit came to pick us up on March 16. Lee and I had been sent out of town for guard duty, and by the time they brought us back to the depot, they had to send out other replacements in our place. On March 19, Lee and I were chosen as members of an advance detail to establish a new location for the replacement depot in Aachen, Germany. Again, there was a call for us that night, and others had to be substituted. On March 22, two vehicles arrived at the depot (now located in Aachen) to pick up replacements. The First Infantry Division wanted riflemen, the other unit needed someone who could speak German. Lee and I shook hands. He went to the First Infantry Division; I was taken to the 196th Field Artillery Battalion, Battery B, Detachment E.

It was not necessary for me to know anything about artillery. Yes, this battalion had fought hard as Fifth Corps artillery in their drive across France and Belgium. But as they were about to enter Germany, the "batteries" were converted from artillery to Military Government Security Guard, MGSG. Their function was now to move closely behind the armored divisions. Whenever a German town was taken by our tanks, MGSG would move in to consolidate the area, while the armored column moved on. Occasionally, there was still sniper fire or artillery action when we moved in, and some houses were still on fire. Consolidation consisted of rounding up prisoners of war, transporting them to the rear, replacing the Nazi mayor with an anti-Nazi or at least an apolitical man, disbanding Nazi organizations and reestablishing orderly procedures, utilities, flow of food, etc. After three or four days, we would load up all our gear on our trucks and rush up to another town that had just been taken. There were fifty men in our detachment. Only three of us could speak German. Evidently, my linguistic abilities were more important to the army than my skills as a rifleman.

The 196th Field Artillery Battalion had originally been formed from a Tennessee National Guard unit. They were an upbeat, hard-working group of men, always helpful and friendly, except when the subject of Blacks came up. I could never comprehend their blind hatred for millions of people whom they had never met. It was amazingly similar to German anti-Semitism. Several times I was told to change the subject of my conversation. "A nigger lover is just as bad as a nigger," I was warned.

Our detachment of MGSG crossed the Rhine River just two weeks after the first U.S. troops established their famous bridgehead at Remagen. We also crossed at Remagen, but on a pontoon bridge built by the U.S. Corps of Engineers. Our starting point was Sinzig/Nieder-Breisig, our destination Limburg on the Lahn. After a few days at Limburg, we leap-frogged to Fritzlar, then Göttingen, then Querfurt.

I remember guarding two trains during this period. The first train was loaded with German small-arms ammunition, and it was burning. Someone must have decided that letting it burn was a good way to dispose of it. No attempt was made to extinguish the smoldering fire, but we had to make sure that the Germans would not grab the remaining ammunition. So, we stood guard on both sides of the train—but not too close. Every second or so, several rifle shells would explode in the fire, presumably shooting casing and bullet in opposite directions. We could not see their trajectory, but we could hear them whistling and bouncing. We stayed until the train was completely consumed.

The second train was loaded with German army food supplies.

Someone had the foresight to park it in a tunnel. All we had to do was to guard the two ends of the tunnel. The local population knew that there was food on the train. When our shift reported for duty, the guards we relieved warned us to be prepared for various attempts at larceny and persuasion.

A group of women approached. I could hear them talking loudly. "Let's try it again." "Hey—I think these are not the same men any more." "Maybe one of them can speak German." I gave a running translation to the other guards, but in a way to make it sound like random conversation. "Can we have some food please?" one of the women shouted in German from a reasonable distance. We responded with dumb stares. She repeated her request more loudly. One of the guards shrugged his shoulders. "*Nix farstay*," he shouted back—the standard GI-German phrase that meant "I don't understand." The women discussed the situation among themselves. "You can speak English," they said to a young girl. "Only a few words," she protested. "Well, tell them that the other guards gave us food, and it's all right for them to give us some too." By the time the girl had built up enough courage to talk to us, I had already told my buddies what to expect. The girl's knowledge of English was very poor. It was easy for us to respond with the same claim of not understanding. The women returned to their caucus. "Ask them when they will change guards," one woman suggested. "Are you crazy? That's a military secret! They'll shoot you if you ask that!" "Can we just run past them?" "Sure, if you like to get shot." "Should we offer them money?"

I listened and translated surreptitiously for a few minutes. Finally I stepped forward and addressed the women in perfect German. "You can't have this food," I explained. "We need it to feed the concentration camp prisoners and the foreign laborers. They have been starving for five years while you were eating." The women stared at me in silence. Then they turned around and scurried away without another word. We did not have any more visitors on that day.

I was back in Germany—the only way I ever wanted to come back. My family had experienced the hatred of this nation. The other men in my outfit had lost good friends in bitter fighting and had witnessed the pain and destruction Germany had inflicted on England, France and Belgium. We could understand why our commanders had forbidden us to fraternize with the Germans. As we advanced across Germany, we learned more and more about the horrible atrocities the Nazis had committed against the people under their control. Still, we tried to be objective in doing our job. Not every German was a murderer.

While we were stationed in Querfurt, a badly injured man dragged himself to our station. His head, arms and shirt were covered with blood. Captain Bate called me in to translate for him. The man was Russian, but he spoke some German. He was one of millions of people from occupied countries who were forced to come to Germany during the war to work as slave laborers. He and his wife had been doing farm work in the neighboring village of Alberstaedt. On that morning, when he realized that American troops had taken over the area, he refused to work any more. His master and several neighbors now attacked the Russian with clubs and knives. When the Russian's wife tried to stop the fight, they stabbed her with a pitch fork. The Russian was able to run away and make his way to Querfurt. He did not know whether his wife was still alive. Did he know the names of his attackers? He only knew his master's name. I wrote it down.

Captain Bate turned to me and said something like "Go get 'em!" About a dozen men had seen the Russian come in and were standing around outside the room. I filled them in on what I had just heard. We grabbed our weapons, helmets and flashlights and jumped into two trucks. All the other men were combat veterans, while I was a rookie. Some of them were corporals and sergeants, I was only a private. But it became instantly clear to them and to me that I would have to lead this activity because I was the only one of the group who could speak German.

We arrived at Alberstaedt after dark. The village was pitch dark because blackout rules were in effect. We stopped at the first house, and I asked for directions to the "master's" house.

The "master" was not very masterly. His arms were raised high, and he was hysterical with fear, seeing a dozen rifles pointed at him. When

I asked him who had stabbed the Russian woman, he immediately called out a name. "Take us to him," I shouted. We ran to a nearby house, where we picked up our second prisoner. "Who else was involved?" The new prisoner called out another name. I slammed my rifle barrel against his ribs and yelled, "Let's go!" We ran on. We came to a house that was surrounded by a high steel picket fence. There was a huge German shepherd dog in the yard, barking and snarling at us.

In retrospect, I cannot justify what I did next; but apparently, my adrenaline was running as fast as the dog's. Without a moment's hesitation, I opened the gate, marched right up to the front door of the house and pounded on the door, ignoring the dog completely. The dog followed me, barking loudly. He never touched me. A man came out, pulled the dog into the house, then joined us as our next prisoner. We continued running.

After the second prisoner had taken us to the twelfth suspect, one of them turned to me and said calmly: "I'd like to have permission to explain something to you." "Go ahead!" "What happened this morning was terrible. There was no excuse for that. You have rounded up all the guilty men, but the last three men you arrested had nothing to do with it. If you keep asking him, he'll keep calling out names until the whole village is rounded up." Naturally, he was the tenth of our prisoners. But the "master" voiced his agreement, and I had noticed that the last three men reacted differently than the previous ones when they were accosted. So I was ready to believe that our mission was nearly complete.

We located the Russian's wife. Someone had crudely bandaged her stab wound. She was much more concerned about her husband's condition than her own. We invited her to come with us, and she took a friend along, another Russian woman.

We loaded our prisoners on one of the trucks, and I gave them a little speech—that we would let the police and court at Querfurt decide who was guilty of what. I did not bother to explain why I spoke German like a native. We dropped the Russian women off at the Querfurt hospital, then we took the Germans to the local police station. The German police were operating under the supervision of the

U.S. military police, who had already received a preliminary report from Captain Bate.

I could tell that all my buddies were impressed by the way I took charge of the situation. I was more surprised than any of them. Perhaps it was a coming of age for me. More likely, I needed to release 12 years of stored up anti-Nazi feelings that night. It felt good.

The Allies were driving Hitler's forces into submission and the rout was on. Our next stop was Leipzig, one of Germany's major cultural and industrial centers. On the morning after our arrival, our detachment was driven to a small camp outside the city. Camp Erla (I have also heard it called Camp Thekla) had been built by Germany to house 300 slave laborers from Poland, Belgium and France. This was not a concentration camp. There were no political prisoners, Jews or criminals here, only people who had to work in German factories or farms during the day and sleep in the camp at night. Still, it was surrounded by an electrically charged barbed wire fence with guard towers.

We learned that the S.S. guards were replaced by teen-aged Hitler Youth members about two weeks before our arrival, probably because the S.S. men were needed at the front. On the day before Leipzig fell to U.S. troops, the young guards herded all 300 laborers into the barracks, nailed boards over the doors and windows, poured kerosene over the building and set it on fire. Eight or ten of the prisoners found the only way to escape from the inferno: they jumped into the latrine pit and crawled to the outside, where they became targets for the guards.

What we saw when we arrived at the camp has been permanently etched into my memory. There was a pile of ashes where the barracks and some 290 people used to be. Several bodies were lying along the fence. I remember one of them. He was middle-aged, wore wire rimmed glasses. He had a wooden leg and was using his crutch to raise the bottom strand of barbed wire. A hail of machine gun bullets extinguished any desperate hopes he may have had.

There were three or four foxholes dug out within the enclosure, possibly for use by the guards in case of an air raid. Bullet-riddled bodies were now lying in each of them. In one of these holes, I saw two boys, probably brothers, 15 or 16 years old, with similar appearance. They were embracing each other and looking up with a fearful or pleading look when they were killed. These were the faces that were staring up at me with sightless eyes on that day and during several nightmares since then. These were the faces that had looked up at the guard, himself a boy. And yet, the guard was able to pull the trigger in a senseless act of murder. How was it possible?

The civic leaders of Leipzig were taken to the camp by the U.S. Army. We were told later that the mayor of Leipzig committed suicide after viewing the remains. We were learning at this time that Camp Erla was only a small sample of the atrocities committed by the Nazis and their many willing helpers. How was it possible?

We stayed at Leipzig for eleven days, and our procedures became more formalized. We stood guard and walked on patrol around the clock. We worked in pairs, four hours on/eight hours off. The easiest shift was 8 to 12 a.m. and p.m., i.e. from breakfast to lunch and from supper to midnight. From 12 to 4 was difficult. Sleep was interrupted by meals at 6 p.m. and 7 a.m. Shifts were rotated for fairness.

My patrol partner was Bob Nolta. He came from southern Illinois. Patrol partners get to know each other quite well: they have many hours of conversation, and there are times when their lives may depend on each other. We found that our views of the world were very much alike, although our backgrounds were entirely different. We became close friends. We were a Mutt-and-Jeff pair, he being unusually tall and I exceptionally short. When people joked about it, we would laugh along with them.[9]

We had just started the "graveyard shift" (12 to 4 a.m.) one night, when we heard the clatter of a hand-pulled wagon on a cobblestone street. We had orders to enforce the curfew. Civilians were not permitted on the street after dark. We ordered the person to stop and approached cautiously. We found a man pulling a cart that carried a boy, about four years old, wrapped in a bloody sheet. The man, a Pole, told us in broken German that their kerosene lamp had exploded, shooting pieces of glass into their son. Could we help? We had noticed a German hospital just two blocks away, and we led the distraught father to it. We went in with the two. A German soldier stopped him in the lobby. "Sorry," he said. "This is a German army hospital. All our patients are now prisoners of war. We are not permitted to admit any civilians." I translated for Bob. "Tell him we want to talk to the man in charge—immediately!" The receptionist left and returned a few minutes later with a German officer, who was wearing an army overcoat over his pajamas. "I am sorry," the officer pleaded in good English. "We have our orders..." Bob loaded a bullet into the chamber of his carbine. "I just changed your orders," he announced. "You will treat this child right now!" "Ah, this is an emergency, isn't it?" the officer exclaimed. "Of course! Bring him in here." We made sure that the boy received good care before we returned to our patrol duties.

The shortage of gasoline was quite evident in civilian transportation. Many trucks were provided with wood burners. Carbon monoxide produced by incomplete combustion of wood chips was piped into the carburetor as a fuel. Often we would see a truck crawl up a hill and suddenly stop. The driver would climb up to the top of the truck bed, open the lid on top of the burner, empty a bag of wood chips into the burner, tamp it down, close the lid, and jump back into the cab. He would be good for a few more miles now. Occasionally, we could see a car pulling its wood burner and spare fuel (chips) along on a trailer. Most civilians rode bicycles around town. If they needed to move a load, they would use a hand-drawn cart.

U.S. Army jeeps and trucks had a design modification added in Germany. A steel angle or I-beam was mounted vertically in front in order to cut through deadly wires stretched across the road by retreating German soldiers. Many army vehicles had clever names or slogans painted on their side. An ambulance was named "*Fleisch-Wagen*." Many vehicles that promised "Berlin or bust" later had the first two words crossed out. One driver had converted his wire-cutting angle into a gallows, with a likeness of Hitler's head dangling from it. There was a tank I saw once with the inscription "Bashful."

Napoleon recognized that an army moves on its stomach. Our

MGSG detachment enjoyed good food. We had hired two young Italian cooks back in France and reassigned the mess sergeant to other duties. These men were artists in their profession. They converted perfectly dull, bland army food into gourmet meals. Occasionally, they would cheat a little—trading canned or dehydrated army food for fresh produce and fruit from a local farmer. They failed to meet our expectations only once, when our supplies were cut off. For four days in a row, we had Spam three times a day. The cooks tried valiantly to disguise their raw material. But whether it is fried, baked, or poached, Spam is still Spam. I have not been able to eat Spam since then. If I just see it or smell it, I get nauseous.

A news bulletin arrived: President Roosevelt had died. How sad, when victory was no doubt just days away. One of the men from Mississippi sang happily, "Old man Roosevelt kicked the bucket!" How could he be so heartless? To me it was like the death of a close relative. Our family always saw FDR as the man who let us come to the United States, as the man who directed the campaign against Hitler. It was not until many years later that people started asking disturbing questions about some of Roosevelt's actions and inactions.

By this time it was obvious to everybody (except Hitler) that Germany had lost the war. For some time now, the Allies had undisputed control of the air, and the Germans were running out of supplies and manpower. There was bitter fighting for every village, for every house when the battle lines were drawn in France or Belgium. Once we had crossed the Rhine River into Germany, however, the German soldiers tended to make their stand between towns, rather than defending a town and having it reduced to rubble. The fanatical S.S. units were still blowing up bridges. Generally, this practice did not slow us down much, but it caused serious problems for the German population, who were not permitted to use our pontoon bridges. Many people found themselves isolated from food supplies or garbage collection. I remember one town where the funeral parlor was on one side of the river, the cemetery on the other. Bodies were transported on row boats.

When Allied troops first set foot on German soil, Hitler called on his people to form underground terrorist gangs—the Werewolves—and to keep fighting to their death for the glory of the Third Reich. For once, the Germans chose to ignore their Fuehrer's instructions. They had had enough. We were on our guard, but nothing happened.

German soldiers were surrendering in droves, creating a logistics problem. Nazi slave labor camps were sometimes converted into prisoner-of-war camps. The newly liberated foreign laborers also placed a heavy burden on our administration. UNRRA, the United Nations Relief and Rehabilitation Administration, accepted responsibility for support and repatriation of Allied displaced persons.

Our MGSG detachment received orders one day to transport a group of prisoners of war (POWs) from Leipzig to a camp in the rear. POWs were generally loaded into the bed of a truck. One U.S. soldier drove the truck, while another sat on top of the cab of the truck, facing the rear and holding a rifle. I was assigned to be the guard on this day. I sat on top of the cab, staring down at the POWs, wondering if any of them had been concentration camp guards, or if any of them were former schoolmates from Constance. The truck raced through the city streets. Suddenly, several POWs yelled at me, pointing at something up ahead, which was behind me. I ducked instinctively, barely avoiding decapitation by a low-hanging streetcar wire. It felt very strange having had my life saved by my enemies.

9 Peace at Last

We moved from Leipzig to Weiden on April 30. We were near the Czechoslovakian border now, having driven almost completely across Germany. Still, some German army units continued to fight. At last, on May 8, 1945, Germany surrendered unconditionally. V-E Day (Victory in Europe) had arrived, and Hitler was dead! Hundreds of millions had been wishing, praying, fighting for this day, but many millions lost their lives before our goal was reached, before success could even have been predicted. I had met many liberated foreigners in the last few weeks, but not one of them was Jewish. Now we heard of concentration camps being liberated, and we also became aware of the horrendous magnitude of the slaughter the Nazis had carried out, especially against the Jewish people.

I was loaned out for a day to a military intelligence unit that had requested a man who could speak German. After I received a typhus vaccination, I was driven to Flossenbürg Concentration Camp. Only now was I told that I would be questioning two Kapos there.

Kapos were "privileged" prisoners who were appointed by the camp commander to be in charge of a group of regular prisoners. Very often, chronic offenders with long, violent criminal records were chosen for this honor. They were among the first inmates of concentration camps, right after Hitler came to power. The two Kapos I was to question had that kind of record.

I had never seen a concentration camp before. Under overcast skies, I now saw a number of plain barracks surrounded by two electric barbed wire fences. A big stone quarry and an airplane factory adjoined the camp. At the main camp gate, a big stone tablet spelled out the standard lie of all Nazi concentration camps: "*Arbeit macht frei*," which meant, "Work will make you free." It was part of a systematic propaganda campaign to make the entering prisoners think they were just going to a labor camp, and that they would be freed again if they worked hard and kept out of trouble.

Before I arrived, most of the bodies of former inmates had been removed. Former guards and local Nazi activists had been forced to bury them in the center of town. Prisoners who were strong enough to leave the camp had already been moved to a hospital or to a new residence. Those who remained were dying like flies, mostly from typhus.

I was taken to a small room containing only a small table and two folding chairs and was given a pad of paper and a pencil. I had the first Kapo brought in. I asked him for name, date of birth, etc. He responded calmly, deliberately. What was his job in the camp? He supervised a group of prisoners who had to work in the stone quarry.

"Did you ever kill any people who worked for you?"

"Yes."

"How many?"

"Oh, about eight or ten—maybe more. I don't remember."

"How did you kill them?"

"With rocks. Sometimes with a club."

"Why would you kill a man?"

"Always for a good reason. They didn't obey the rules."

"What rules, for example?"

"They didn't work hard enough, generally. Some didn't keep clean."

"You killed some people because they didn't keep clean?"

"Yes, that is correct."

"Do you think a man deserves to be killed if he doesn't keep clean?"

He stared at me quizzically for a few seconds. "Of course. The rule was to keep clean. They didn't obey the rules." He obviously wondered why I could not understand such simple logic.

"How long have you been a concentration camp prisoner?"

"About eight years."

The second Kapo gave similar answers. Both confessed their crimes without hesitation, but neither of them thought he had done anything wrong. There was not the slightest trace of guilt or remorse. They seemed unable to judge any proportionality between their victims' offense and the resultant penalty. Taking a life was completely trivial to them.

I translated the dialogue for the officer in charge and asked if he had any other questions. He seemed satisfied. I never found out what happened to the Kapos. Their perverted sense of values may well have been the result of their own suffering as concentration camp prisoners, I couldn't know. Still, I felt that their degradation was total and irreversible and that they should never be returned to society. My opinion, however, was not solicited, and I did not offer it.

I learned a few facts about Flossenbürg Concentration Camp. It held as many as 26,000 prisoners. About 50 percent of the camp population died each year. The occupants were mainly career criminals, political prisoners, and foreign nationals. Jewish prisoners were added near the end. A group of 5,000 prisoners were marched from Buchenwald Concentration Camp to Flossenbürg shortly before V-E Day. It took twelve days. About 3,000 were killed along the way when they were unable to keep up with the others. Only 2,000 reached their destination, half-starved and sick.

I met a 12-year-old Gypsy boy who had survived the march. Before Buchenwald, he had also been at Dachau and Auschwitz. His parents were killed at Auschwitz. He had no-one left, no place to call home. He was alive, but what would the future hold for him?

Every time I saw new evidence of the systematic murder carried out by Germany, my thoughts would turn to our French relatives. What had happened to them? Was it at all conceivable that someone could deliberately have hurt a sweet girl like Gilberte? Someone like the Kapos? Of course not. We will hear from them soon, I told myself. Please, God!

UNRRA asked for help. They were not able to keep up with the tremendous number of liberated foreigners that needed to be registered for repatriation, and so I was loaned to UNRRA for a few days.

DPs (displaced persons) had come from all parts of Europe, but at least one-half of them were from the Soviet Union. Most of the Soviet DPs had been enslaved by Hitler, but a good number of Russians came to Germany voluntarily. They saw the German invasion as an opportunity to escape from Stalin's slavery. These DPs did not wish to return to their country.

Most of the DPs spoke some German, some did not. I spoke some French, but no Russian. When I met a Russian DP who spoke German fluently, I asked him to stay briefly and help me out prior to his own repatriation.

I got along well with my Russian assistant. He had been a medical student before he got caught up in the war, and I had been an engineering student. We had many stimulating conversations, but we generally avoided ideological controversy. I asked him once whether he had any problem as an educated person living under a totalitarian regime. My question caught him off guard. He paused for a few seconds, then explained: "Americans may not be able to understand this. My father was a peasant under the czar; so were his parents and their parents. They could not write their names. They had no property, no leisure, no future. The only ambition they ever had was to stay alive, to keep from starving by working hard during all their waking hours. My government sent me to college, and some day I am going to be a doctor. I shall always be grateful to my government. Most of my generation feels that way, too. We may not enjoy all the privileges that you do. That's not important. What counts for us is that we are much better off than our parents were. We are willing to give our lives in defense of the government that did that for us." Forty years later, a new generation would judge their government more severely, perhaps also in terms of comparing their own life with that of their parents. It would be the end of the Union of Soviet Socialist Republics.

Our unit had a lively celebration on V-E Day. Four *Fräuleins* were hired to serve our dinner that evening. There was no shortage of liquor. A month earlier, when we were stationed in Fritzlar, we were ordered to guard a German army warehouse, which contained thousands of bottles of delicious apricot brandy. After we left Fritzlar, one of our trucks was always pulling a trailer behind it. We no longer needed the trailer after V-E Day.

The time had come to move on again. We drove through beautiful country to the picturesque town of Marienbad in the Sudeten part of Czechoslovakia on May 10, 1945. Marienbad was once a world-famous resort, a playground for royalty. During World War II, Germany converted all the big hotels into army hospitals and declared Marienbad an open city. It was never damaged during the war.

The Sudeten area had played a critical role in Hitler's expansionist policies. Most of its population was ethnically German. A belligerent Nazi movement was organized among the Sudeten Germans, strongly supported by Hitler's agents. About 60 percent of the ethnic Germans in Czechoslovakia voted for their Nazi party in 1935. They challenged the Czech government. When order was restored, the Nazi puppets accused the Czech government of persecuting its German minority and demanded secession. Hitler now jumped into the ring and threatened to go to war unless Czechoslovakia ceded the Sudetenland to Germany. The leaders of Great Britain and France wanted to avoid war at any cost. They met with Hitler in Munich in 1938 and agreed to "give" him Sudetenland as the price for peace. It was morally indefensible, politically short-sighted, and militarily stupid. Czechoslovakia was the soundest, strongest democracy on the mainland, the perfect place for the western democracies to stand their ground against Hitler. But Czechoslovakia's defenses were all in Sudetenland, the part of the country closest to Germany. When Chamberlain and Daladier invited Hitler to help himself to Sudetenland, his troops accepted the invitation. A few months later, they took over the rest of Czechoslovakia. At last, the democracies came to realize that war was the only way to stop Hitler. But they had waited too long, they had given him too much.

Back to MGSG in Marienbad. We were lodged in Hotel Panorama, on a hill overlooking the town. Our cooks were now able to take over a well-equipped kitchen and to function at their highest potential. Meals were delicious, especially since we could eat them on hotel dishes rather than aluminum mess kits. There was even a swimming pool on the grounds. I reported some excitement in my letter of May 22, 1945.

We made a good catch on May 20: the president of the so-called National Turkestan Unity Committee. From the Turkestan region of the Soviet Union, the organization provided the Nazi army with 200,000 troops, including Waffen-S.S., shock troops, engineering units, etc. Aside from the president, we also grabbed his wife (who was working as an interpreter with U.S. military government), the military commander (in charge of all their troops), their propaganda chief, and a half-dozen associates. The president had 76,000 marks in his pocket, and he carried jewelry worth many thousands of marks.

I do not know what happened to the Turkestanian soldiers and their leaders. Russian nationals who had fought for the German army during the war were being forcibly repatriated to Russia at this time. It meant certain death for them. But if they held out for a few months, the U.S. "intelligence" service (a gross misnomer) may have spirited them to the United States, as they did a number of murderous Nazi officials, to be honored and well paid as consultants in the Cold War against the Soviet Union.

There was not much more to be done in Marienbad during the one-and-a-half months we spent there. We were told to be on the lookout for certain Nazi officials, including the local *Kreisleiter* (regional leader). There was little chance that we would find any of them.

A civilian corpse was reported to be lying next to our hotel's driveway, a man who had shot himself. That was not our problem. We notified the local police. The member of our detachment who had found the body kept the pistol that was used for the suicide. Another GI got the wallet and the watch. The civilians now moved in and absconded with the shoes and suit. After three days, the police finally removed the bare body and identified it as the local Nazi *Kreisleiter*.

Groceries were quite scarce among the civilian population, just as they had been in other towns where we had previously been stationed. Cigarettes were more in demand than food, even among hungry families. Cigarettes could be used to purchase any commodity or service. I had never realized before how powerful a nicotine addiction could be. American soldiers walking through town while smoking cigarettes would often be followed by two or three men, who would fight over discarded cigarette butts. Several women came to our hotel and offered to wash an individual soldier's laundry, if it was accompanied by a cake of soap. The left-over soap was all the payment they expected for the service. Military garbage cans were sifted for food scraps and cigarette butts by many scavengers.

Bob Nolta and I were patrolling a street one day, when we witnessed the conclusion of a wedding between two U.S. medical corps members, a physician and a nurse. Their mess sergeant had provided 40 or 50 pounds of rice for the occasion. The happy couple was showered with rice, thrown by their fellow medics, as they walked from the makeshift chapel to their jeep. The sidewalk was covered with a layer of rice, up to one inch thick, after all the personnel disappeared.

Bob Nolta and I watched from across the street. A couple of townspeople came along, looking puzzled. They stooped down to see what they were walking on and chewed a few kernels of rice. They looked around to see if the owner of this treasure was watching. Then they rapidly scooped up as much of the rice as would fit into their pockets. A dozen more people came running over to them. After a few minutes, the sidewalk was perfectly clean again.

The population of Marienbad was 100 percent Sudeten German. The ethnic Czech minority had been evicted from the Sudeten area and their belongings were confiscated after Hitler took over the country. It was now announced by the new Czech government that the former Czech residents would return, that the town would be renamed Marianske Lazne, and that the Germanic residents would have to move to Germany without their property. The local people were shocked. Their families had lived here for generations. Maybe only some of the families, the Nazis, would have to move. They started accumulating letters purportedly proving anti-Nazi activity or at least absence of Nazi activity during Nazi rule.

There was another request for a soldier who could speak German. I was assigned to work with the town administration as the military liaison person. It was an easy job, sitting behind an impressive desk in an impressive office and generally telling people whom to contact for action on their problems.

A group of soldiers from a medical unit came in one morning, pushing four boys—about 12 years old—in front of them. The boys had been hanging around the medical headquarters for several days, and a number of items disappeared from jeeps and ambulances during the time. They chased the boys away several times, but the boys kept coming back.

I walked over to the civilian police chief's office. He decided to hold the boys in the local lockup for the rest of the day "for questioning" and to turn them loose with a stern warning in the evening.

About mid-afternoon, a man asked to talk to me. "The police arrested my son this morning," he complained. "But he didn't have anything to do with the guns."

I was about to ask, "What are you talking about? What guns?" But I restrained myself and decided to bluff.

"If he didn't, who did?" I asked pointedly.

"It was Albert who found the guns and hid them," he declared. Now I realized that he was talking about the boys we had locked up that morning.

"But your son *knew* about the guns, didn't he?" He agreed weakly. I thanked him for the information and promised to look into the matter.

I had Albert brought into my office. "Albert," I said slowly. "I want you to tell me all about the guns." Albert did not seem surprised. Apparently, he had also assumed that "the guns" were the reason for the boys' detainment. He now explained that he found five pistols when the four boys were playing in an abandoned house. The policeman who had escorted Albert to my office was still present.

"Where are the pistols now?" I asked.

"In the attic of the empty house," Albert replied.

"Take us there!" I ordered.

Albert took us to the house and pointed out where the pistols were hidden. None of them were military weapons, and there was no ammunition in them. The items the U.S. medics had reported missing that morning did not include any pistols. I turned the pistols and the case over to the civilian police.

A woman came into the office one day, walked up to me and asked: "Are you Mr. Ottenheimer?" I admitted that I was.

"Excuse me for asking," she continued. "Are you Jewish?"

"Yes, I am."

"I am Jewish, too," she announced.

I was stunned. She was the first Jewish survivor I had met since my return to Europe. "May I sit down?" she asked. I regained my speech.

"Of course! I want to know all about you! What is your name?" It was Mrs. Walter. She was a native of Marienbad, married to an auto mechanic. She was able to avoid deportation during the war because her husband was Christian (Sudeten German) and had some good connections through his work. But their food rations were low, and they were constantly harassed and frequently threatened.

I became a steady guest at the Walter home during the following weeks. They were lovely people and had three beautiful children. The oldest, Susi, a girl of 14, was a talented young artist. I still enjoy looking at numerous drawings she made for me. Mr. Walter was a very quiet, simple man with tremendous inner strength, completely devoted to his family. He had been more jovial in his younger days, but the stress of sheltering his wife from the hatred of his peers apparently turned him into a serious man. Mrs. Walter was much more outgoing. She was a warm, enthusiastic woman with a quiet sense of humor.

Marienbad was only a few miles away from Pilsen, the beer capital of the world. Under Nazi rule, beer production was reduced, and the total output of the breweries was sent to the German army. "Beer" sold to civilians looked and tasted like rusty water. Mr. Walter had fond memories of the delicious beer he used to drink, and his greatest wish at this time was once more

Susi and Hanna Walter, 1945

to enjoy a glass of real pre-war-quality beer. I was not a beer drinker, but I noticed that a number of men in my unit regularly bought cans of American beer via Post Exchange channels. Mr. Walter's eyes gleamed when I brought him a can of beer, opened it ceremoniously, and poured it slowly into a tall glass. With the whole family watching respectfully, he took a sip of beer from the glass. He stopped abruptly and looked at me in bitter disappointment. "I thought you said this was beer," he moaned. Evidently, war-quality American beer was not much better than rusty water.

My parents and relatives had sent me packages while I was in basic training. Now that army mail was catching up with me, letters and packages were again arriving regularly. Uncle Sieg's daughter wrote frequently. I asked my parents to change the contents of their packages from cake, candy and chips to groceries for my civilian friends. The Walters were the first recipients of these shipments. I also gave them cigarettes. Cigarettes were issued monthly to all GIs. In a local store, I traded one pack of cigarettes for a huge box of colored pencils, artist quality, which I gave to Susi. The Walters were deeply grateful. The army's ban against fraternization with Germans did not specify an exemption for German Jews. I assumed, however, that the rule's intent was to have us shun the supporters and followers of Nazism, not the victims. I never tried to conceal my friendship with survivors.

The Walters introduced me to several other Jewish survivors who were now living in Marienbad. I shall quote a letter I sent to my parents on August 20, 1945:

A year ago, a concentration camp death march passed through Marienbad. A half-starved Jewish girl escaped. She asked the first person she met whether there were any Jews living in Marienbad. Instead of turning her in, he sent her to the Walters, who hid her in their house and shared their meager rations with her until the U.S. Army arrived. Well, last night, I took this same girl, Medi, to a concert, which we both enjoyed very much.

One can see that these people don't have a need for material goods any more, only love. Another camp survivor told me at the Walters' home the other day: "First we were hungry. After that has been taken care of, our greatest need is to feel like a human being again, to be treated as a human being. It is not so much sexual love that the survivors crave, but the understanding, the respect, yes—the love—that everyone should feel for fellow human beings." When I see how happy these poor people are when we give them a little compassion, how they thrive in response to it, I can see how important my visits are.

After the concert, Medi and I visited a Dr. Loebner, who had spent six years in concentration camps. We kept returning to the same subject: How many tragic memories there are and how small the number of people who have true sympathy for the victims. All European Jews are suffering from a psychic ailment. They may well be getting enough food now to avert physical illness. But they have a serious deficiency of love, the only remedy for their illness. We must show them that they are not just living among enemies. Letters and packages from friends and relatives can save lives. Suicides are quite numerous these days.

Incidentally, Medi originally came from Russia. She was miraculously reunited with her brother and her father. She was 16—haggard, bald, flea-infested—when she came to the Walter family. When I met her, she was a beautiful girl of 17. She married an American soldier a few months later.

I mentioned the importance of letters and packages from overseas. Unfortunately, there was no civilian postal service in Europe at this time. The only way a survivor could locate a relative, initiate immigration, receive letters and packages from anywhere was by finding an American soldier who was willing to use the army postal service (illegally) for this purpose. At various times, I transmitted mail for more than 20 survivors at a time. The mail clerks probably thought I was running a lucrative black-market business.

Fritz and Medi, 1945

When I wrote the above letter, Japan had already surrendered, and World War II was over except for some formalities. Only a month earlier, my redeployment to the Pacific war was still a distinct possibility. Points were assigned to each soldier to reflect the number of months of active duty he had served, the number of dependents he had and other factors considered relevant. A man who had more than fifty-some points would be sent to the United States for discharge. Anyone with fewer points would be either kept in Europe or redeployed to the Pacific area. I had about 20 points.

I remember when the two atom bombs were dropped on Japan early in August 1945. There have been many questions asked in subsequent years by many people (including myself) about the moral justification for pulverizing two densely populated cities. At the time, though, there was no question, no regret—only wild elation. The war against Japan was a tough, bloody war. We believed the Japanese when they swore to fight on to the last man. If technology could come up with any way to avoid the brutal process of attacking island after island, everybody was in favor of it. It was only later that we allowed ourselves to think of the death, the pain, the innocent residents, the children of Hiroshima and Nagasaki.

MGSG was terminated on June 25, 1945. Its task was completed, and most of its men had enough points to qualify for discharge from the armed service. But we had to have a final farewell party. I wrote home about it.

I managed to buy 300 bottles of pre-war top quality wine—100 bottles of port, 100 bottles of vermouth and 100 bottles of Moselle white wine. The captain added some liquor to our supply. Music was provided by a band that I dug up through my local connections. By 3 a.m., everybody was pretty well stewed, including the band and the waitresses. I thought that I was just feeling happy; but several of my buddies swore that at 1 a.m., they saw me watering the flowers with Italian vermouth, vintage 1929.

I found it very painful to say good-bye to my good buddies. Our experiences of just three short months had forged strong bonds of friendship. I watched sadly as the trucks drove away.

Those of us who were short on points, mostly the interpreters, were now assigned to headquarters of the 16th Armored Division, supposedly for military government work. When we arrived at the small town of Plan (or Plana), just a few miles from Marienbad, we were told that there was no military government work available right now. We were ordered to do clerical work—collating and counting brochures, rubber stamping letters, licking envelopes and—most challenging of all—addressing envelopes. All this took no more than four hours per day. On the second day, I used my leisure time to rush back to Marienbad and complain to a captain in military government about my plight. He assured me that he would take care of the problem. On August 5, I was transferred back to my former job in Marienbad.

In a manner of speaking, World War II started with Hitler's seizure of Czechoslovakia. It was Hitler's first major victory. The war ended at the same location. A few days before V-E day, there was still fighting in Czechoslovakia after most hostility in Germany had ceased. I learned about this chapter in military history while I was assigned to the 16th Armored Division.

The 16th Armored Division was organized and thoroughly trained in the United States during 1944. As the war was winding down in Europe, the division commanders were getting nervous. Were they going to miss out on the glory and the career opportunities available during a war? They accelerated their preparations, got all their men and equipment shipped to Europe, and rushed across France and Germany in a desperate effort to catch up with the war front. They met the enemy in Czechoslovakia.

At this time, the main objective of the German troops was to make contact with any American unit for the purpose of surrendering to them rather than to the nearby Soviet forces. The first unit of the 16th Armored Division to arrive on the scene was a maintenance outfit. It scored brilliant successes! A colonel was riding in a Jeep through the town of Pilsen. When he rounded a corner, he found himself looking into the gun barrels of a huge German tank. Not knowing what else to do, the colonel pulled his 45-caliber pistol out of its holster and bounced a bullet off the tank's impenetrable armor. Much to his surprise, the hatch on the tank opened, and a white flag waved back and forth above the hatch.

The 16th Armored Division ran into a problem after V-E Day. They had a number of medals to hand out. Bronze stars were normally awarded to soldiers who showed exceptional courage in the performance of a death-defying act of heroism. Who would qualify for that honor in the 16th Armored Division? We witnessed a ceremony of bronze stars being awarded to the division chaplains—for exceptional effort in maintaining high morale among the troops. It was embarrassing.

One of the primary objectives of the Allied military campaign was the liberation of the various countries and restoration of their legitimate governments. This was now going on in Czechoslovakia, but it did not give me a happy feeling. Were my expectations too simplistic? Yes, Hitler had evicted the Czech nationals from Sudetenland in 1938 and allowed proven Nazis from Germany to move in and take over their property. These Germans were now ordered to return to Germany empty-handed. OK so far. All ethnic (Sudeten) Germans were also expelled from Czechoslovakia and ordered to leave their property behind, unless they could prove that they were victims or active opponents of Nazism. The Walter family was able to prove this with difficulty; but their friends, who had supported them during Nazi occupation, were not granted exemption, although they had never been Nazi collaborators or sympathizers. The Czechs who moved in were not the families that had originally lived there. Rather, they were young adventurers. And the houses they picked for themselves were not necessarily those of former Nazi activists, but simply the houses they liked best. No differentiation was made between those residents who had supported the Nazis (there were quite a few) and those who chose not to (there were quite a few of those, too). More than three million people were booted out of their ancestral homes solely by ethnic selection.

The Czech government tried to justify their policy by accusing the Germanic population of committing acts of sabotage and terrorism. The charges were pure fiction. But we had strict orders not to interfere in Czech internal affairs in any way.

The human vultures were moving in on the evicted Germans. I heard of several members of the U.S. military police who offered—for a fee, payable in advance—to move a family's possessions illegally to their new location in Germany. On the day of the family's departure, they would load the goods onto their army truck, drive to the next town and sell everything for additional profit. The family was now irreversibly deported to Germany without furniture and without recourse.

Injustice has always upset me, even when it happened to Germans. In hindsight, though, sometimes I wonder: How many Sudeten Germans were actually better off rebuilding their lives in West Germany rather than living in Czechoslovakia after the communist takeover? And would the schism between the Czech Republic and Slovakia in 1993 have passed through a further ethnic conflict if the Sudeten Germans had not been evicted in 1945? We will never know.

The Czech central government was situated in Prague, which was in the part of the country occupied by Soviet troops. It was supposed to be a democratic government like the pre-war Czech government. But the Soviet authorities were the real power. It was they who wrote the definition of what constituted democracy.

We were receiving reports from reliable sources in the Russian-occupied part of Czechoslovakia that many democratic (non-communist) leaders were being murdered or kidnapped. We even had several cases in our own zone of anti-Communist Czechs being kidnapped and driven into the Russian zone, never to be seen again. Over the past several years, U.S. soldiers had developed feelings of respect and admiration for the Soviet army in the process of fighting against a common enemy. Those feelings were now fading rapidly. When time came for the occupying countries to turn Czechoslovakia over to its own people, the United States simply pulled out. The Soviets converted many of their soldiers into political agents, who stayed behind to maintain control. We had witnessed and, by our tacit acceptance, participated in the second betrayal of Czech democracy—only seven years after the Munich sellout. Czechoslovakia was now a part of the Eastern Bloc.

I left Marienbad—and Czechoslovakia—on September 3, 1945. I was transferred to the Fourth Armored Division, stationed in Landshut, lower Bavaria. On my arrival, I was dismayed to discover that I had been assigned to the Adjutant General department for office work. I reported subsequent developments in two letters to my parents.

An officer interviewed us to determine which office we would be best suited for. I inquired casually if there were any openings in Military Government. He thought they might be looking for a driver, but he wasn't sure. Why not run across the street and ask? I ran across the street to Military Government, found the lieutenant in charge and announced, "I'm the new interpreter, Sir!" He asked a few questions: Could I read and write German? How did I learn it? What was my service experience? Did I know how to drive? I answered all but the last question satisfactorily, and I will probably get my assignment tomorrow.

September 6, 1945

Dear Folks,

I started my new job today. It went like this: A soldier drove me to the County Courthouse in Landshut. He led me into a room, where about 20 people were standing in line. Five tables were manned by three pretty girls and two gentlemen. The soldier called out to the five workers: "Hey, everybody! Here is your new boss!" Then he ran out.

My "staff" welcomed me. When the line got a bit shorter, they explained the work I would be supervising: This is part of the UNRRA organization. All displaced persons (DPs) presently residing in the county are required to be registered here for favorable food rations (Allied countries only), repatriation to their home country (if they want it), transfer to a DP camp, or continued local residence. The employees are themselves non-German from Hungary, Estonia,

Lithuania, Soviet Union, but they speak German fluently and English in various degrees. They have fallen way behind in their work. Hundreds of forms are stacked up, waiting to be processed. I snooped through some of their files and found all kinds of confusion. An American's form was filed under "Austria," an Englishman's under "Chile." A five-year-old Brazilian girl refuses to be repatriated "until she can find her husband." The girls who work for me look like models. I can see why my predecessor hired them—and why he never did any work: Too many distractions.

The staff members were delighted when they realized that I was taking my job seriously. They recognized the need for someone who could assign tasks, who could make quick decisions when guidelines were vague or non-existent, and who could speak German to them and the clients. Morale and efficiency improved significantly.

I called in all the DPs whose records did not make sense. How could there be an American DP in Landshut? She turned out to be a chubby, cheerful black woman, who had lived in

My staff at UNRRA

an isolated Bavarian village for over thirty years. She was the only black person, other than U.S. army personnel, I had ever seen in Germany. She spoke Black-American dialect as if she had just come over from Georgia, and she also spoke the Bavarian dialect of German like a native. "Do you consider yourself American?" I asked. "Heck, no!" she replied. "Then why are you registered as a DP?" "The soldier who used to work here said I had to. I didn't want no part of it." We let her revert back to German status.

A young Hungarian man was sent to me for a decision. Hungary was considered an Axis power, an ally of Germany. Hungarians were not to be registered. But this man claimed to be Jewish. "Can I see your identification papers, please?" He gave me a Hungarian army certificate. It did not specify religion. "Any other papers?" None. "Were you imprisoned, interned in a camp?" No. He was kept in a special army unit that had to walk across areas that were thought to be mined or booby-trapped. "I would like to help you," I assured him, "but how do I know you are Jewish? Can you recite a Hebrew prayer or blessing?" No, he was raised in a completely assimilated secular family. "You don't know even one word of Hebrew?" No. He decided that DP status was not worth the effort. "Don't worry about it," were his parting words.

A young German showed up. He had just been discharged from Dachau Concentration Camp. I looked at his papers. His name was Hindemith. This was also the name of a composer of modern symphonic music, relatively unknown among the general public. I asked the young man: "Are you related to Paul Hindemith, the composer?" His face brightened.

"You know him?" he asked in astonishment.

"I have a recording of 'Mathis der Maler'," I replied.

"That's my Uncle Paul! Is he still alive?" I was unable to answer that question. But I did register him as a DP.

Alexander Postoiev was one of my staff members. He was an intelligent, dignified, middle-aged man from the Ukrainian area of the Soviet Union. He was once a professor of astronomy at a Russian university, lost his job and his freedom when he was accused of making bourgeois remarks and having appearance unbecoming a Soviet educator. Like many thousands of other Soviet nationals who were still living in Germany at this time, he did not wish to return to his motherland. I was still trying to think of the Soviet Union as our close ally, but the many cases of Soviet atrocities reported by Russian expatriates were starting to sink in. When Alexander confirmed the previous reports, based on his own experiences and observations, I finally accepted them as truthful.

I asked Alexander to write down his feelings in English for me. I copied the document verbatim (complete with spelling errors) and

passed it on to my commanding officers, to my parents and to several
friends in the United States. Stalin's excesses are well known today;
but at the time, these revelations were quite shocking. It should be
understood that nearly all Soviet nationals who wanted to be repatriated had been returned to the U.S.S.R. Alexander pleaded the cause of
those who wanted to stay in Germany.

The terrible news has reached us, Russian citizens, that we might be
all forced to go "home." There being no official announcement, and
having heard from several American officials statements to the contrary, we cannot believe it. We would like, however, to make the reasons of our refusal to be repatriated once more quite clear to the American Authorities.

The results of registrations of (Russian) displaced persons give to
understand that far less than one percent only want to go home. All
other expressed more or less definitely (depending on the grade of
fear to speak) their invariable intention to live anywhere else in free
countries or even to remain here in Germany.

Great many of them have wives, children, parents there ... Nearly all
don't speak any foreign languages. The young people have no possibilities of education and study. Nobody has any money or other means
to live and very few have some relatives somewhere in the world to
rely upon ... And, nevertheless, they all don't want to return and would
oppose to it by all possible means. Why?

The first reason is the general policy of Soviet Government: the
reign of awful terror, oppression, fear and lies, no trace of any free-
doms, no justice, forced labor, constant need and hunger. The now so
well known stories about Nazi's atrocities are children's tales in comparison with all that has been going on in USSR (in "quality" as well as
quantity). Who has once got out of a prison, does not return there
willingly!

The second reason: everyone in the USSR knows what has been the
fate of unhappy war prisoners, which had come to their country from
Finland after the war of 1939-40. Nobody has returned home and
who lives, toils somewhere in one of the uncountable concentration
camps. Very many are dead and nobody knows the exact number of
them ... "There are no prisoners of war of the Red Army, only traitors"

has been the official slogan! But then it were thousands, now millions … civilian as well as war prisoners.

The third reason is the direct consequence of the first two. Everyone of us has personal experience of "living" in USSR and of its "justice" system and everyone already knows what "cordial" reception have had those unhappy which had already reached the Soviet camps. Some were lucky to escape and to come back to the American occupied territory. Those witnesses are unanimous in their reports, which make the hair raise up on our heads … Their experiences are briefly as follows: The huge camps containing hundreds of thousands of human beings, citizens of the "most free and democratic country of the world" are being guarded by barbed-wire fences and a good armed watch. All personal belongings of the arriving people are being at once confiscated (including clothing, they got from the Allies). The families are being separated (quarantine!). All are being questioned and cross-questioned about their life and doings since 1941 and the answers sent to their respective places of former residence to be proved and complemented by NKVD (the Soviet edition of Gestapo). It seems that all their "crimes" have been registered for this highly "respected" institution in due time by a well organized enormous net of espionage which covered and covers the whole Europe. Only persons younger than 18 are being sent somewhere to the East (nobody knows where), others are being shot without much delay or are sitting there since May or June waiting for their sentences and starving on 200 gr. of bread and some soup daily. It is said, that the hair of some girls has been cut short because of "German fashion" of hair dress!

The vilest and the most injust wholesale manslaughtering campaign the world has ever seen is going on and we know its reason quite well: Nobody, who has once been abroad and seen a better life and happier countries is to be permitted to relate his experiences (Especially after having made acquaintance with the Americans). They all are traitors and "people's enemies" and must die or have a long term of imprisonment.

We know, that many Americans believe all this to be only propaganda of some anti-Soviet minority. Yes, it all seems to be too horrible to be true, but have you some prooves to the contrary, except lies from Soviet papers and radio? Do you know a single American who has been ever permitted by Soviets to visit the country quite free and to speak with its people without any interpreters or "guides" (from

NKVD)? Have the American newspapers now their correspondents in the Russian Zone and are they free to see what is going on?

Remember the murders, robbery and destruction of the first years of the Revolution, the deliberately planned hunger of 1933 and death of 8 millions of peasants in the Ukraine alone (only because they did not want to enter the collective farms), the awful wave of terror in 1937-38 and 15 millions (minimum!) toiling and dying now in prisons and huge concentration camps in tundras, forests, and deserts of our un-happy country. Is that all only propaganda? No it is not! That knows everybody, who lived in USSR or was there only once with his eyes open. That know all Lithuanians, Latvians, Estonians and Poles, who had once the opportunity to live under this regime and who don't want now to go to their native countries. They too know the value of Soviet justice and democracy.

More than that: Several terror attempts by Soviet officers are known and even cases of kidnapping in broad daylight here in the American Zone, the victims having been in some cases saved by the Americans. That is here…One can picture to himself what happens there …. Is there no bottom to the depths to which human atrocities and suffer-ings can sink?

The worst, never heard of before, the most blood-thirsty and unsatiable tyranny of the history of the mankind … Is it going now to be fed by new many hundreds of thousands of innocent martyrs, who are ready to toil heavily in any other country under any conditions, who are ready to die sooner than to be tortured again to the end of their lives?

Is that true that now, when all the world hopes for a new, better, happier and peaceful existence, we all should be against the elemen-tary principles of the international law and customs delivered by force as common criminals to the new martyrdom?

We cannot believe that "the land of the free and the home of the brave," which had been fighting for the liberation of the world from tyrannies and despotism would do such a terrible act of injustice!

I could not accept Alexander's reference to Nazi atrocities as com-parable to "children's tales;" but there was no longer any doubt in my mind about Stalin's brutality. Stalin and Hitler were two of the very worst kind.

Russian DPs were not forcibly repatriated at this time or later. Earlier, however, immediately after V-E Day, there had been an agreement between the U.S.A. and the U.S.S.R. that all Russians who had fought for Hitler against their own country would be forced to return to the U.S.S.R. This practice was stopped when it was discovered that nearly all returnees on a train had committed suicide rather than face torture and certain death on their arrival in the U.S.S.R.

Our file of registered DPs was arranged by nationality. The thinnest file was the one labeled "Jewish." I found out that only two of the DPs in this category were still living in the county—Lilly Marcuse and her daughter, Lore. I went to their home and introduced myself. They were delighted to receive my offer of friendship. My next letter home included a request for more groceries.

Mrs. Marcuse must have been about fifty years old at the time, Lore in her early twenties. Their past was tragic, their present condition unhappy, their future uncertain. The family was apparently fairly wealthy when Hitler came to power. They lived in Stettin, a city in the northeastern part of Germany. Mr. Marcuse died—a result of Nazi harassment or imprisonment, I do not remember which—leaving Lilly with two children. Her son, a talented college student, became seriously ill and died. Lore, the daughter, was deaf, and her speech was hardly comprehensible. The two women were on their own.

When the war started, Lilly and Lore packed up what was left of their money and valuables and took a train to Bavaria. They made an offer to Christian acquaintances, who lived in the country: "We are willing to give you all of this and to be your servants if you will hide us in your house." Their offer was accepted, and Lilly and Lore spent the war years in hiding. They were not happy years. There was a strong personality clash, and what seemed like a lot of money was soon used up on black-market food. The hosts might have turned the women in, except for the knowledge that the hosts would have been punished just as severely as the fugitives. They were all very happy to see the American troops approaching, bringing their hostile and dangerous coexistence to a conclusion.

The town government of Landshut permitted the Marcuses to take over a house that had been confiscated from a former Nazi official. All subsequent requests by Lilly for missing furniture, tools and supplies were either denied or ignored. The neighbors rejected all gestures of friendship. Lilly ascribed this to latent anti-Semitism. She changed her mind after she became more familiar with others who were treated the same way. It seems that the local Bavarians hated the North Germans. They regarded Lilly and Lore as unwanted North German immigrants rather than Jews. But the effect was the same. I voiced my disgust about German attitudes in a letter to my parents about this time:

> I am so glad that I don't have to live in Germany any more. Aside from the Jews, who still haven't learned to hate, every German hates his neighbors. All this cheating, tattling, bickering, envy and greed make me sick. Everything has changed! If you know of any refugees who want to return to Germany, tell them they're nuts!

In a letter dated October 17, 1945, I told my parents about another group of Jewish survivors.

> I spent a very pleasant evening with six young Jews from Poland, who came yesterday to be registered as DPs. They are quiet, intelligent men between 25 and 35 years old. Each one of them lost his whole family the same horrible way: murder by the Nazis. The men themselves were lucky to be liberated just in time. They were facing certain death by starvation within days, perhaps within hours. Their skeletal remains were converted back to human bodies in a U.S. army hospital. Then they were "employed" by a friendly unit of medics to do practically nothing. Little chores were rewarded with hundreds of cigarettes, chocolates, watches, fountain pens, etc. All the dirty work was done by captured S.S.-men. When the medics were sent back to the United States, they left the house and a load of good things to the six survivors. The six now want to move to Austria to join their friends, who claim that the population there is exceptionally friendly.

In yet another letter, I reported meeting two other Jewish camp survivors.

...They were compensated by the Military Government for their suffering by being given a textile business that formerly belonged to a Nazi official. One of the men was trained as a carpenter, the other had been a student in a technical school. Neither knew anything about textiles or about running a business, but both were very proud of their new status. They showed me their store: Buttons in all sizes, colors, shapes; threads in all colors and quantities; fabrics of all kinds, buckles, ribbons, wrapping paper, a typewriter, six night gowns, and hundreds of shirts. The carpenter, Abraham, was very excited as he showed me the prettiest buttons in the store. He was even more excited when he found a box of embroidered monograms. Moritz, his companion, was examining a bolt of lining material. He felt it between his fingers, like an expert, and suggested that it was probably good for making shirts. An old sales clerk, who has been in the business for over twenty years, is still there. I saw him gulping nervously. He looked as though he was ready to burst into tears.

Abraham looked suspiciously at a cabinet filled with letters, forms and folders. Should he throw them all out—or keep them to make a good impression? Abraham and Moritz speak only Yiddish, and they like to just sit around on the counter. But that does not matter: Anyone who has merchandise to sell will get customers, even if he lacks basic knowledge and experience of the business. And if the business fails, the two men will have lost nothing, maybe gained a little experience.

Very few Jewish camp survivors were set up in business. A fair number were given apartments from which Nazi activists had been evicted. The majority flocked to Jewish Displaced Person camps, where they hoped to be able to find relatives or friends or to discover a way to immigrate to another country.

Jewish soldiers from all over Bavaria assembled in Kehlheim for high holiday services. Local Jewish camp survivors were invited to share this experience with us. We felt as though six million Jews, who had been murdered so recently not far from there, were also participating. It was deeply moving.

Chaplain Eugene Lipman made us aware of the significance of the time and location. The main emphasis of his sermon, however, was placed on the fate of the living survivors. Despite the good intentions of the U.S. Army and UNRRA, there was a serious lack of warm clothing and blankets for the approaching winter season. Food was barely adequate. The Chaplain urged every soldier to immediately write to his family, friends, home congregation etc., requesting that packages be sent (via army mail) to the Chaplain. By marking the packages "RELIGIOUS SUPPLIES," there would be no limit as to size or weight of the packages.

The response was very dramatic. It was estimated that nearly 180 tons of clothing and food were received. The army unit to which the Chaplain was attached had to rent several warehouses to hold the packages until they could be distributed. Many of the packages fell apart, spilling the supposed "religious supplies" all over the postal facilities. But the job was done.

A soldier named Goldberg was able to borrow a Jeep for a day. He picked me up, and we invited Lilly Marcuse to come along for a trip to Deggendorf DP camp, about 50 miles from Landshut. My letter of October 14 described the experience.

> Since I came back to Europe, I never saw more than six Jewish people at a time, and those were generally timid and fearful, as if they had just woken up from a bad dream. Here, it was different: Nearly 1,000 Jewish people live here with a joy of life and a pride that would be unusual even among people living in normal circumstances. It was good to see healthy, cheerful children noisily kicking a soccer ball around; men and women chatted excitedly on benches or while strolling; and the colorful bulletin board announced an election, religious services, a dance, sports, scholastic and training courses, and a meeting of the youth club.

> I was told that until three or four weeks ago, Deggendorf was run like a dirty prison camp. But now, there is complete freedom, and everything is clean and orderly.

> Between 200 and 400 of the residents are German Jews, the rest mostly from Poland. I was happy to find out that there were two weddings last week; but I was devastated when I realized that among the 1,000 survivors living in the camp, there were only about 50 children, all of them teenagers. What happened to the others?

Lilly Marcuse was happy to meet an old friend from Stettin at the camp. I met a woman from Gailingen, my grandfather's home town. She had been a close friend of my mother's cousin, Mery, until Mery was deported to an unknown destination. We never heard from or about Mery any more.

Eddy and friend

On October 20, Eddy appeared on the scene. Eddy was the most beautiful, most affectionate, most fun-loving puppy who ever lived. He was a wire-hair terrier. When I saw him on the street, it was love at first sight. I offered the owner two cartons of cigarettes, an offer she could not possibly refuse. (I probably could have had the owner for that price.) My mother was upset when she heard about the name. How would my Uncle Edwin feel about that? I changed the name to Teddy. Eddy did not mind.

The first time I took Teddy to work, he brought the whole operation to a screeching halt. Everybody—DPs, staff, county employees—wanted to play with him. Teddy loved it. Teddy became an important part of my life. In many of my letters, the train of thoughts would be interrupted by such statements as "Teddy is trying to tell me something," or "Teddy just stole my pen," or "Teddy just bit my nose." He made friends with everybody—soldiers, civilians, other dogs, even cats. But he was always happy to come back to me.

There was an announcement that American soldiers stationed in Europe would have an opportunity to take a furlough in Switzerland. I applied immediately and was accepted. I dropped Teddy off at Mrs. Marcuse's house, along with a batch of food and a bag of dirty laundry, and I was on my way. The details of my furlough were contained in two letters, which are combined below.

A group of us took a short ride by truck to Munich Sunday evening at 8 p.m. We sat around in Munich (with coffee and doughnuts) until 2:30 a.m. We boarded a train, third class. The seats were hard, and it was cold and crowded. We were given field rations for breakfast. We had lunch in Karlsruhe (after standing on line for 1½ hours), had supper in Strasbourg, and arrived in Mulhouse, France at 11:30 p.m. We slept there, and processing started on the following day (October 30, 1945).

This is said to be the first time in the history of Switzerland that foreign soldiers in uniform are permitted to visit the country officially. That is why a lot of red tape has to be unraveled. Prearranged guided tours are not so bad. But if a soldier wants to travel freely, as in my case, there are regulations regarding entry and departure at the border as well as police registration (coming and going) in each town to be visited.

I entered Switzerland at Basel on the morning of October 31. This is an overwhelming experience after traveling through hungry, barren, heavily damaged European towns. All the houses are well-maintained here, streets are clean, and all the stores are filled with meat, vegetables, pastries, fruits, clothing, beverages, all kinds of household goods and many luxury items. It is strange to see store owners not holding hordes of people out of their premises, but instead trying to entice customers to buy from them rather than from the competition. You can't imagine how that affects a GI—also the fact that everyone looks healthy and well dressed and that so many young men walk around unperturbed in civilian clothes. I marvel at all that and the fantastic beauty of the country. I can't help thinking: What have these people done that God loves them so much?

It is not surprising that business with GIs is booming in Basel. The soldiers, all of whom enter Switzerland in Basel, don't want to miss this heavenly opportunity to buy up everything that they have not been able to get for years. There are some limitations, though. Milk and milk products (including the heavenly Swiss chocolate), fat, meat, bread, eggs and shoes are rationed. But nobody is starving.

I left Basel at noon for Zurich. Railroads are absolutely clean, fast, quiet, warm and on time, in contrast to the rest of Europe. I could still remember the Zurich railroad station. After a short ride on a modern streetcar, I rang the bell at Metzgers. Uncle Sigmund [father of Julius and Richard; brother of my grandfather] was very confused. I had awakened him from his nap, and he had no idea what this foreign soldier might want from him. When he finally realized who I was, he was overjoyed—so were Julius and Richard. They asked me a thousand questions. During long conversations, they kept interrupting:

"Are you hungry, boy?" "Are you tired, boy?" "Act as if you were at home!" ... Often I felt as though I were talking with you, dear Opa, because Uncle Sigmund's voice, humor, expressions and appearance are very much like yours.

After two days in Zurich, I took a train to St. Gallen to visit another family of cousins. Once more, there was a joyous welcome. In my boyhood years, I had spent several vacations in St. Gallen. Now we had a wonderful reunion. I also took the opportunity to telephone my mother on her birthday, November 4.

On the way back to Basel, I made a quick side trip to Kreuzlingen, a small Swiss town located next to my former home town of Constance. I looked across the border creek (now drained or rerouted) to my old neighborhood. It would not have been easy any more to cross the border illegally. There was a tall barbed wire fence on the Swiss side of the creek, a long trench with barbed wire on the German side. I talked to a Swiss border guard for a while, but I had no desire to visit Constance. My feelings of attraction and repulsion were hopelessly entangled.

The return trip to Landshut on November 8 was just as strenuous as the earlier one to Mulhouse. When I arrived at Marcuses, Teddy gave me a hysterically happy welcome, yelping and jumping for an hour. Mrs. Marcuse said that Teddy pulled a sock out of my dirty laundry right after my departure and kept it in his makeshift bed until I returned. Teddy was only two months old when I left for my furlough, and I had owned him for only eight days.

I stayed in Landshut for two months. While I was on furlough, an order arrived directing me to report to a transient camp in Augsburg on November 14 for assignment to the Third Military Government regiment. A soldier is always ready to move on, but I found it hard to say good-bye to my staff and the Marcuses.[10] I refer to my letter of November 15, 1945.

My trip to Augsburg was somewhat eventful. My lieutenant arranged for a closed Jeep with driver to take me there. A few minutes after our departure at 8 a.m., the engine conked out. We discovered that one of the fuel cans the driver had used to gas up the Jeep was filled with water. By 12:30 p.m., all the water had been removed from the tank, fuel line and carburetor, and we tried it again. All went well until we got close to Munich, when a tire blew out. The spare tire was very anemic and would not have survived the trip to Augsburg or even back to Landshut. The driver cruised slowly through the streets of Munich until he spotted an empty Jeep trailer (U.S. Army equipment) that was endowed with the same size tires as our Jeep. He hitched the trailer to our vehicle and quickly drove about a mile away. A few minutes later, we were able to replace the defective tire and acquire a very good spare. The rest of the trip was pretty routine.

A transient camp is a dull place. I was there for a month. I managed to visit Landshut twice. In Augsburg, I met Dr. Muhlhauser, an elderly, blind Jewish camp survivor who had originally lived in this city. As a chemist, he had made significant contributions to German military strength during World War I, and he lost his vision as a German soldier during a poison gas attack. Evidently as a reward for his World War I record, the Nazi government sent him to Theresienstadt, a relatively benign concentration camp. He survived and returned to his home after the war. He lauded his former friends and neighbors, who were now taking care of his needs every day.

While I was at the transient camp, I kept my candy bars and other food items in a box on the window sill. That was the coolest part of the generally overheated room. I woke up one night hearing strange sounds right next to my cot. I looked intently in the darkness and finally saw several mice climbing up my barracks bag (which contained all my worldly possessions), jumping toward the window sill, missing it, landing on the floor, and starting the process over again. I watched for a while with genuine interest. Then I reached quietly to the lower part of my cot, where Teddy was sleeping. I picked Teddy up and placed him softly on the floor. The mice never stopped. Teddy stretched, still half asleep, and looked around. When he saw the mice, he let out a frightened yelp, jumped up on the cot and slipped into the sleeping bag with me, but crawled all the way down to my feet. I learned that Teddy was not a hunting dog.

As soon as mail service had been restored in France, I had written a letter to Uncle Léon's employer and friend, asking if he knew anything about the family's whereabouts. I promptly received an answer: "They were deported in July of 1942. We do not know where they were sent. We have not heard from them since."—My parents heard from other relatives in France—Cousin Sylvain and his father, Aunt Louise and her son. They had been in hiding and survived the war. My parents asked Sylvain to find out what he could about Uncle Léon, Aunt Martha and Gigi.

We were all deeply worried by this time. My mother, particularly, was sick with apprehension. Every day brought news of "liberated" concentration camps and of the horror that was revealed when the gates were opened. Survivors and perpetrators now told the world about gas chambers and mass shootings, about starvation and disease, about torture and medical experimentation, about millions of bodies being burned or buried or utilized. Our worst fears were being confirmed; the most preposterous, unbelievable rumors of the past years turned out to be understatements of actual facts.

A letter from Sylvain broke into the trivia of transient camp life with shocking news: Aunt Martha, Uncle Léon and Gigi were gone! They were killed on July 23, 1942—the day of their arrival at Auschwitz Concentration Camp. I read and re-read the letter, hoping that I'd somehow missed a word or sentence that would set everything right. But through the blur of watery eyes, I realized that the inevitable, ugly truth would not be denied. When would the pain and suffering stop? How much longer would we be subjected to the horror cast by one madman? I slept sporadically that night, wanting to go home, wanting this war to be done, wanting to be at peace—with myself.

10 SIFTING THROUGH THE RUBBLE

My orders had finally arrived. I was to report to the Third Military Government Regiment, Special Branch, headquarters for Lower Bavaria. I made the short trip from Augsburg to Regensburg on December 3, 1945.

My new living conditions were luxurious. I had a small hotel room all to myself. Meals were served by waitresses in the hotel dining room while a live pianist maintained a relaxed atmosphere. A bar served beer, wine, sodas and snacks free of charge until late every night. Live entertainment was presented every Sunday night, with standard drinks and snacks still offered free and French champagne available at $1.00 per bottle. Conveniently, the Military Government offices were located in an office building across the street from the hotel.

I found out what the term "Special Branch" meant. It was the department of Military Government responsible for denazification of the German government. Anyone holding or applying for a job in government, civil service, teaching, or working for a U.S. Army unit had to be screened for prior Nazi affiliation or activity. Every candidate had to fill out a questionnaire that asked about membership and rank in each of nearly 100 specified Nazi organizations, about police records, annual income since 1932, and many other questions. Depending on the degree and type of activity, Special Branch had certain options, as I explained to my parents in my letter of December 18, 1945.

...We arrange to have 10 to 20 people arrested every day (for falsification of questionnaires, or by automatic arrest category, such as membership in S.S. or Gestapo or high leadership in the Nazi party). We have detailed information about everyone who lived in or near Regensburg. We have military records, complete with biographical information, political inclination, etc. We have party, S.A., S.S. and Hitler Youth records. There are police reports that indicate whether a person was sent to a concentration camp for criminal activity or political action. We have complete newspaper files. We took over a large number of employment files from local industries and utilities, where job applicants had bragged about their Nazi activities in order to gain preference—generally signed and notarized. Every single questionnaire we receive is first evaluated as written, then it has to run the gauntlet through our document center. Processing generally takes from 1 to 2 weeks, although a "rush job" can be pushed through in 2 hours. We handle many cases. Last week we made 1,900 determinations! The verdict can be quite stiff. Party membership prior to May 1, 1937 results in dismissal from the position and seizure of the applicant's property. Any position of leadership in the Nazi party, no matter at what level, is similarly punished. These men can only work as laborers. It has happened, however, that some of these people moved out of the U.S. occupation zone and were immediately appointed to a high position. Contrary to general opinion, we are much stricter against Nazis (not against other Germans) than the Russian, French or British occupation forces are.

As thorough as our investigations were of people from the Regensburg area, we were completely ineffective in dealing with Germans who had been evicted from Sudetenland or Silesia. Czech and Polish authorities were totally unresponsive any time we requested information about any of their former residents. Russian authorities were similarly impassive to any inquiries about former residents of their zone. Anyone who moved in from any of those areas was exonerated by default, unless he was a major war criminal or top Nazi leader—or denounced by someone who came from the same region.

Denunciations were common. We had an investigation department that was kept busy following up on many leads. American intelligence agents also intercepted letters and phone calls from suspected Nazis and forwarded transcripts of supposedly incriminating information to us. Most of the suspects were apparently aware of the practice. They defeated our tactics by making phone calls to their friends in which they falsely accused anti-Nazis or personal adversaries of Nazi activity or war crimes, causing innocent people to be subjected to prolonged, stressful investigations. We decided to ignore the intelligence reports after a while.

There were four U.S. soldiers and some 60 civilians working in our Special Branch. Two sergeants were in charge of investigation and the document center, respectively. Les, a former psychology student from California, was in charge of the whole group. I was his assistant. Les was only a sergeant, but he was carrying out a program under the direction of a U.S. general in Munich. A lieutenant of the Public Safety department was nominally in charge of our group. He signed letters. Occasionally, a major or colonel would try to "pull rank" in an attempt to reverse our adverse finding on his German girlfriend. We would stand our ground, suggesting politely but firmly that he take it up with the general. We were never overruled as far as I know.

When business was slow, I would sift through the many unusual documents available in our building. I studied the military record of a certain Waffen-S.S. unit one day. I noticed that one of the combat actions credited to this particular unit was "Cleanup of Bialystok Ghetto." Unlike the political S.S., whose members were subject to automatic arrest, Waffen-S.S. members were in a less severe category. This particular unit, however, was evidently involved in some actions that deviated considerably from conventional military combat. I made a note of this fact.

A week or so later, a major from a local U.S. Army unit appeared in my office, accompanied by a young German. "There seems to be a mistake here," the major complained. "I received instructions to fire this man who is working for our unit. He is an excellent worker, and he tells me that he was never politically involved."

I pulled out his file. "I see that he was a member of the Waffen-S.S.," I pointed out.

"That was strictly an army unit," the German replied quickly in fluent English. "We had nothing to do with the S.S. We were just soldiers fighting on the Eastern Front against the Russian Army."

"Never any action against civilians?" I asked.

"Never!"

"What unit were you in?" I asked.

He told me.

"I know for a fact that your unit carried out the liquidation of the Bialystok Ghetto," I declared slowly.

"Oh, wasn't that terrible?" he countered instantly. "I was home on furlough when that happened, but my comrades told me about it when I came back. No, I had nothing to do with it! I never liked Hitler ," he added for good measure. "If the war hadn't ended when it did, I probably would have gotten into trouble because of my views."

The major was still convinced of his protege's innocence. I was not. I suggested that he could take it up with the general. Until then, the man would not be allowed to work for the U.S. Army.

I experienced many variations of the above conversation. My job was to field all requests for exceptions from Military Government laws. Most appeals were without merit: "Yes, I became an officer in the SA—but I was forced to accept the position or they would have locked me up."

"The Nazi Party was just a social club. We had drinking parties."

"I was never a Nazi in my heart. I wish Simon Goldberg were still around. He would tell you that we were good friends once."

I remember only one man who had a valid case. He had been a Social Democrat leader before 1933, joined the Nazi party to avoid being sent to a concentration camp, then helped a number of Jews and others that were persecuted. A thorough investigation confirmed his claims, and he was cleared.

I was amazed how often a priest or minister would show up in defense of an ardent ex-Nazi.

"Herr Schmidt was a good Christian! He was very active in church, never missed a service!"

"But he was an S.S. officer. Do you think that was all right? And he was a party member."

"He was very good to his family. He was a diligent worker. He was forced to join the party in order to keep his job."

"But he joined the Nazi party in 1928, five years before Hitler came to power."

"Maybe so, but he never really believed in all that Nazi stuff."

"It seems that nobody did. Thank you for the information."

The disturbing alliance between Christian clergy and former Nazi activists was undoubtedly abetted by the politics of the Christian Social Union at the time. I wrote home about that in March 1946:

> The CSU is by far the strongest party in Germany. All the militarists and Nazi followers find a haven there. It is a very effective organization: All the priests and ministers, from the largest cities to the tiniest villages, are fervent spokesmen for the party.

The German humor magazine, "*Simplicissimus*" commented in May 1946: "Local elections having been concluded, the church altars will now be available once again for religious functions."

I shall always remember one refreshing exception to that pattern. In a letter to my parents, I quoted an unusual note we had received from a local priest:

> Herr Müller asked me to write to you on his behalf. Be advised that Herr Müller always came to church every Sunday. For the rest of the week, however, his conduct was so despicable that no punishment could be severe enough for him.

We did not penalize Germans who joined the party after May 1, 1937. Party membership became mandatory after that date for civil service workers and a number of other positions. Refusal to join NSDAP at that time would have resulted in immediate dismissal. We chose to be less lenient toward one specific group. A number of American families of German extraction migrated to Germany in 1939, generally joined the Nazi party or the German army, and remained in Germany for the duration of the war. Their explanation of these events was invariably that they came to Germany to visit a sick aunt (or mother or grandmother) and were trapped there by the start of World War II. They "had to" join the party to counter anti-U.S. feelings. Actually, they responded to Hitler's call earlier that year for ethnic Germans all over the world to come back to their homeland in its hour of (military) need. We were not very sympathetic to their plight, but knowing the

State Department of those days, these "misguided" people were probably welcomed back to the United States with open arms.

A serious problem developed in screening applicants for teaching positions in German public schools. We had a poorly defined category of "militarist," which was primarily applied to teachers. The next generation of Germans should not be educated by professional soldiers, it was reasoned. We soon came to realize, however, that we had to dismiss a significant number of active teachers because they had served in the German army for 20 to 30 years prior to teaching. It was, in fact, the credits they had earned in their military career that gave them an open door when they applied for a teaching position under Nazi civil service regulations.

The local school director complained bitterly to us. "The only way we can establish a sound democracy in Germany is through education," he pointed out. "It will not be an easy task. But you are making it impossible by telling us to fire all the experienced personnel and to replace them with unqualified newcomers or questionable Silesians. Do you really think this is a good policy?" We saw his point but refused to back down, especially since the "experience" he valued so highly included the teaching of racism and other Nazi propaganda during the previous 12 years.

Falsification of a questionnaire, such as failure to list an important Nazi rank or activity, was considered a crime against U.S. occupation forces, punishable by stiff fines and prison sentences. The violator would be questioned by one of our investigators and turned over to the police for prosecution in a Military Government court. All our investigators were foreign nationals, whose enthusiasm was generally higher than their competence.

I have a rather painful recollection of one of the court cases.

"I see you made a written confession of your guilt," the judge, a U.S. army captain, observed.

"I was forced to sign it," claimed the defendant. "This man," pointing to the investigator, "pointed a gun at me!"

"I did not!" shouted the investigator. "I only laid it on the table.

And it wasn't a real gun. It's made of wood."

The case was instantly dismissed.

The most important step in the processing of questionnaires was evaluation, i.e., assigning a final determination to the case. This was done by three or four highly qualified, trustworthy civilians under our constant supervision. One of them, David Wiener, invited me to his home a few days after my arrival on the scene. It was the beginning of a warm friendship, which lasted until the Wieners died some 45 years later.

David and his wife, Hannah, had spent four years in concentration camps. He was born in Silesia, his wife in Poland. They had a baby boy before the war started. He was killed at Auschwitz concentration camp. They also lost most other members of their immediate families.

For the first time, I found out in detail the horrible happenings of the Holocaust—not the statistics, but the fear, the pain, the hunger, the helplessness of the victims, and the brutality, the hatred, the joy or indifference of the murderers in the act of killing. We talked for hours; and all the time, I thought about Aunt Martha, Uncle Léon and Gigi: How did they die? What horrors did they endure before the end?

Hannah and David Wiener

What were their last thoughts? Why did they—and all the others—have to die? Why, God, why?

The Wieners introduced me to many of the other Jewish survivors living in Regensburg. One of them, a former dentist, had been given the job at a concentration camp of extracting gold teeth from bodies being removed from the gas chamber. He told of the time he was overcome with abhorrence at what he was doing, causing him to vomit. An S.S. guard noticed it and laughed hysterically. "Was that your mother you just took care of?" he shouted gleefully.

Some 700 Jewish survivors lived in apartments in various parts of Regensburg. Most of them were originally from Poland. It was ironic that they now had to live in the land of their persecutors. Those who returned to Poland after the war encountered open hostility from the local population. But nobody wanted to stay in Germany. The Wieners and the former dentist were among the few who wanted to emigrate to the United States.[11] The vast majority were determined to go to Palestine, which was still a British mandate at that time.

"We must have our own country," they would often exclaim. "We can no longer live in somebody else's country, where we are just tolerated. Look at what has happened to us. This must never happen again!"

As we approached the festival of Passover, I "ordered" packages with specified contents from my parents. I was invited to the Wieners for the Seder ritual, and I wanted to make a major contribution to the Passover meal. Some six or eight local camp survivors were also invited.

Tradition tells us that certain post-biblical rabbis stayed up all night on the eve of Passover, discussing God's miraculous rescue of the ancient Israelites from Egyptian slavery. We spent half of the night discussing the most recent history, when God failed to intervene in the annihilation of six million Jews. Of course, the fact that we started the evening with the Seder ceremony showed that, despite our pain and bitterness, we still had to cling to God. This may sound contradictory, but it was a common dilemma among survivors. Several years later, my own father would cry out: "Can there be a god who would let Hitler come to power? What kind of god would permit Auschwitz to exist for years?" But he continued to keep the kosher laws, to observe the Sabbath, and to go to synagogue several times a week.

My religious education depicted a personal God who rewards the good, punishes the bad, and responds to requests (prayers). However, this concept was shattered by the Holocaust, where so many good people were allowed to be slaughtered by callous murderers, some of whom were permitted to enjoy a full life. I could no longer expect rewards for my good behavior or pious prayers. Millions of desperate prayers by good people went unheeded during the Holocaust. My prayers couldn't claim greater urgency or higher merit than theirs. (Yet, many years later when I was rolled into an operating room, I prayed. After the operation I was told that all the malignancy had been removed from my body, and I thanked God. Did it make sense? Of course not. Theology has to make sense; religion does not.)

I had become a frequent guest at Dave and Hannah's apartment, just about every Friday evening. My parents sent more packages now. I still made frequent trips to the Marcuses in Landshut, which was not far from Regensburg. The Deggendorf DP camp was also within easy commuting distance of Regensburg, enabling me to continue my mail deliveries to a number of people there.

My daily schedule was quite full, and I was not being a good "father" to Teddy. The hotel maids were happy to take care of him during the day, but they spoiled him terribly. Teddy had become everybody's pet. I found a veterinarian who was willing to take Teddy temporarily as his family pet and to train him properly. He already had a huge, friendly German shepherd dog that got along beautifully with Teddy. I visited them every couple of days for a few minutes.

Karl was the sergeant in charge of the investigation group at Special Branch. He was born in New York City. His Lutheran parents had come from Germany and had taught him to speak German like a native. Karl was violently anti-Nazi. He was very competent and conscientious as long as he was sober. When he got drunk, which happened about every third or fourth Sunday night, he seemed to accept the blame for all the evil Hitler had done and cried tears of guilt and shame. He would also cry bitter tears of grief about the love of his life, a young prostitute whom he often met at a bar. Les and I never met her, but it appeared that she disliked Karl intensely and did not want to have anything to do with him. That's why Karl was crying into his beer at the Sunday night party.

"She's not worth it! Forget her," Les and I would plead with Karl.

"You're too good for her."

"You don't know her," Karl would sob. "I know she's just a prostitute on the outside. But deep inside her, there's a wonderful human being! Oh, how I love her."

Karl could not be consoled. After a while, we gave up and just let him cry by himself. By Monday morning, he was sober, sensible and pleasant again.

Shortly before returning to New York for discharge, Karl met and immediately married a very sweet, pretty German girl. When I visited them in New York a year later, they were the parents of a new baby girl. The next time I called, I was grieved to hear that they were divorced.

My work schedule allowed me to do a bit of sightseeing around the area and to take a couple of boat trips on the Danube River. Regensburg is a beautiful historic town. The only buildings destroyed by our Air Force during World War II were the railroad station and the Messerschmidt airplane factory. All the bridges spanning the Danube River were blown up by the S.S. as the U.S. Army approached. A large group of townspeople demonstrated publicly against suicidal plans to defend the city. The S.S. seized the leader of the group, a minister, and hanged him in full view of the group. But then they left Regensburg without offering any resistance to our troops. The war ended a few days later.

A man applied for a job as guard at a Displaced Persons food warehouse. In his questionnaire, he admitted that he had been convicted six times for fraud and document falsification. He had paid his debt to society, however, having spent a total of eight years in jail. In view of the fact that he *never* engaged in *any* Nazi activity, he felt that he should get the job. Our document center confirmed his police record, but also reported that he was a long-time member of the Nazi party. He now had to face his seventh conviction for document falsification.

We were justifiably proud of our work in Special Branch. Ours was a regional office with many resources. Local offices were generally not so well endowed. As a rule, a local Military Government office would consist of a lieutenant and two or three other soldiers. Typically, none of them could speak German.   They would desperately look for a German secretary (preferably a pretty one) who could speak English. After they found one, they would be completely at her mercy. She would decide who could see the Americans, and she would control communication into and out of the office.

A local MG office sent us a man with instruction to teach him the denazification business, so he could set it up in their district. He spoke English very well, because he had lived in the United States for seven years. During casual conversation, he admitted joining the Nazi party after his return to Germany. We sent him back home empty-handed.

There were German civilian denazification boards in action at the time, screening business owners. Anyone judged to be a Nazi was ordered to sell his business immediately—well, eventually...to his wife or his son.... It was a farce, a whitewash. It was an omen of what would become of our denazification program after it was turned over to German authorities two years later.

A surprise visitor showed up: Mrs. Walter from Marienbad. It was six months since I had left Czechoslovakia. Mrs. Walter had sent me a letter once, complaining about conditions there and asking me if I thought they should migrate to Germany. I advised strongly against it. But now she had come to Regensburg to find out for herself how things were in Germany, possibly to make arrangements for the move. My letter of March 26, 1946, gave some details.

> Mrs. Walter gave me a sad report: "As far as the Czechs are concerned, Sudeten Jews are simply Germans. The harassment of the past six and a half years is continuing now under new management. Economic conditions are not bad, but each of us is treated as a personal enemy by the Czechs. We also fear, any day now, that all our possessions will be taken over by a local trustee. We've got to get out!" I helped Mrs. Walter as well as I could and introduced her to some of the local refugees, who could provide her with practical advice and information.[12]

Little Teddy got sick. He came down with distemper, although he had been vaccinated against it. The hotel maids offered a different diagnosis: They had seen him lick up DDT powder at the hotel and suspected that it had poisoned him. He lost weight, and his pretty fur became matted. When he became paralyzed and blind, the veterinarian recommended that we relieve him of his suffering. I held Teddy in my arms while the injection was administered. His body trembled, stiffened slightly and then relaxed. My lovable Teddy was no more.

My depression was relieved a short time later when my good buddy, Lee, suddenly appeared. We had exchanged letters quite often since our paths diverged at the replacement depot exactly a year earlier. How much had happened to both of us in that one year!

As radio operator with the First Infantry Division, Lee was thrown into some of the heaviest fighting of the war. Men were killed all around him. During one engagement, his walkie-talkie was shot out of his hand while he was directing mortar fire. He had to run back under enemy fire to get a replacement set, then return to his position in front. A few minutes later, the new transmitter was hit, probably by shrapnel from his own mortar fire, and he had to repeat the replacement process. All but three men of his platoon were killed, but Lee survived with just a few scratches. Lee earned three medals, including the coveted Silver Star.

Lee was sent to Regensburg by his unit in order to take some courses. He had not slept in a real bed for a year, so I let him have my bed for his first night in Regensburg, while I slept on the sofa. He could not fall asleep for a long time but then slept until 11 a.m., according to my letter of March 25, 1946. I also reported in the same letter:

> Lee played poker with some of my friends this afternoon. While I sat next to him, he won about $15. After I walked away, he lost all that plus some more. He told me later that he kept all my letters during the war and always carried them on his person. He thinks they brought him good luck. Strange!

Lee and I spent a lot of time together during his three months in Regensburg. When he was redeployed for discharge, he visited my par-

ents in New York. Lee and his wife, Patsy,
visited us in November 1996.

Many of the Jewish survivors were involved in black market activities. The German policemen were not permitted to arrest
any concentration camp survivors, so they
turned the job over to the MPs, the U.S. military police. There was only token punishment, but it was deeply resented. When I
visited the survivors, wearing my U.S. Army
uniform, all their anger was directed at me.

J.L. Lee with Tillie

"What kind of liberators are you? You lock us up and let the Nazi
murderers go free."

I tried to explain calmly that we did try to catch the real Nazi
murderers. (Survivors who had just departed from a concentration
camp were not likely to appreciate that distinction. In their minds, all
Germans were murderers.) But MPs have a duty to maintain law and
order. Black market operations violate the law.

"How can you defend them?" they would protest. "Can you compare what we are doing to the Germans with what they did to us?"

"Of course not. There is no comparison," I admitted. "But I hate to
see the Germans and the American soldiers get the impression that
Jews are crooked financial manipulators. That's what Hitler accused
us of. You don't want to tell people that Hitler was right, do you?" We
were both hitting below the belt with our arguments.

"Only a Yecka (German Jew) would worry about what the Germans
think of us," they sneered.

I would try to laugh it off. But we were still as far apart as ever on
this issue. Fortunately, only on this issue.

Les and Karl were redeployed to the United States, leaving me in
charge of the Special Branch program. I was given a token boost by
being promoted to technician 5th grade, equivalent to corporal. But
everyone knew that my discharge was imminent, and I proceeded to
train a couple of recently arrived occupation soldiers to be my replace-

ments. They had no trouble understanding the technical require-ments, the logistics of the system. I was not so sure about their judg-mental capabilities, their historical sensitivity. I suppose I had become a bit possessive about my job.

A letter from home informed me that my paternal grandmother Fanny had died. She was healthy, alert, and knitting right up to the last day. She helped to celebrate her great-grandson's birthday party, went to sleep that night and never woke up. She was 94.

I applied for another furlough to Switzerland. It seemed like the perfect way to end my stay in Europe. The trip to Mulhouse was more comfortable than the first time; and the processing there went smoothly, since I agreed to go on a standard vacation tour this time.

I found that I had an extra day to spend in Mulhouse. My cousin, Sylvain, and his wife, Ninon, lived in Dornach, which was a suburb of Mulhouse. I decided to pay them a surprise visit.

Mulhouse is located in Alsace-Lorraine, in the north-eastern part of France. Germany took Alsace-Lorraine from France after the war of 1870-71, France got it back after World War I (1914-1918). After France fell to the Nazi army in 1940, Germany proceeded to reabsorb the area, but it returned to France at the end of World War II. Under-standably, most of the residents spoke both French and German—and, in daily conversation, a delightful blend of the two. Between my native language and the French I had learned in school, I had no trouble understanding directions on how to get to Dornach.

Physically getting to Dornach was another matter. Recovery from the ravages of World War II was much slower in France than in Ger-many. The rubble of wartime destruction was still present, rationing of food and clothing was still tight, and public transportation was chaotic. I hung on to the outside of a mobbed streetcar, then changed to another one in the same mode—trying also to hold on to a bag that contained a valuable gift for cousin Sylvain, two cartons of cigarettes. My arrival was a complete, joyous surprise. We had never met before, and we now had to really get to know each other.

I had picked a good day for my visit, July 14—Bastille Day, the

French national independence day. Sylvain and Ninon had been saving up their ration coupons for this day and had baked a delicious cherry cake. Sylvain did most of the talking. He was fluent in French, German, Yiddish, and English. Ninon spoke only French.

Sylvain told me how he survived World War II. He and his parents were helped by friends in the country, who were willing to share their meager rations with them. After the war ended, the friends' daughter, Ninon, converted to Judaism and married Sylvain. They were now trying to regain possession of the family business, a Kosher butcher shop, and their former house, but French bureaucracy was very sluggish. Sylvain's mother (my father's sister) died during the war, his father shortly after the war. On the way back to the processing center, the streetcars were not too full; I, however, was stuffed.

The Swiss tour I had selected was fantastic. It swept me through Lucerne, Lake Lucerne, Mount Rigi, the Schöllenen Gorge, and Andermatt, with several days available at Flims and Zurich. I was able to spend some time with my cousins in Zurich and St. Gallen.

At Chaplain Lipman's request, I called on the U.S. Consul in Zurich to find out how survivors' immigration to the United States could be facilitated. The consul indicated that there was no relaxation in the procedures. His interest in our conversation picked up when I mentioned that I was an immigrant myself. He asked how my family was managing in America and was visibly pleased when I indicated that we were holding our own. "And now you are an American soldier," he observed happily, "and you don't have a trace of an accent! This makes me feel good," he continued. "You see, I used to be the consul in Stuttgart until the war started. So, I'm the man who approved your family's visa! Evidently, my judgment was sound." I indicated that he must also have been the man who turned us down after our first visit to the consulate. But then we parted with a friendly handshake.

After my return to Regensburg, I resumed preparing for my departure from Europe and army life. I received an unexpected offer of civilian employment that would keep me in Germany. It was a civil service position, inspecting Special Branch departments in the U.S.

occupation zone and helping to upgrade the flawed ones. I was anxious to get back to school, but this job would pay $5,000 plus all living expenses for a year's work—a high salary compared to my parents' income. Wasn't it time that I started to contribute financially to the family? And my education would only be delayed for one year. I decided to find out how my parents felt about it. I wrote them a detailed letter and asked for immediate advice. A telegram arrived a week later: "Come home." I took their advice.

The U.S. denazification program has sometimes been criticized as having been too mechanical. Its emphasis on membership and rank in various organizations penalized the poor laborer who joined the party without conviction in order to advance himself; but it exonerated the shrewd industrialist who made a fortune by supplying and supporting the Nazi regime—without ever joining any organization. What other option did we have? Should we have investigated a million Germans by psychoanalysis or by mutual denunciations? Should we have conducted a million jury trials in a year? Or should we just have kept the Nazis in their positions as judges, teachers, police officials, mayors, etc.?

Most of our decisions were reversed by German review boards after they took over. Still, I have always felt that our work was not in vain. During the twelve years of Hitler's rule, the Nazi activists had strutted around proudly in their uniforms, hung giant swastika flags out of their windows and marched in numerous parades. They were the elite, the role models, the heroes, especially when the Nazi-led armies swept across Europe. The people were stunned when their moment of glory was followed by the pain and chaos of a lost war and when they had to consciously acknowledge the atrocities that had been committed in their name. The denazification program, which was initiated at this point, may not have achieved all its objectives; but it did force every German to privately evaluate, with fear and regret, his or her own involvement in Nazi activities and to publicly deny any Nazi sympathies. Prior Nazi activity or orientation became a matter of shame and contempt among the German people, a subject they refused to discuss with their children. And for a majority of the population, it is still that way today.

11 REBUILDING MY LIFE

I sold my pistols to newly arrived occupation soldiers. I had acquired the guns from German POWs. After the war ended, a pistol was handier to carry than a rifle. It was also fun to do a bit of target practice at times. But I wanted no part of gun play as a civilian. Symbolically, this sale constituted my separation from military life.

Like every other GI, I was looking forward to my discharge. But once again, it was difficult saying good-bye to friends whom I would probably never see again. Some had become dependent on me—for extra food, for mail service, for encouragement. And in the process, they helped me to satisfy a need of my own.

I don't remember anything about the long trip north to Bremerhaven. After our arrival, there was a perfunctory medical examination for venereal disease (referred to as "short-arm inspection"), then we were admitted to our troop ship, the M.I.T. Victory. The name of the ship meant nothing to me. I had no way of knowing that I would some day have a son who would some day be a student and, briefly, instructor at the Massachusetts Institute of Technology.

The M.I.T. Victory, like all other victory ships, was a small freighter, mass-produced during World War II. It was converted into an army transport vessel. It was much smaller than the ship that had carried me to Europe one-and-a-half years earlier, but accommodations were more comfortable and spacious. Three hours out of Bremerhaven, there was a noticeable pounding noise. The ship turned around, and we had to return to harbor for diagnosis of the problem. Everyone stayed on board while a diver went down to examine the underside of the vessel. He reported that a part of the rolling chock, a vertical plate welded to the bottom along the length of the ship, had torn loose in front and pulsated when the ship was moving. We lay at anchor for another day while the diver cut off the disjointed part (15 feet) of the rolling chock with an acetylene welding torch—under water. Finally we were on our way.

Fort Dix, New Jersey, which had been my initial induction center, had now become my separation center. The separation process was mostly paperwork plus a physical examination and a dental check. My military career ended on September 10, 1946, with a bus ride to New York, followed by a subway ride to my home. There were no fireworks, no flags, no brass bands—but the greatest war hero could not have received a warmer, more loving welcome. My father seemed to feel that I had won World War II single-handedly. My mother had worried and prayed for my safety for 695 nights and was now happy to find that her forebodings had been groundless. My sister (Ilse) and Opa were just glad to have me back.

Returning to civilian life as a student at City College seemed easy and pleasant at first. I did well in all courses except electrical engineering. That was an important exception, however, since electrical engineering was to be my major field. I reexamined my plans and decided that I would rather pursue a career in industrial engineering, a field which was not available at City College.

I found myself sinking into depression. My vocational wavering was only one of the factors. There was also the let-down from military responsibility and excitement to the blandness of a student's life. I was deeply affected by what I had seen of the Holocaust, by the murder of our relatives and by the knowledge that our family barely avoided that fate. My social life was not very good—and I hated New York City; actually, any big city. I decided that I needed a change, a drastic change.

As a veteran of World War II, I was entitled (under the "G.I. Bill of Rights") to receive payments from the government for tuition, supplies and living expenses at any college in the United States. I was no longer tied down to City College, to New York City, to living with my parents. I could choose my own path.

I was admitted to the School of Industrial Engineering at the Oklahoma Agricultural and Mechanical College in Stillwater, Oklahoma, starting in Spring 1948. It was exactly what I needed—a blank slate: new environment, new friends, new situations that required me to make my own decisions. Cousin Idi in Switzerland once described me as "uncomplicated." She was right. And I was now happy among friendly, unsophisticated students in a quiet campus atmosphere.

I enjoyed my courses at A&M. My grades were excellent, despite the fact that the temperature was as high as 112 degrees at times—with no air conditioning.

During my second summer at A&M, I became a staff writer on the student newspaper, the O'Collegian. When there was not much news to report, I decided to ask students around the campus the "Question of the Day," printing their answers along with some (generally humorous) editorial comments. It became a popular feature of the newspaper.

A number of local students told me that I was the first Jew they had ever met. They seemed surprised to find that I was a "nice guy" and joked about the weird stereotypes they had picked up in Sunday school or from hate mongers. It was disturbing to find that their bias against blacks and Catholics was more deep-seated.

I graduated in August 1949. The oppressive heat kept me from appreciating the ceremony and graduation speech, but it was still a very happy day for me. I was aware of the fact that I was the first, the only member of my family to ever receive a college education. I prayed that my ancestors were looking down at me from up there.

Jobs were scarce. I had sent out applications prior to graduation. The only firm offer I received was for a non-engineering job—as a field supervisor for Southwestern Bell. I was not interested, but found the offer interesting: I had been advised not to apply to Bell because, supposedly, they never hired Jews.

As a student, I made occasional trips to Tulsa to visit the Rothschild family. They had come from Constance about the same time we did. They had a daughter, about Ilse's age, who was married to an engineer, Eric. The latter had come down with multiple sclerosis. He was bound to a wheelchair and was now losing the use of his hands. Would I want to be his helper? I would not have any responsibility, would not get much pay—but it might be a good educational experience. I agreed. I went to work for Midwestern Constructors, Inc. at $225 per month as Eric's helper.

Midwestern was a construction company specializing in installation of oil and gas transmission systems, i.e., transmission pipes, oil pumping stations and gas compressor stations. Eric was the only engineer and took care of any design work that was needed. My job was to do the manual work for him—writing, sketching, calculating per his instructions.

When Eric was working, he drove himself to complete exhaustion. All his muscles were dying gradually, but he tried to ignore his horrible illness. He avoided taking pain pills during working hours because they made him drowsy. He was generally in good spirits and had a fine sense of humor. He knew that his life was ending. It made him get all he could out of every hour that remained. He was able to do this because his wife had the same vivacity and boundless energy.

A time came when Eric was no longer able to work. The multiple sclerosis had weakened his diaphragm and chest muscles. Every breath became a strenuous task for him. Eric and his wife spent his final days in seclusion. I think he was less than 40 years old when he died.

I was told by Midwestern Constructors that Eric would not be replaced. I was transferred to the cost estimating group with a clear indication that there would not be much of a future for me there. I proceeded to send out new resumes that were similar to the previous ones, except that I now had a year of work to brag about—that all-important first experience.

There was not much industry in Oklahoma other than oil and gas. I decided to move back east. One of my managers referred me to a friend of his who was running a pipeline construction project in New Jersey. I inquired by phone and was offered a job as equipment time clerk. It would be a temporary job (3 or 4 months), would not involve any engineering work, but would pay nearly three times as much as I was earning at Midwestern. I decided this would be a good way to pass the time while looking for a permanent job. My job was to keep track of which piece of equipment was used for how many hours each day. It was a simple bookkeeping job. We worked nine hours a day, six days per week—hence the good pay.

I had moved in with my parents again and was commuting to the job site in New Jersey every day. This was my first chance to get acquainted with my little nieces. Margaret, Ilse's first daughter, was three years

Henry and Ilse with Helen and Margaret

old when I returned to New York. Helen was one. Both girls were very sweet, and we got along beautifully with each other. I also came to know and like Ilse's husband, Henry.

My mother had been working at a cousin's doll factory for several years. My parents were able to save enough money from their meager pay to buy a house on Loring Place in the Bronx. It was a two-family house with two garages and parking spaces in the back yard. My parents moved into one of the apartments and rented out everything else. Around this time, my father's World War I disability pension was restored, and my parents started receiving monthly restitution payments from Germany as compensation for the loss of their business and wrongful imprisonment under the Nazi regime. They were now able to take a little vacation every year and still save more money. When Social Security was added to their income, they were able to retire very comfortably.

One day, Ilse picked up her clothes and her two girls and moved into my parents' apartment. We were not aware of any advance indication, but she now expressed an intense hatred for her husband for "reasons" that did not make sense to us. She demanded a divorce. We persuaded her to see a psychiatrist, who diagnosed her condition as postpartum depression that supposedly was brought on by the birth of the second daughter. There were other psychiatric diagnoses and treatments in subsequent years, but Ilse's mental health was never

restored. The divorce was carried out. Ilse was able to continue working, but a major part of the task of raising Margaret and Helen now fell
to my parents. They performed it remarkably well. Ilse died suddenly in
1977 at age 55.

When I returned to New York, I registered with an employment agency.
The Blaw-Knox Company of Pittsburgh offered me a job in piping design
with their Chemical Plants division. I was happy to accept it.

I had never been to Pittsburgh, and I knew no one living there. It
was exciting to jump into a new environment, into a new experience.
It was November 1950.

My initial work for Blaw-Knox Company was drafting rather than
engineering. I was grateful for that many years later. Knowing how to
make—and read—a complicated piping drawing turned out to be
very valuable in my subsequent career, even when draftsmen were
available to do the work for me. There were many times when I could
solve a design problem only by working it out myself on a sheet of
paper or a sketch pad.

A co-worker at Blaw-Knox introduced me to a young chemist named
Henry Gruen. After some conversation, Henry asked me if I would like to
share a furnished apartment with him. It seemed like a good idea, having
lived in a furnished room for a year. We looked around and selected an
apartment on Darlington Road, not far from my previous residence.

Henry's background was similar to mine—Jewish immigrant from
Germany. He was a lively conversationalist and had many interests
that were similar to mine. Discussions were fun, even when we disagreed. We started double-dating with compatible girl friends.

Henry and I were invited to a party. When we indicated that we did
not have dates, the hostess offered us two phone numbers to call. My
blind date was a girl named Goldie Beruh. We decided to get acquainted before the party.

Goldie had just returned from a week at Brandeis camp and was
religiously inspired. We decided to attend a Sabbath service at Poale
Zedek synagogue to initiate our first date. On December 28 of the
same year, 1952, Goldie and I were married—in the same synagogue.

I had worked extensively on the Savannah River Plant design. In the process, I learned quite a bit about nuclear plant design. Blaw-Knox was awarded several contracts for nuclear test "packages." Each package was an extremely compact system, entirely self-contained and mounted on its own platform, with precisely defined external connections and support points. I became a specialist of sorts on nuclear test package design. We were also expecting our first baby.

The Wedding Party

As Goldie's due date approached, we became the conventional nervous parents-to-be. We did not require an emergency race to the hospital. Goldie's water broke. We had time to make final arrangements and drove leisurely to the hospital. Marcie was born at 1:20 p.m. on September 4, 1954. I had always considered newborn babies to be rather ugly for the first week or two. Marcie, of course, was different. She was the most beautiful newborn in the world, complete with the proper number of fingers, toes and other vital parts. I guess I really did not think that we would be able to perform this miracle. But somehow we did. Bringing the baby home also seemed like too much responsibility. But Goldie apparently knew what to do. Her mother helped a lot, and I was determined to learn and do my share. Little Marcie thrived.

I had been designing two high-pressure nuclear test loops for CAPA, Commercial Atomic Power Activity, of Westinghouse Electric Corporation of Pittsburgh. My contact was with Ed Goldsmith, manager of their test engineering group. I asked Ed if there were any openings in his group. Contractor-client ethics required that I notify my own management of my intentions before Westinghouse could respond. The chief engineer called me into his office to offer me a raise if I were willing to stay with Blaw-Knox. Two weeks later, I was interviewed by a department manager at Westinghouse. A generous job offer followed by mail. I had been with Blaw-Knox for seven years. It was time to move on.

My work with Westinghouse started on January 15, 1957. As part of the initial orientation session, they explained their pension plan to me. I remember smiling impatiently. I was not quite 32 years old. I never suspected that I would remain with Westinghouse until I was ready to invoke that same pension plan exactly thirty years later.

A Westinghouse division working for the U.S. Navy was a pioneer in the use of nuclear power for submarine propulsion. A new division, the Commercial Atomic Power Activity, was created to develop commercial plants that would produce electric power from nuclear energy. It was in its early stages when I joined it. CAPA was located in Forest Hills, another one of those suburban communities of Pittsburgh.

It is exciting to be a member of a pioneering, expanding organization. There are many opportunities for innovation and originality. At the same time, there is a need for caution and setting of limits in uncharted areas. Opportunities and needs abounded among the highly-motivated, highly-qualified staff at CAPA. Politics and bureaucracy did not enter until much later.

We were expecting another baby when I changed jobs. Now, the time had come. Goldie's water broke again, as with the first delivery. But this time, labor pains started right away. We drove to the hospital, where Goldie was rushed to the delivery room and I went to the waiting room. In those days, the only role the father played in childbirth was to wait. The obstetrician arrived at the hospital just in time. After a short time, he came to the waiting room to congratulate me on the birth of a healthy son. Danny arrived at 2:44 a.m. on May 15, 1957. Once more I had a feeling of awe and gratitude. Once more, bonding was instantaneous.

Opa, my maternal grandfather, became terminally ill. There were no high-tech diagnostic tests. Opa kept losing weight, strength and continence, and his doctor just gave up. My father took care of his father-in-law day and night for about two years, feeding him, washing him, lifting him as necessary. During one of my visits, Opa started to talk to me about dying. I wouldn't hear of it. I have always regretted my refusal to let him talk about death. I hope someone will be able to talk and listen when my time comes. Opa was 93 when he died.

One of our neighbors had a son, age 18, who invited me to join him and a group of friends on a caving trip to West Virginia. I had crawled through a small cave once and enjoyed the experience. This was to be a whole weekend of "spelunking."

There seem to be only two ways to react to the caving experience: You love it or you hate it. I became an avid caver and have remained that way for life. Perhaps it was a delayed revolt against the sanitary, sheltered atmosphere my mother imposed on me during my childhood. I was now able to satisfy an innate craving to climb, jump and slide over muddy rocks and through subterranean streams in a strange, dark world. I emerged after hours of frolicking—soaking wet, covered with mud, and happily exhausted. I noticed with pleasure that the other members of our masochistic group were equally exuberant. As I recall, we "did" three big caves on that weekend. At age 73, I still "do" one occasionally, generally in the company of my children and grandchildren.

I had started going to night school at Carnegie Institute of Technology. Westinghouse had an education program that paid for my tuition. My bachelor's degree was in Industrial Engineering, but all my work since graduation had been in mechanical engineering. It was not easy, with two small children in the house, to work all day and take classes or do homework in the evening. My grades were not the best, and Goldie was stuck doing practically all the housework. In June 1963, I was awarded a Master's degree in mechanical engineering.

Since my high school days, I have always been fascinated by biology. When I was undecided about my career choice, engineering won out only because medical school would have taken too long. Now, I heard of an opening in the Bioengineering group at the Westinghouse Research and Development (R&D) Laboratory. I applied for a transfer to R&D and was accepted.

Bioengineering is the application of engineering principles (any branch) to biological systems. It is very humbling for an engineer to realize how clumsy and bulky his methods and devices are compared to nature's ways. "The mountain labored and produced a mouse" is a popular expression to indicate tremendous efforts yielding worthless results. Well, if the greatest engineers and scientists of the world were given an unlimited budget to create a mouse, they would come up with a contraption as big as a truck that would not do one-tenth of the things that a mouse can do, and the period of gestation would be measured in years rather than days. Still, to the extent that we can augment nature, no matter how awkwardly, bioengineering is a fascinating activity.

My first and most interesting activity at R&D was to develop the mechanical parts of an intra-aortic balloon pump, also known as a diastolic augmentation device. It is used in hospitals all over the world today.

In 1968, Westinghouse sent me to Europe for an evaluation of municipal garbage grinding machines. I arranged my itinerary to give me a weekend in Constance. It was my first time back since 1939. My parents had given me the names of some former local friends, and I spent a pleasant evening with them, talking about old times and about the bad things that had happened to so many good people. Most of the people we talked about were of my parents' generation, relatively unknown to me since I was 14 when we left Constance.

I spent hours just walking through the streets and alleys, retracing the steps of my childhood, reabsorbing the atmosphere of this beautiful town, being completely ignored by the current residents. There had been no damage in Constance during World War II. When the war started, German towns were blacked out at night, while Swiss towns were lit up brightly to let Allied bomber pilots know not to drop any bombs on them. Constance took advantage of its position on the border by keeping its lights turned on at night to blend in deceptively with its Swiss sister town. It was a clever trick — while it lasted. In November 1940, yielding to German demands, the Swiss blacked out their country until shortly before the end of the war. But fate served Constance well in that there was nothing worth bombing there.

It was January 1970 and there were indications that the Bioengineering group was about to be reduced or phased out. The timing was right for me. Ed Goldsmith, the manager who had originally brought me into Westinghouse, had just returned from a long assignment in Belgium. He asked me if I would like to join his new group, and I accepted his offer.

Westinghouse also had a volunteer tutoring program. They urged employees to drive to an all-black elementary school during working hours to tutor individual students on a one-to-one basis. It was one of many educational programs the company has supported all over the country. I signed up as a tutor, but generally worked late on my tutoring day. I was doing it on my time, not on company time. I also took my tutees on occasional trips to a science museum, to local caves, on a nature hike, and—once a year—on a guided tour of my work place, where a number of employees would demonstrate their work and explain what kind of training or education they needed. The tour included a sumptuous lunch (pizza or hamburgers) and a bag of souvenirs for each student, donated by Westinghouse. I arranged the same tour for whole classes on several occasions. After ten years of tutoring, I was officially honored by the president of the Westinghouse Electric Corporation for my efforts. I received the Minority Communications award, a framed lithograph by Romare Beardon. More important, some of my former students (including one I tutored 20 years ago) still call me to tell me of their accomplishments or to have me meet their new family.

I only spent about 35 minutes a week with each of the children I tutored at Crescent Elementary School. That is a small fraction of the time they spend in school, an even smaller fraction of their lives at home and on the street. I was surprised to find that in many cases, my brief association with them influenced their classroom behavior and scholastic achievement appreciably. Our educational institutions are expected to overcome the effects of the violent, abusive environment in which many of these children live. We cannot do this in the classroom alone. Our only chance of success is on a one-to-one basis, in a program that combines tutoring with outside activities and, most importantly, a heavy dose of sincere caring.

Goldie and I were introduced to square dancing and round dancing in 1968. We took to it right away. We took lessons for nine months, memorizing 100 different steps. Following graduation, we joined the Greengate Twirlers Club. It was a joyous activity, fairly strenuous, requiring some skill, and allowing us to meet some of the friendliest (uncomplicated) people in the world. We danced every Saturday night for 17 years.

Our children grew so fast. Their school work was very good. Marcie placed high demands on herself and worked hard to achieve them. Her grades were excellent. Her social life was hampered by her shyness and lack of self-esteem. Dan was more casual. Learning came easy for him. His major effort in school was applied to extracurricular activities. Too much learning did not earn peer approval. This changed dramatically when he went to high school. He associated with a group of very bright kids who were not ashamed to be bright. Learning now became a competitive game. But his involvement in outside activities continued. He was very busy.

Boy Scouts was one of Dan's major activities. He worked his way up to the rank of Eagle Scout. I also became involved as committee chairman of Troop 42 and leading its members in caving, hiking and rappelling activities.

Goldie had not gone back to work after our children were born. When the latter entered their teen years, Goldie felt the need to become active outside the house. She decided to become a teacher. She had never gone to college. A friend of ours was skeptical. "You'll be an old woman by the time you graduate," he warned. I made a quick calculation. "Goldie will be 44 when she graduates," I pointed out. "How old will she be at that time if she doesn't go to college?" The answer, of course, was the same. "Well, if she'll be 44 either way, she may as well be 44 with a college degree." Goldie did very well in college and earned a degree in teaching home economics and social studies. She found a position as a long-term substitute, which turned into a permanent staff position after a year. She taught home economics and social studies at Woodlawn Middle School until she retired 19 years later.

Goldie and I decided to take a vacation trip to the old country in August of 1984. Our first stop was Leigh on the Sea, outside London, for a visit with Goldie's cousin, Sonja.

Sonja and her sister, Gerda, were whisked out of their native Austria into England just before the Holocaust started. Their last-minute rescue was part of the *Kindertransport*, when England agreed to permit 10,000 Jewish children from Germany to enter England. Similar legislation was introduced in the U.S. Congress but was voted down. Gerda and Sonja subsequently migrated to Israel. Their mother survived the Holocaust and was reunited with her daughters. The three of them were the only ones of Goldie's many European relatives to survive the Holocaust.

We flew from London to Cologne, Germany, to meet my former roommate, Henry Gruen. Henry was one of the very few German Jews who returned to Germany after the war. He did research work in radiochemistry at the Max Planck Institute for many years.

There was a passport check at the Cologne airport. When the officer noticed on my passport that I was born in Germany, he had to make a phone call to have my name checked against some list—probably of war criminals. Goldie grew increasingly tense while we were waiting. "Why does he keep staring at me like that?" she demanded to know. "Ask him." I did my duty as an interpreter, and the officer assured me that he was just waiting for his call to be returned and was not staring at anyone. Goldie evidently had a bad case of nerves, not uncommon among Jews entering post-war Germany.

We took a luxury train—
"*Das Rheingold*"—along the
scenic Rhine River on our
way to Mulhouse, France.
There, we spent two days
with cousins Sylvain and Ninon. Having returned to his
normal environment, Sylvain
came through as a human
dynamo: He was a masterful
cook and baker, sometimes

Cousins Sylvain and Ninon

cooking and baking for 200 people. His large garden was filled with
fruits, vegetables and prize-winning flowers. He raised pigeons and
was in great demand for giving massages. He was one of the top
leaders of the local Jewish community, being especially helpful to elderly and foreign people. He collected stamps and co-taught Yiddish at
a nearby university. He had recently turned over his kosher butcher
shop to his son, so he could devote more time to his other activities.
He used a three-wheeled 1926 Citroen car (he called it his Cadillac)
and a light motorcycle for transportation. Ninon was at his side—or
not far behind him—in all his endeavors.

We took a train to Constance and checked into the Insel Hotel.
This hotel is located on its own little island in Lake Constance, but
only a few steps away from the town park and a five-minute walk from
the center of town. It is a majestic building, formerly a monastery,
with beautiful landscaping, good food and excellent service. I showed
Goldie all the places that were important to me in my childhood.
Liesel Veeser, her daughter and granddaughter were our personable
companions on various excursions. Liesel had been an apprentice in
my parents' store when she was a teenager, and we reminisced about
some of the events and people of the 1930s that we were able to recall.

We were able to take this trip to Europe because our children were
grown and established. On previous trips Goldie's parents had taken
care of our children. In fact, Goldie's parents had a privilege that

Goldie and I never enjoyed—having grown children and growing grandchildren living in the same town. Of course, we and our children also gained important benefits from this arrangement. Marcie and Danny enjoyed being spoiled by their grandparents, and we enjoyed having a tasty meal or willing baby-sitters available on a moment's notice.

Goldie's parents were both born in Poland. They came to America early in life. Dad worked in a dry cleaning plant for many years; but it was the praying, studying and communal work he did for a small Chassidic congregation that gave real meaning to his life. I loved to hear him sing the traditional prayers. Dad developed poorly defined digestive symptoms in 1963 and quickly succumbed to cancer of the pancreas.

Goldie's mother seemed to enjoy her chores as a housewife. She was always ready to serve a meal or a piece of cake, all prepared in the Polish-Hungarian-Jewish tradition. But she also included a most delicious pizza and a tasty chow mein in her repertory. After our children were born, they became the center of Mom's world. They brought pleasure to what turned out to be her last 20 years. Her sudden ailment was diagnosed successively as arthritis, then osteoporosis, then bone cancer. She died in July 1974 at age 75.

Goldie's older brother, Joe Beruh, was a prominent producer of plays on and off Broadway until his death in 1989. Her younger brother, Edgar, and his wife, Judy, still live in Pittsburgh.

My parents took many bus rides to Pittsburgh, and we drove to New York regularly. They loved their grandchildren. We were not able to be with my mother on her 83rd birthday in 1975, but my parents would be with us for our daughter Marcie's wedding, just two weeks later. We had a long, cheerful phone conversation with Mama on the evening of her birthday. She described the new dress she had bought for the wedding. Early the next morning, our niece called to tell us that my mother had died during the night. When my father woke up, he found Mama lying in the bathroom. Had she gotten sick during the night? Had she called for help and not been heard? We rushed to New York, but Fate had taken its course.

Papa decided to move into Kittay House, a residence for seniors. He moved into a small efficiency, keeping some of his own furniture. Among the residents at Kittay House were Aunt Celia (his sister-in-law) and a number of old acquaintances. He had a bowl of cereal every morning; the other meals were served in the communal dining room. His granddaughter Helen (Ilse's younger daughter) was a teacher at a nearby high school. She visited Papa every day for coffee and cake on her way home from school. Other relatives lived nearby and also visited frequently. Papa adjusted beautifully to his new conditions and assured all of us that he was happy there.

It was 1981 and my father's 95th birthday was approaching. One month earlier, he let me know that he had a special wish: to hear from a member of the Hacker family in Reutlingen, Germany. He explained. After my parents lost their store in Constance, Papa became a sales representative for a tie manufacturer, visiting clothing stores all over southern Germany. Some customers objected to being served by a Jewish salesman. In response to a few complaints, the manufacturer visited a number of Papa's accounts to gage their feelings. When he called on Mr. Hacker, the latter got very angry, as he later reported to my father. "I don't care for your ties," he stated frankly. "The only reason I still do business with you is because I like Mr. Ottenheimer. He is an honest, hard-working man who knows his business. His religion has nothing to do with it. If Mr. Ottenheimer leaves your company, don't bother sending anyone else." My father's friendship with Mr. Hacker continued after Papa lost his job. Now he wanted to greet Mr. Hacker one more time.

I quoted Papa's request in a letter to the mayor of Reutlingen, who personally tracked down the specific Mr. Hacker. The latter was 93 years old, living in a nursing home, mentally incompetent. But a few days before the big birthday, Papa received a long, friendly letter from Mr. Hacker's son (who remembered him) and a congratulatory letter from the mayor, along with a book about Reutlingen. He was very pleased.

We had a big celebration for my father on his 95th birthday on

December 3, 1981. He had been living in a nursing home adjoining Kittay House following the amputation of his leg. His granddaughter, Helen, still enjoyed coffee and cake and conversation with him every day. The whole family and many friends showed up for the party, and Papa was smiling happily as he looked over all the assembled guests in the community room.

"You need me to hold the family together, don't you?" he asked me.

"We sure do," I replied. "You're the big boss!"

Papa passed away quietly in his sleep on May 3, 1983. He was 96 years old, the last of our parents to leave us.

A few years later I received a letter from the mayor of Constance. All former Jewish residents of Constance were invited to come to their old hometown for a week's vacation, a reunion, in September 1986. We were expected to pay for our own transportation, but the town of Constance would pay all expenses while we were there. I accepted the invitation.

The week was well organized. There were delicious meals served at good restaurants. There were tours and discussions and short speeches. We were honored like royalty.

The mayor of Constance set the tone for the week in his welcoming speech. He described the once harmonious relationship between Jews and non-Jews and how it was scuttled after 1933. "What happened then must never be forgotten or repressed ... The manner in which we live with our past tells a lot about our approach to the future ... We do not wish to salve a bad conscience, and we do not see this invitation as an act of absolution. It is to be understood as a gesture by a new generation that seeks to learn from history, that wants to teach the next generation about the consequences of hate and intolerance ... Our only wish is that you will rediscover your old home town. Even though you now live in distant lands, may you feel yourselves as that which you once were and which you have remained: respected citizens of Constance."

About 40 guests participated; but the only ones I had known in our previous life were Marianne, whose late husband, Eric, I had worked for in Tulsa; and Beatrice, the daughter of our former cantor/rabbi. We remembered and talked for hours.

There was another evening of reminiscing. Two former schoolmates found out that I was among the highly publicized visitors. They picked me up and took me to a little neighborhood inn for a dish of *Käsespätzle* and a few hours of conversation. I was saddened to hear how many of our class had died, most of them killed in the War. The German army, though generally apolitical, fought vehemently under Hitler's command and delivered the countries of Europe to the *Führer*, to do with whatever he wanted. I had welcomed reports of German army casualties during the war—not so now when I was told about individual former friends by name. I could not be happy about their destruction and loss.

We had Sabbath services with the new Jewish community of Constance. There were about 100 Jews living there now, but only one elderly couple had originally lived in Constance and returned there after the war. They were Dr. and Mrs. Bloch. He was the author of the book on the history of the Jews of Constance.[13]

One of our guided tours took us to a massive tower located on the shore of the Rhine River. It had been an important part of the town's defenses for several centuries. A historical marker indicated that the tower was built by the Jews of Constance in the 13th century as a gift to the town; and that in 1430 and again in 1443, the Jews of Constance were imprisoned for ransom in the same tower. All Jews were expelled from Constance in 1548. None were permitted to live or trade there until the mid-1800s.

I visited the cemetery and was impressed by its good condition. The town administration continued to maintain the Jewish cemetery during and after the war. My grandmother's grave was immaculate. On Aunt Emma and Uncle Jonas's stone, several letters had fallen off. I made arrangements with the cemetery administrator to have the stone repaired.

Erhard (Roy) and Mirjam Wiehn were instrumental in initiating and running the week's activities. Roy, a sociology professor at the

University of Constance, and his wife, Mirjam, an elementary school teacher, have devoted their life to creating understanding of Jews and Judaism and teaching Holocaust history to those who would rather forget about it. Roy is author of several books

Celebrating with Mirjam and Roy Wiehn

about the Holocaust and editor of collections of survivor and eyewitness reports, including a German translation of my book. He has written many columns and articles for newspapers, conducted public programs and presented speeches—all on the same subject. Roy was founder and president of the German-Israeli Friendship Club of Constance. He was largely responsible for forging a cooperative exchange agreement between the Universities of Constance and Tel Aviv. He drew attention to and organized support for small struggling Jewish communities in Eastern Europe. I considered it an honor to have met and earned the friendship of this dedicated couple.

At the end of the week, I took a train to Freudenstadt in the Black Forest region. My former roommate, Henry Gruen, and Irmgard, his companion, were attending a convention there. We had a happy reunion, then they returned to a professional seminar, while I attended a concert of Robert Stolz music.

This was not a routine concert. A woman, accompanied by a pianist, alternated between telling the story of Robert Stolz's life and singing his pretty songs. It was a heroic story of a popular German composer of light, folksy operettas, who was sufficiently outraged by Hitler's policies to leave Germany, although he himself was not being persecuted. I admired the sensitive way the singer discussed Stolz's ideals. Looking around, I could see mostly men and women older than myself. Many of them undoubtedly had been those same Nazis that were being condemned by the singer. I am sure that I was the only Jew in the hall.

I found out that we were very near to Rexingen, the little village where my father was born and where Uncle Isi, Aunt Celia and my grandmother used to live. Henry and I took a short bus ride there.

The village had become a bit modernized since I had spent a couple of vacations there as a boy, but I was still able to recognize a few landmarks. Our former family home had been completely renovated, the dirt road was now paved, and there was not a trace of the big linden tree, the stable and the manure pile that were once located next door. Other than that, it just seemed that everything was smaller and closer together than it used to be.

We visited the Jewish cemetery. It was generally in good shape, except that the Black Forest was re-invading the old part of the cemetery, where some grave stones of the 1700s were being pushed aside by trees growing on or between the graves. We were intrigued by a monument erected in memory of a Jewish flight lieutenant from Rexingen, who had lost his life as a pilot in the German "air force" during World War I.

There were no Jews left in Rexingen. We had a long talk with an old woman. She told about the good times Christians and Jews used to have together when she was young. She showed us an old photograph of a group of youngsters of both religions taking dancing lessons together. What I learned about Rexingen from the old woman motivated me to also find out what I could about Gailingen, the village my mother's family came from.

A subsequent trip to Constance in July 1987 was a family project. Our son, Dan, and his wife, Sara, wanted to come with us to see where I had grown up. We spent the first few days in Switzerland with our cousins. But our goal, which was my mission as well, was to return to Constance.

In Constance, we took a long walk, touching the memorable places of my youth. I introduced my family to the mayor, to Dr. and Mrs. Bloch[14] and to my former classmate. We had dinner at the homes of the Wiehns' and another friend, Professor Dirk Pette and his wife,

Fanny. Liesel and her family accompanied us on a pleasant boat trip on Lake Constance. Dan and Sara took some side trips, but Goldie had to slow down. She had caught a cold.

Goldie was plagued by chronic bronchitis in those days. Anytime she caught a cold, she was instructed to go on antibiotics. But here she was in Constance with a cold and sore throat—and she had not brought any antibiotics.

I called Dr. Bloch and asked him to recommend a local doctor. He recommended his own physician, Dr. Jung, whose office was only a few blocks from our hotel. When we called Dr. Jung's office, we were told that there were no openings that morning, but that they would try to squeeze us into their schedule.

As soon as we arrived at the waiting room, Dr. Jung called us right into his office. He spent a good half hour examining Goldie, reviewing her medical history, explaining her condition to us, writing two prescriptions, condemning excess use of antibiotics and vitamins by American doctors—and questioning me about my own background. Then he escorted us back to the waiting room. When the receptionist asked us where she should send the bill, Dr. Jung said: "That won't be necessary. There will be no charge for a former Constancer."

Before we had time to recover from our shock, he asked us who had recommended him. When we told him, he said, "Ah yes—Dr. Bloch is a patient of mine—and his parents were patients of my father." This statement rang a bell in my mind. It reminded me of an event that happened nearly 50 years earlier, involving the fathers of Dr. Bloch and Dr. Jung.

It was November 10, 1938, the morning after *Kristallnacht*. Our beautiful synagogue had been blown up, and all the Jewish men were being rounded up by the Gestapo, to be shipped to Dachau concentration camp. A fanatical S.S.-man with a grudge had his sights set on the father of Dr. Bloch. The older Dr. Bloch, 70 years old at the time, was a highly respected attorney and president of the Jewish congregation of Constance. The S.S.-man and two of his associates pulled Dr. Bloch out of his house, drove him to the Rhine River, dragged him onto a boat, rowed him to the middle of the river and dropped him overboard. A number of people on their way to work had watched this from the shore, were highly perturbed, and proceeded to untie another boat in order to rescue the old man. The S.S.-men now hauled him back into their own boat and rowed him to shore. They drove him to Gestapo headquarters, where they tortured him and beat him with wire whips, blinding him in one eye.

There were many witnesses to the happenings at the river. A wave of shock and indignation swept through the town. It apparently reached the Gestapo, because they released Dr. Bloch after dark—on the condition that he show himself in public daily for a week—while all the other Jewish men were sent to Dachau.

At this time, the father of the doctor who had treated Goldie offered his services to the elder Dr. Bloch and nursed him back to health. He was warned by the Gestapo that it was against the law for a non-Jewish physician to treat a Jewish patient. The elder Dr. Jung ignored the threats, and the Gestapo did not interfere.

In my opinion, this incident was extremely important. It is generally held that opposition to Hitler's policies was useless and dangerous after the first few months of Hitler's rule. But here was a time in 1938, nearly six years after Hitler came to power, when the local Gestapo had to release a prisoner in response to public revulsion. The course of German history could well have been changed had there been such a wave of revulsion across all of Germany following the excesses of *Kristallnacht*. Evidently, there was hardly a ripple—and fate moved on.

I had entered the nuclear power activity in its embryonic phase and watched it grow into a giant industry. Thirty years later, I could now see it come to a screeching halt. In order to avoid massive layoffs, Westinghouse offered its long-term employees an early retirement bonus: a full year's pay if they retired as of January 1, 1987. I was not quite 62 years old and had worked for Westinghouse for not quite 30 years. I qualified for a good pension. But was I ready to quit? The work I was doing now—had been doing for the past eight years—in Test Engineering was the most exciting, the most satisfying of my entire professional life. Was I ready to give it up? Then came another announcement: The Test Engineering and Operation department would be disbanded. It made my decision very easy: I would retire.

I had reached a stable time in my life. Our mortgage was paid off, and we were not anticipating any significant expenditures. Dan and Sara were both in managerial positions in small computer firms. Marcie had established her own highly rated business in computer training, and Ed was marketing manager for a computer company. Goldie intended to keep on working as a teacher following my retirement. I was in excellent health and had many interests that I never had enough time to pursue. There would never be a better time to retire. My manager gave me one final raise and I attended a retirement seminar and a retirement party. That was it—the end—the beginning.

Dan with Sara and David

My retirement years began with diverse activities. The "Over-Sixty" program at the University of Pittsburgh provided many stimulating, enjoyable hours for Goldie and me. I've audited more than 50 courses of all kinds since I retired. We also derived much pleasure from attendance at plays and operas. Our favorite diversions, however, are visits with our children and grandchildren.

I was privileged to interact with six young German volunteers at the Holocaust Center over a period of ten years. 'Action Reconciliation Service for Peace' formed by the Protestant Church of Germany, sends high school graduates for 18-month stints to work with people who suffered most under Nazi terror.

Yet, I can't help but think about my link to the past. In 1982, I was asked to be a speaker for the Holocaust Center of Pittsburgh, and I still do that today. From 1990 to 1994 I was also coordinator of the

Holocaust speakers bureau. I became familiar with many Holocaust survivors living in the Pittsburgh area, and in 1993
they elected me to be president of their
organization. I have been very proud of
this honor.

A neighbor also introduced me to the
Rehabilitation Institute right after I retired.
I joined their volunteer engineering group.
We designed and built various devices for

The author at the Holocaust Center of Pittsburgh

the Institute's patients and students, as requested by the staff members.
We had a little machine shop in the basement of one of their buildings,
and we met periodically to discuss needs and progress.

I came to know some of the teachers of the Rehabilitation Institute's
day school, and I became a volunteer assistant to Su Stenger, one of the
teachers. All Mondays during the school year have become "Rehab"
days for me since 1987. Working with brain injured children has
become one of my most meaningful retirement activities.

I have always been involved in the leadership of our congregation,
Temple Sinai. This activity has continued in recent years. For a few
years I was also a volunteer speaker for the Pittsburgh Science Institute, and I did some tutoring in the school where Goldie used to teach.

Goldie's job as a teacher was getting frustrating and her health was
deteriorating. She had developed chronic asthmatic bronchitis. It was
set off whenever she caught a cold, which now happened with increas-
ing frequency. In March 1990, she requested and was granted a year of
medical sabbatical leave. At the end of the year, she retired. Her health
has improved significantly since then, and so has her peace of mind.

Our daughter's marriage to Ed ended after 19 years. A few months
later, Marcie met Jim Miller. They have been happily married since
April 19, 1997.

There has been no time for boredom in my retirement. I wrote this
book mostly during the summer months, when my other
activities slowed down. I completed it while recovering from successful

Marcie with Jim, Claire, Sarah, Elise

activities slowed down. I completed it while recovering from successful surgery for prostate cancer. It's been a good life, and now there seems to be a good chance for more.

In fact, the purpose of my fifth post-war trip to Germany was to present my book—this book—to the public of Constance. Professor Roy Wiehn had read the manuscript, liked it, and asked me to have it translated into German. He edited the German version and had it published by his friends, Drs. Hartung-Gorre, in December 1996.

The German government has designated January 27 as an annual Holocaust commemoration day. The formal presentation of my book on January 26 was to be the opening event of the 1997 Holocaust commemoration in Constance. The town government paid for two-thirds of my air fare, Dr. Wiehn paid the rest.

I visited my old friend, Henry Gruen, and my cousin, Sylvain, before heading for Constance. Sylvain's wife, Ninon, had died in May 1995. As my train approached Constance, familiar buildings came into view: The Rhine tower, Insel Hotel, town theater, Konzil building. These structures still looked as they did 60 years ago. That should not have surprised me, since they were built centuries ago. I found myself getting excited. Why? These are only shells, I told myself. What was I expecting to find? My parents? Old friends? My youth? I ascribed my strong feelings to the fact that I had come alone, without a connection to my American life.

Mirjam and Roy Wiehn greeted me as I stepped off the train. Their elation reflected my own feelings. We took a short walk through the town park to the Wiehn residence, where I had been invited to stay during my visit in Constance. We took another walk along the beautiful lake. Somehow I felt right at home with these people.

We took a leisurely walk to the Swiss town of Kreuzlingen on Saturday. Crossing the border, which had been a matter of life or death at one time, seemed so trivial now. We just walked past some bored looking guards. We did a bit of shopping in a modern, well-stocked supermarket. There was no trace any more of the family-owned stores, where customers used to be greeted by name.

Fritz and Goldie, 1999

Saturday afternoon, only hours before my scheduled public reading, a lens fell out of my reading glasses. Mirjam rushed the glasses to an optician in the neighborhood, who repaired them immediately, free of charge. Roy and I selected the specific passages I was to read from the book on the next morning.

Sunday was the big day of my presentation. Roy, Mirjam and I arrived at the Seniors Center early enough to set up 50 chairs, a book table and a speaker's table. Roy did not expect a good turnout. The local newspaper had printed only a terse announcement on page 23 rather than the big splash of publicity anticipated by Roy. He was surprised when he had to set up 30 additional chairs.

Guests started arriving, greeting me or introducing themselves. There were professors, my publishers, former classmates and friends of my sister, Ilse. One of them gave me two class photographs showing Ilse standing next to her favorite teacher, Miss Kirn. My cousin Jack from St. Gallen, Switzerland had to cancel out because of a back problem; but his two sons, daughter-in-law and grandson arrived just before the program started.

Roy started the proceedings by reading the greater part of his preface to my book, then called on me to continue. I gave a brief introductory talk, then read selections from the book, mostly about my experiences as a boy in Constance. Dr. Renate Gorre made some concluding remarks, after which I had informal conversations and signed books. The audience seemed interested and appreciative. Roy, Mirjam and I took my cousins from St. Gallen out for lunch at a historic hotel across the street from where my parents' store used to be located. Now it was time for the Wiehns to prepare for an informal reception in my honor at their home for 10 friends. After the guests departed around midnight, Roy and I talked until about 2 a.m. It was the end of an exciting day, a singular experience.

The Constance edition of the Monday morning *Südkurier* carried an article about my reading session. It concluded with the following paragraph:

> Ottenheimer points out that his book was not written in bitterness, and that is how it reads. Suspensefully written, it holds a balance between amusing anecdotes and experienced horrors. In the process, it offers an important and commendable contribution to the reconstruction of events of those days.

I was highly gratified with the article and with the reading session itself. I was amused and puzzled by the respect—even awe—with which I was received by some of the people at the presentation and subsequently on this trip. It occurred to me that I was being regarded not as Fritz Ottenheimer, but as a symbol of the former Jewish community of Constance. Hardly any such symbols exist today.

Arrangements had been made for me to read to a class of 50 twelfth-graders at a local high school on Monday morning. The students were well informed about the history of Nazism and the Holocaust, if only to explain the school's name, the Scholl School. Brother and sister Hans and Sophie Scholl were leaders of the White Rose, a German student organization that produced and distributed leaflets advocating resistance against Nazi despotism. They were caught and executed by guillotine in February 1943.

Following a respectful introduction by the school principal, I chose to talk freely rather than read from the book. It was a very moving experience for me. I was that little Jewish boy in Constance again as I shared the pain and humiliation of persecution with these young people of Constance. I talked for an hour, in German of course, and fifty young minds were hanging on every word I said. There followed thirty minutes of thoughtful questions and answers. When the class was dismissed, several students came up to shake my hand and thank me for coming. I had given similar talks (in English) to student groups in the Pittsburgh area on many occasions, but they had never touched me so deeply. I was drained.

Mrs. Homburger, co-owner of a local book store, had driven me to the Scholl School. Now she took me for a short ride to the cemetery. I visited the graves of my maternal grandmother and my aunt and uncle. Next, we had lunch at the Homburger's home, overlooking the lovely Lake Constance. After lunch, she walked me through the quaint winding alleys of the oldest district of Constance to my next appointment at St. Stephan School.

Pursuant to my request, Dr. Wiehn had arranged for me to visit my former school after school hours. When five former classmates learned of my plan, they decided to join me for this activity, and so did a local newspaper reporter. The young school principal, Dr. Hipp, offered his services as our guide.

The school building dates back to the year 1255. The outside still looks the same as in my student days. Internally, it has been spruced up, but very tastefully, with antique features, such as the old wooden beams, actually more prominent than before. St. Stephan is a very progressive coeducational public school now, with special education classes, "international" remedial classes for foreign students, Montessori classes, after-school child care, co-op agreements with local industry and cultural organizations, and high-tech tools and computers.

It turned out that for my classmates, this was also their first return visit to the school. They had graduated shortly after I was evicted by the Nazi government. I am sure that Dr. Hipp soon realized that recognition of old features excited us much more than admiration of the pedagogical advances, but he continued to enlighten us. He also listened with interest to our recollections.

"Why did the Jewish boys sit together in the last row?" one of my classmates asked. I had forgotten about that. We decided that it must have been decreed by the administration, because the friendship between the Jewish boys was not as close as with other boys who sat in front.

Reunion with German classmates

"Whatever happened to Leo?" the Jewish boy I had known.

"Didn't you hear? He joined the French resistance. He was at the head of the French army that occupied Constance. He gave me a big 'hello' when he saw me."

"This is the room where Bach used to teach. He wore SA uniform pants in class."

"Do you remember how this room used to smell? Old Angus always kept cigars and Limburger cheese in his desk."

"Teacher Eisenreich got a high position in the Nazi sports organization."

"Do you remember how Henrich whipped us when we misbehaved?"

"Yes, I can still feel it. But I also remember him telling me— privately—that the government was wrong in its treatment of the Jews. That meant a lot to me."

After a while, the conversation focused on people who became active in Nazi activities. How much of it was unavoidable? Why did some exceed normal bounds? "We still can't understand how those horrible things could have happened."

"For most men of our age, the war years were spent in military service. One-third of our class were killed in action, another one-third have died since. Only 9 or 10 are still alive, and six of us are here right now. How good it is that we could meet this way."

We thanked Dr. Hipp and walked over to a nearby café, where we continued the conversation over a glass of wine. One question came up with deep concern: "Did any of us, as kids, ever hurt you or hurt your feelings?"

"I may be repressing unpleasant memories, but I don't remember even one incident. And I said so in the book, too."

"I didn't think so. I'm glad."

By the time we parted, we agreed that we were closer to each other now than we had ever been as boys. An article with photograph about our reunion appeared in the local newspaper two days later.

Tuesday started with my traditional solo walk through Constance, retracing all the streets and alleys that I frequented as a boy. It is a pleasure to do this in Constance. When I was a boy, I never realized how beautiful my hometown was. But I also needed this walk in order to restore my sense of reality—that to the vast majority of the population, I was still a stranger.

I had a formal appointment with Dr. Horst Frank, the new mayor of Constance, on Tuesday afternoon. The *Rathaus* (city hall) building is very old and very beautiful, like so many other buildings in Constance. Dr. Wiehn and Dr. Gorre accompanied me. We found Dr. Frank to be a very likable, uncomplicated man. He had campaigned as a member of the "Green" (environmentalist) party, astounded everyone by defeating the major party candidates. He had previously been an attorney specializing in restitution cases for Holocaust survivors in various countries. We chatted for half an hour.

Former classmate Heini Roek and his wife, Irmgard, insisted on driving me to the train station on Friday. "When you left Constance in 1939, there was nobody to wave good-bye to you," they pointed out. "We don't want that to ever happen to you again!" They also gave me a bag lunch to enjoy on my trip to Augsburg. I had previously sent my big suitcase on to a hotel in Munich, where I would be arriving on Sunday. And I had exchanged emotional farewells with Roy and Mirjam before they left for work. Now it was time to leave Constance again. But how different it was from 1939.

The Walter family were the first Jewish people I met after World War II. In 1945, when my army unit was stationed in Marienbad,

Czechoslovakia, I spent much time with the family. Hanna, their youngest child, now lives in Augsburg, Bavaria. Susi, the older sister, has returned to the family home in what has been renamed Marianske Lazne, Czech Republic. Augsburg and Marianske Lazne were the next two stops on my itinerary.

Hanna had offered to pick me up at the Augsburg railroad station. She was only two years old the last time she saw me (*see picture, Page 83*), but I had sent her a recent snapshot of myself. She addressed a gray-haired man from Turkey as "Fritz?" He looked confused, but then she spotted me right behind him. Following introductions, Hanna drove me to the Augsburg synagogue, where she works as a secretary. A friend, Pavel, guided me through the building. It was magnificent. The synagogue, which had been burned out on *Kristallnacht* (November 1938), was rebuilt to its original condition by the city of Augsburg after the war. It is not being used for its intended purpose, however. While there are numerous Jewish residents in Augsburg, many from the former Soviet Union, they generally lack the religious education and tradition on which religious practice must be based. Present leaders and teachers evidently are unable to provide the missing ingredients. There is a congregational cadre that maintains the building—as a museum for school groups and other visitors—and tries to satisfy the ritual and social needs of a handful of orthodox Jews in a small chapel.

Hanna told me about a teacher who brings his classes periodically to the synagogue. He ordered his students to ask their grandparents what they could remember about the Jews of Augsburg. All responses were written out on the blackboard and carefully analyzed: What kind of people were these Jews? What kinds of citizens were they? What was done to them? How much did the grandparents know about their fate? Where are they today? Why were they treated that way? What did the grandparents do to help them? Hanna observed that the students that come with this teacher always show the greatest interest and ask the best questions when they tour the facility . I was pleased to see several copies of my book (for sale) in one of the show cases.

I was happy to meet Hanna's daughter and grandson. Hanna filled me in on some of her parents' history: After the Nazi takeover of Czechoslovakia, the gentile spouse of every intermarried couple was urged to divorce the Jewish partner. Mr. Walter was the only one in Marienbad who refused to comply, despite proddings from his own relatives. After the war started, Hanna's father was the only member of the family permitted to enter an air raid shelter. He declined the privilege.

Hanna drove me to the railroad station on Saturday. Although I was stationed in a transient camp in Augsburg in 1945, I was not able now to recognize any structure in this lovely city. On the way to Marianske Lazne, I enjoyed a delicious fish platter in the dining car. Customs and passport inspection at the border was perfunctory. Susan recognized and welcomed me immediately when I left the train, probably because I was the only gray-haired passenger. Susi was only 14 years old the last time she saw me in 1945.

When my MGSG unit was stationed in Marienbad in 1945, we were quartered in the former Panorama Hotel for two months. In preparation for my current trip, I had written to Susi that if there was still a Panorama Hotel in Marianske Lazne, that is where I would like to spend the night—for old times' sake. It turned out that during the Communist rule in Czechoslovakia, the Panorama Hotel had been converted into a vacation home for Czech railroad workers and their families. Susi explained my request to the director of the home, who agreed to let me have the executive suite as a paying guest. He led me to a small apartment: living room, two bedrooms, and bathroom. He apologized for having to charge me 250 crowns for the night, including breakfast, i.e., a little more than $9. I found out later that a roast duck dinner in a nice little restaurant cost about $4. It appears that the Czech Republic is a good place to visit for a vacation.

It was fascinating to be able to walk through and around the Panorama building. The director even allowed me to enter the guest room where I had slept when I was stationed there. I wondered: Where are my old buddies now? How many are still alive? The building's interior had been well maintained; furniture was plain but in good condition. The outside of the building appeared to have been patched and repainted many times. This seemed to be typical of all the hotels and villas that used to be the pride of Marienbad. The international vacation atmosphere was missing during my visit, perhaps because it was winter; but the Germans, who were hated and evicted in 1945, were now being welcomed with open arms as well-paying tourists.

Susi and I walked through many streets that I used to patrol in 1945, and we talked for several hours about the family I used to know and about our lives since those days. "If only Mother could be here now," Susi lamented several times.

On Sunday afternoon, I headed West to Munich. I checked into a small hotel near the main railroad station. This was the city my parents had visited on their honeymoon in 1921. Most of the city was destroyed during World War II, reconstructed during the immediate post-war years. It is a beautiful, active city today.

I took a commuter train to Dachau early Monday morning. I wanted to visit the memorialized remains of Dachau concentration camp, where my father was kept for a month after *Kristallnacht*. When I arrived, I discovered that Dachau, like all "museums" in Germany, was closed on Mondays. I did not have the option of returning on another day since I was to return to Pittsburgh on Tuesday. I entered a cab, asked for a drive around the camp and encouraged commentary. The elderly driver pointed out where various parts of the camp were located: the main gate, the firing squad, the post-liberation burial ground, the SS-barracks. He related that as a boy, he used to stand at the main gate with a hand wagon and offer—for a price—to take baggage of discharged prisoners to the train station. Most of the early inmates were criminals and political prisoners, and local businesses and industries could lease them for labor at 1 Mark per day. Jews were incarcerated later. He remembers when his Jewish neighbors were committed to the camp.

"We really didn't know what went on inside the camp," the cabby assured me. "We thought it was just a prison camp!" A woman in Constance made the exact same statement to me a few days earlier. I got the impression that there was nothing wrong with sending Jews to Dachau as long as it was "just a prison camp." But now we know that it wasn't just a prison camp.

"Well, you know," the driver observed, "during a war, you can't avoid cruelty."

"What kind of war was going on in 1938, when they took my father to Dachau?" I asked him. He did not reply.

I took the next train back to Munich. I walked around for several hours. Now I was ready for my return to Pittsburgh.

12 Remembering and Repairing

November 9, 1998 marked the 60th anniversary of Kristallnacht. The mayor of Constance invited me to visit my hometown once again, this time as the main speaker at their public commemoration of this event. More than 300 residents crowded into the newly built Culture Center that night. A choral group sang Jewish songs before, between, and after speeches. Mayor Frank spoke briefly, followed by Mr. Nissenbaum, head of the new Jewish community of Constance. Now it was my turn.

Ladies and gentlemen. I am grateful to my old hometown for this invitation. If my parents were still alive, they would also be pleased, for Constance was once their beloved home, their life. Unfortunately, their love of home was converted into pain during the 1930s — into deep pain, but never into hate.

The 1930s were difficult years; but our friends and classmates remained decent despite the vicious Nazi propaganda. We figured as long as the people didn't go along with all that agitation, we had nothing to worry about. But then the customers stayed away from our store, and we had to give it up. And gradually some friends stayed away from us, and we drew away from the others so they wouldn't be endangered.

The year 1938 was a fateful one. Is it possible that 60 years have passed since then? I can still remember it clearly. I was 13 years old. It was the year of my Bar Mitzvah celebration. It was also the year of Kristallnacht. (I recounted in detail what I remembered about Kristallnacht.)

In May of 1939 we were summoned to appear at the US consulate for a second time, and this time we received our papers. My family and I (at age 14) left our hometown. It was a sad day, it was a happy day. It was our salvation. If we had had to wait any longer for our visas, we would have been condemned to death — like six million others — for the 'crime' of being Jewish.

The title of my autobiography asks despairingly, 'How could it happen?' Sixty years after Kristallnacht, I am still looking for an answer.

So many things still cannot be explained today.

Some of you may remember Richard Tauber, the magnificent German tenor. He sang opera, operetta and contemporary hits. He was once Germany's favorite singer. The women were in love with him. When the Nazis came, however, Tauber wasn't allowed to sing any more, and he had to leave the country. How could this happen? Richard Tauber and his parents were Catholic, but one of his grandparents was Jewish. But surely the German people would understand and stand behind their beloved Tauber? We didn't hear a thing from the people.

The music of Richard Tauber was the music of my family. We sang, we played piano, we played records — the old German folk songs, operetta arias, Viennese songs, children's songs — these were the sounds of my happy childhood. Sixty years ago tonight the songs died away, and with them, my happy childhood. We immigrated to America and were able to form a new, happy home there.

But, today, whenever I hear a Tauber CD, I realize that I have lost something valuable, that something beautiful was stolen from me. Similarly, when I visit the beautiful town of Constance, my joy is mixed with sadness. It cannot be avoided: The past cannot be changed.

The German people were obedient in those days. 'Fuhrer, command — we shall obey!' was their motto. I think that people would not be as obedient today. I talked to a group of students at the Scholl High School this morning. You can be proud of your children. They are intelligent and sensitive. I had the impression, though, that 'blind obedience' and 'silence' are not their major subjects. And that's as it should be, even if it's inconvenient at times. These young people have their ethical values, their own thoughts, their own opinions, which gives me hope that the future will not repeat the past. True, I recall my parents' conviction back then that the German people would not stand for Nazi injustice. My parents were unrealistic in their optimism. Will my optimism prove valid? We can only hope.

Ladies and gentlemen, your attendance tonight has shown me that the past has not been forgotten, and your interest has shown me that you share my feelings. I thank you for both."

There was sustained applause for a full minute and I felt gratitude and encouragement from the many nameless faces in front of me. The mayor then invited a number of friends and officials to a nearby cafe for snacks and conversation with me. It felt good to be back in Constance.

During the week ahead I talked with four groups of high school seniors, a gathering of doctoral candidates, and a class of 8th grade students. It was the last group who moved me most. They were students at St. Stephan School, the same school I had once attended. Most of the 20 or so children came from poor families, and nearly half of them were foreign immigrants. They could identify with my experiences and feelings as an immigrant boy, as a member of an unwanted minority. Yet, I could see a sense of hope in their eyes, a connection with my survival and success.

Later I participated in a book presentation at the university and conducted a reading session at the town library of Radolfzell, a small town near Constance. I spent an afternoon with my former classmates and a few hours with other friends, some of whom had traveled considerable distances to meet me. Two television crews interviewed me for several hours to produce a videotape for an exhibit on the history of Jews in Constance. On Saturday morning, I attended services with the present Jewish community of Constance. It had been a busy week, but I was thankful for every moment.

I often think about the two mutations that Germany has passed through during my lifetime: A highly civilized nation was abruptly converted into a black hole of history; a mere twelve years later, this same country (now in ruins) was transformed into a vibrant liberal democracy.

How could it happen?

Epilogue

I am holding a strange book in my hands. It looks like a phone book, and it contains a listing of 80,000 names along with corresponding dates and places of birth and nationality. It has 664 pages. The title of the book is *Memorial to the Jews Deported from France, 1942-1944.* It is a list, assembled by Serge Klarsfeld, of 75,000 Jews deported from France to Auschwitz death camp, plus another 5,000 killed in France. This book, more than any other, has helped me to understand the immensity and atrocity of the Holocaust.[15]

The pages of the book glide through my fingers. I stop randomly on page 194, and my eyes rest arbitrarily on a name: Manfried Burghardt, born July 15, 1925, in Halle, Germany. He was deported on August 21, 1942 in Convoy 22. There are no other Burghardts listed on this convoy. What happened to Manfried's parents? Were they hauled away on a previous convoy? Did he have any brothers, sisters, girl friends? What did he look like? Did he like to play soccer, hate to brush his teeth? Was his mother worried when he had measles 12 years ago? Could he play an instrument? Was he hoping to be a dentist some day—or an archeologist? His 17th birthday was just one month before his departure to Auschwitz. Did he have a happy celebration with his family—or was he starving among strangers in a filthy detention camp?

We are told that of 1,000 people on this convoy, 892 were gassed as soon as they arrived at Auschwitz, while 90 men and 18 women were shunted aside temporarily for forced labor. Only seven men were still alive in 1945. Manfried was not one of them. Is there anyone alive today who knew Manfried? Is there any indication anywhere outside this book that Manfried Burghardt ever existed? What were his thoughts when he stood for hours, for days in a hot, crowded, stinking cattle car among strangers; and when he started gasping in the "shower room" at Auschwitz? And what about the other 79,999 names in the book— every single, individual, significant, pitiful one of them?

I was born in the same year as Manfried. If Aunt Flora had waited 4 months before issuing an affidavit for our family, we would probably have been deported to Camp Gurs, France, along with the other Jews who remained in Constance. My name might have been printed on the same convoy list as Manfried's, with the same final destination.

Convoy Eight left Angers, France, on July 20, 1942 and arrived at Auschwitz on July 23. There were 824 Jews in this convoy. Only 19 men survived. Three names included in the convoy list were Léon Wertheim, age 50; Marie Wertheim, age 46, and Gilberte Wertheim, age 15. They were my Uncle Léon, Aunt Martha, and cousin Gigi.

Why was Aunt Martha listed as Marie? Actually, Marie was her middle name. Did she make a weak attempt to raise some doubt in her captor's mind by using her Christian-sounding middle name? The dates of birth were listed correctly. More likely, it was just a clerical error.[16] I don't know why I was shocked to see my relatives' names on this list. The information was no surprise. It agreed with what we had learned many years before. But the starkness of a bureaucratic document that announces in effect: "These people are to be killed ..." is hard to comprehend.[17]

I have studied the book for many hours, shed many tears. There are so many names. There is so much tragedy, so much despair. I leaf through all 664 pages of small print and pick out a name here and there; yet I still can't fathom the full extent of the anguish recorded here. It is a monstrous book. Then comes another humbling realization: If all six million Jewish victims of the Holocaust could be chronicled in this manner, it would take 75 books of this size just to list their names. How many more books would be needed to record their lives, their hopes and accomplishments, their loves and pains, their final thoughts?

I barely avoided the ravages of the Holocaust, but I cannot forget what happened to others. Chronologically, the Holocaust was only a small part of my life and of this book. Emotionally, its burden is overwhelming. I wish I could have simple answers for the questions that haunt me.

MILITARY GOVERNMENT–GERMANY
SUPREME COMMANDER'S AREA OF CONTROL
PROCLAMATION No. I

TO THE PEOPLE OF GERMANY:

I, General Dwight D. Eisenhower, Supreme Commander, Allied Expeditionary Force, do hereby proclaim as follows:—

I.

The Allied Forces serving under my command have now entered Germany. We come as conquerors, but not as oppressors. In the area of Germany occupied by the forces under my command, we shall obliterate Nazi-ism and German Militarism. We shall overthrow the Nazi rule, dissolve the Nazi Party and abolish the cruel, oppressive and discriminatory laws and institutions which the Party has created. We shall eradicate that German Militarism which has so often disrupted the peace of the world. Military and Party leaders, the Gestapo and others suspected of crimes and atrocities will be tried and, if guilty, punished as they deserve.

II.

Supreme legislative, judicial and executive authority and powers within the occupied territory are vested in me as Supreme Commander of the Allied Forces and as Military Governor, and the Military Government is established to exercise these powers under my direction. All persons in the occupied territory will obey immediately and without question all the enactments and orders of the Military Government. Military Government Courts will be established for the punishment of offenders. Resistance to the Allied Forces will be ruthlessly stamped out. Other serious offences will be dealt with severely.

III.

All German courts and educational institutions within the occupied territory are suspended. The Volksgerichtshof, the Sondergerichte, the SS Police Courts and other special courts are deprived of authority throughout the occupied territory. Re-opening of the criminal and civil courts and educational institutions will be authorized when conditions permit.

IV.

All officials are charged with the duty of remaining at their posts until further orders, and obeying and enforcing all orders or directions of Military Government or the Allied Authorities addressed to the German Government or the German people. This applies also to officials, employees and workers of all public undertakings and utilities and to all other persons engaged in essential work.

DWIGHT D. EISENHOWER,
General of the Army,
Supreme Commander,
Allied Expeditionary Force.

MILITÄRREGIERUNG–DEUTSCHLAND
KONTROLLGEBIET DES OBERSTEN BEFEHLSHABERS
PROKLAMATION Nr. I

AN DAS DEUTSCHE VOLK:

Ich, General Dwight D. Eisenhower, Oberster Befehlshaber der Alliierten Streitkräfte gebe hiermit Folgendes bekannt:

I.

Die Alliierten Streitkräfte, die unter meinem Oberbefehl stehen, haben jetzt deutschen Boden betreten. Wir kommen als ein siegreiches Heer; jedoch nicht als Unterdrücker. In dem deutschen Gebiet, das von Streitkräften unter meinem Oberbefehl besetzt ist, werden wir den Nationalsozialismus und den deutschen Militarismus vernichten, die Herrschaft der Nationalsozialistischen Arbeiter Partei beseitigen, die NSDAP auflösen sowie die grausamen, harten und ungerechten Rechtssätze und Einrichtungen, die von der NSDAP geschaffen worden sind, aufheben. Den deutschen Militarismus, der so oft den Frieden der Welt gestört hat, werden wir endgültig beseitigen. Führer der Wehrmacht und der NSDAP, Mitglieder der Geheimen Staats-Polizei und andere Personen, die verdächtig sind, Verbrechen und Grausamkeiten begangen zu haben, werden gerichtlich angeklagt und, falls für schuldig befunden, ihrer gerechten Bestrafung zugeführt.

II.

Die höchste gesetzgebende, rechtsprechende und vollziehende Machtbefugnis und Gewalt in dem besetzten Gebiet ist in meiner Person als Oberster Befehlshaber der Alliierten Streitkräfte und als Militär-Gouverneur vereinigt. Die Militärregierung ist eingesetzt, um diese Gewalten unter meinem Befehl auszuüben. Alle Personen in dem besetzten Gebiet haben unverzüglich und widerspruchslos alle Befehle und Veröffentlichungen der Militärregierung zu befolgen. Gerichte der Militärregierung werden eingesetzt, um Rechtsbrecher zu verurteilen. Widerstand gegen die Alliierten Streitkräfte wird unnachsichtlich gebrochen. Andere schwere strafbare Handlungen werden schärferens geahndet.

III.

Alle deutschen Gerichte, Unterrichts-und Erziehungsanstalten innerhalb des besetzten Gebietes werden bis auf Weiteres geschlossen. Dem Volksgerichtshof, den Sondergerichten, den SS Polizei-Gerichten und anderen ausserordentlichen Gerichten wird überall im besetzten Gebiet die Gerichtsbarkeit entzogen. Die Wiederaufnahme der Tätigkeit der Straf-und Zivilgerichte und die Wiedereröffnung der Unterrichts- und Erziehungsanstalten wird genehmigt, sobald die Zustände es zulassen.

IV.

Alle Beamte sind verpflichtet, bis auf Weiteres auf ihren Posten zu verbleiben und alle Befehle und Anordnungen der Militärregierung oder der Alliierten Behörden, die die deutsche Regierung oder an das deutsche Volk gerichtet sind, zu befolgen und auszuführen. Dies gilt auch für die Beamten, Arbeiter und Angestellten sämtlicher öffentlichen und gemeinwirtschaftlichen Betriebe, sowie für sonstige Personen, die notwendige Tätigkeiten verrichten.

DWIGHT D. EISENHOWER
General of the Army
Oberster Befehlshaber der
Alliierten Streitkräfte

*Document posted by the MGSG-Military Government Security Guard,
in every German town seized by the US Army.*

References and Updates

1. Eckhardt Friedrich & Dagmar Schmieder-Friedrich, editors, "The Gailinger Jews."

2. Chapter 2—I made an unusual phone call on August 25, 1983. Dr. Moos (our "Uncle" Semi) was the man who, as my mother's obstetrician, had brought me into the world. He was now living in Australia, and I called him to wish him a happy 100th birthday. He was still as witty and exuberant as ever—for one more year.

3. Chapter 3—Erich Bloch, *History of the Jews in Constance: 19th and 20 Century.*

4. Chapter 4—Erich Bloch, *History of the Jews in Constance: 19th and 20 Century.*

5. Eckhardt Friedrich & Dagmar Schmieder-Friedrich, editors, "The Gailinger Jews."

6. Leopold Marx, "Shavej-Zion: Experiment and Promise."

7. Chapter 4—In the process of checking on some details for this book, I found out that we had been misinformed. Yes, Gus was returned to active duty; but he was married before the war, returned to Constance after the war and had three sons. He died in 1961 at age 56.

8. Chapter 5—I asked the U.S. Immigration and Naturalization Service recently why we were detained at Ellis Island. They sent me a copy of a 1939 document that gave the reason as "Likely to Become a Public Charge—Physical Defect." It was the second time U.S. authorities blocked our immigration on account of my father's war injury.

9. Chapter 9—Bob Nolta and his English war bride, Pat, visited us about 15 years after the war, but then we lost contact. Pat wrote me recently to say that Bob died on December 18, 1997, following 20 years of severe mental and physical illness.

10. Chapter 9—I kept in touch with Lilly and Lore Marcuse for a few years. Lore renewed her friendship with a young man, Werner Isaac,

who had immigrated to South Africa before World War II. Werner was also deaf. As I recall, he was a professional photographer in Johannesburg. He arranged for the two women to immigrate to South Africa. Lore and Werner were married in 1949.

11. Chapter 10—David and Hannah Wiener as well as the former dentist and his wife immigrated to the United States. The Wieners opened a hardware store in Monticello, NY. They were blessed with a little girl, Lea, who now became their whole life. Every letter and phone call reported proudly about Lea's accomplishments—as a toddler, in elementary school, in high school, in college. Lea married an Israeli man and they moved to Israel. David and Hannah now sold their store, moved to Israel, and spent the rest of their lives as happy members of Lea's extended family, watching their grandchildren grow up. David died in 1987, Hannah in 1991, both in their early eighties. In March 1995, Lea fell while riding in a bus and died of brain injuries at age 48. Lea's daughter Shoshi visited me in Pittsburgh in August 1996.

12. Chapter 10—I lost contact with the Walters when I left Europe. Late in 1993, about 47 years later, I sent a letter to their old address. It was returned, but someone had written Susi's current address (in Germany) on the envelope. I wrote to her and have received two letters from her so far. Some excerpts follow:

Dear Fritz,

Yes, I am the same Susi. I was very happy to get your letter with the photos. Thank you so much! You haven't changed, except for the hair color. Too bad I couldn't show them to my parents. I don't remember how you met my family—I only remember that you were there and the magnificent colored pencils (which I still have—only they have gotten small). Unfortunately, I was not able to develop my artistic skills: We couldn't speak Czech! Then came the Communists and took away our house and the workshop. My dad was "permitted" to keep working in his shop as a government employee, reporting to an administrator who was in charge. You see, liberation did not bring us pleasure.

Circumstances were always against us. My parents did not have a good life, nor did we children. The Czech "pioneers" who took over the border area were very angry because we spoke German. Later, as Communists, they allowed everything to decay. The houses became ruins—it was terrible. Now, everything is being restored again, but many structures have to be torn down (that's always the easiest way). They wanted to tear down our family home, that's why I fought to get it back. My great-grandfather was born in Marienbad, and he built the house in 1882. I owe it to my ancestors and to myself to fight for it.

There are 8 Jews in Marienbad today. They are not natives—they came from Poland. There is not a single Jew living here [in Bad Wiessee], but there is anti-Semitism. Don't ask me against whom!

Hannerl works in the Augsburg synagogue as a secretary. Her marriage also failed. Her daughter is married and has a nine-year-old son.

Couldn't you come to Europe some time? There is so much to talk about. I am so happy that you contacted me. You are like a relative to me, because there are only very few people around who knew my parents. You only knew them briefly, but at a fateful time.

13. Chapter 11—Erich Bloch, *History of the Jews in Constance: 19th and 20 Century*.

14. Chapter 11—I have been exchanging letters with Erich and Lisel Bloch. Erich was honored by family and friends on his 95th birthday in 1992. His autobiography, *The Lost Paradise*, was published in the same year. His health declined after that, and he died in 1994. Lisel has moved to Israel to be close to her children and grandchildren. She resides in a senior residence at Kibbutz Shave Tzion. Now there are no longer any pre-war Jewish residents of Constance living there, but a new street has been named after Erich.

15. Epilogue—Serge Klarsfeld, *Memorial to the Jews Deported from France, 1942-1944*.

16. Epilogue—Serge Klarsfeld sent me a photocopy of that page of the original Gestapo list. (*See front cover*) Aunt Martha was listed as Marie. Mr. Klarsfeld also sent me a copy of his latest book. It contains photographs of 1,500 of the 11,000 Jewish children deported from France. Each picture is a horrendous tragedy.

17. Epilogue—In response to my inquiry via Red Cross, the International Tracing Service, I.T.S., verified that the three Wertheims were deported to Auschwitz on July 20, 1942. It appears, however, that Uncle Léon

was selected for forced labor on his arrival at the camp. I.T.S. reported that he died at Auschwitz a month later, on August 19. What that tells me is that Aunt Martha and Gigi were separated from him, entered the gas chamber without him, took their last breath without him; and that Uncle Léon had to live for a month without them, being reminded of their fate with every breath he took of the putrid air of Auschwitz.

ABOUT THE AUTHOR

Fritz Ottenheimer is a retired mechanical engineer from Westinghouse Electric Corporation, who lives in Pittsburgh, Pennsylvania with his wife. He speaks widely on the Holocaust in both Germany and the United States, and has authored articles on the subject as well. A German translation of his life's memoirs was published in 1996.

Photo: Joy Berenfield

Fritz Ottenheimer lived the first 14 years of his life in Constance, Germany. One year after his Bar Mitzvah, his family was able to immigrate to the United States, narrowly avoiding almost certain death in the Holocaust. Ironically, Ottenheimer returned to Germany as a member of the US Army in 1945 to help free Europe from Hitler's clutches. This, his second book, chronicles a man's experience during one of the lowest moments in world history.

Fritz Ottenheimer may be reached at fritzott@aol.com